GEORGIA STUDIES SERIES

County Government in Georgia
City Government in Georgia
State Government in Georgia

STATE GOVERNMENT IN GEORGIA

By Lawrence R. Hepburn

INSTITUTE OF GOVERNMENT UNIVERSITY OF GEORGIA

STATE GOVERNMENT IN GEORGIA

Editor: Emily Honigberg

Design and production: Reid McCallister

Typesetting: Debra Peters

Proofreading: Dorothy Paul

Institute publications editor: Ann Blum

Library of Congress Cataloging in Publication Data

Hepburn, Lawrence R 1940-
State government in Georgia.

Includes index.

SUMMARY: Traces the history of Georgia's state government, examines the importance of politics and elections, and discusses the various components of the legislative, executive, and judicial branches of the state's government.

1. Georgia–Politics and government–Juvenile literature. [1. Georgia– Politics and government] I. Title.

JK4325 1981.H46 320.4758 80-24403
ISBN 0-89854-067-4

FOREWORD

Teachers in Georgia school systems, in recent years, have expressed to us an increasing interest in an up-to-date textbook on Georgia state government. At the same time, more and more persons outside school systems have voiced concern about the quality of citizenship education in the country. As tests have indicated, many students do not have even rudimentary knowledge of government.

Since the Institute of Government began in the 1920s, persons associated with it have been working with state officials and agencies, using their expertise to further knowledge about Georgia's state government. Accordingly, we thought that the Institute was in an ideal position to provide this textbook about Georgia state government. We hope that it will meet the educational needs of both teachers and students, especially during this period of renewed interest in state government across the nation.

The recent renaissance of state governments in the United States is, in part, a result of a growing awareness that the federal government is limited in the problems it can solve. In part, it reflects a recognition of the strength of our federal system—a system that allows many modifications of government policies to fit varying needs across the country. But state government has yet to get the attention it deserves from the media or from most textbooks.

State Government in Georgia is designed to inform students about what state government does, how it affects their lives, and how citizens may influence what it does. It attempts to breathe life into the institutional structures of government by indicating how the persons who participate in state government affect what it does.

The author is Dr. Lawrence R. Hepburn, educational research associate, at the Institute of Government. For more than 15 years as a high school social studies teacher and as a college professor, Dr. Hepburn has developed instructional materials and conducted workshops for teachers.

We wish to acknowledge the assistance of state officials and employees who contributed their time and ideas to this book. Without their help, it could not have been written. We hope that it will improve teaching and learning about state government in Georgia.

Delmer D. Dunn
Director
Institute of Government

October 1980

ACKNOWLEDGEMENTS

Subject matter consultants: C. David Billings, Douglas G. Bothun, Donald Brewer, Walter A. Denero, David England, Edwin L. Jackson, James E. Kundell, Linda D. Meggers, R. Ernest Taylor, and J. Devereux Weeks, all of the University of Georgia; and William H. Brandon, attorney, Atlanta, Georgia.

Classroom testing: Diane Brook, Jefferson City Schools; John Coen, Fulton County Schools; Mercedes Paxton, DeKalb County Schools.

Photo credits: University of Georgia Library, 6; Office of the Secretary of State, 17, 21; Lawrence R. Hepburn, 23, 88, 93, 109, 119, 146, 151, 155, 178; Edwin L. Jackson, 43, 45, 55, 59, 64, 89, 106, 108, 111, 112, 113, 116; Joseph B. Strickland, 60; William E. Birdsong, 70, 75; Georgia Department of Transportation, 77; Department of Natural Resources, 110; Governor's Office of Consumer Affairs, 123, 124; Georgia Bureau of Investigation, 143; Georgia Supreme Court, 153; Georgia Department of Offender Rehabilitation, Susan E. Morris—Intern, 172, 173.

Story illustrations on pages 2, 15, 26, 40, 48, 100, 118, 130, 160, 162, 164, 167, 170, by Don Smith.

Cartoons on pages 82 and 135 by Clifford "Baldy" Baldowski, reprinted by permission, from the *Atlanta Constitution.*

CONTENTS

UNIT I. FOUNDATIONS OF GOVERNMENT IN GEORGIA 1

UNIT II. THE LEGISLATIVE BRANCH 28

UNIT III. THE EXECUTIVE BRANCH 66

UNIT IV. THE JUSTICE SYSTEM 138

CHARTS, MAPS, AND GRAPHS

NOTE TO THE READER:

In the text, several "**Think About It**" questions are often placed *before* a reading. These questions will help you find the important ideas in the reading. On completing the reading, you may want to refer to the questions to make sure you understand the main ideas.

New words that appear in italics are often defined in the text. If an unfamiliar word is not defined in the text, check the glossary at the end of the book.

I FOUNDATIONS OF GOVERNMENT IN GEORGIA

Beginning of Government in Georgia
Government by the People

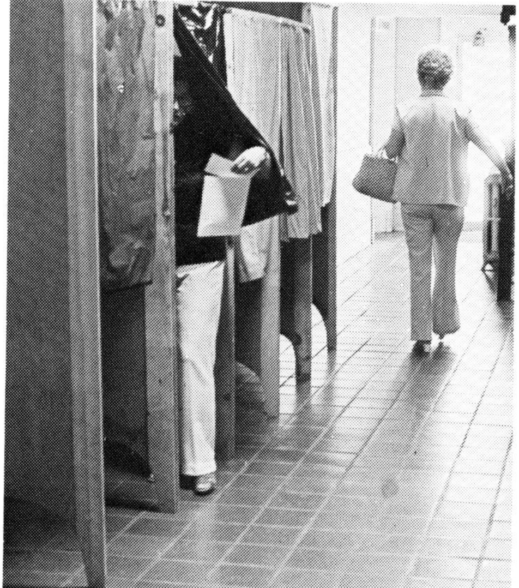

THE CONSTITUTION

OF THE

STATE OF GEORGIA

WHEREAS the conduct of the legiſlature of Great-Britain for many years paſt, has been ſo oppreſſive on the people of America, that of late years, they have plainly declared, and aſſerted a right to raiſe taxes upon the people of America, and to make laws to bind them in all caſes whatſoever, without their conſent; which conduct being repugnant to the common rights of mankind, hath obliged the Americans, as freemen, to oppoſe ſuch oppreſſive meaſures, and to aſſert the rights and privileges they are intitled to, by the laws of nature and reaſon; and accordingly it hath been done by the general conſent of all the people of the States of New-Hampſhire, Maſſachuſetts-Bay, Rhode-Iſland, Connecticut, New-York, New-Jerſey, Pennſylvania, the Counties of New-Caſtle, Kent and Suſſex on Delaware, Maryland, Virginia, North-Carolina, South-Carolina, and Georgia, given by their Repreſentatives met together in General Congreſs, in the city of Philadelphia.

AND WHEREAS it hath been recommended by the ſaid Congreſs on the fifteenth of May laſt, to the reſpective Aſſemblies and Conventions of the United States, where no government, ſufficient to the exigencies of their affairs, hath been hitherto eſtabliſhed, to adopt ſuch government, as may, in the opinion of the Repreſentatives of the people, beſt conduce to the happineſs, and ſafety of their conſtituents in particular, and America in general.

AND WHEREAS the Independence of the United States of America has been alſo declared, on the fourth day of July, one thouſand ſeven hundred and ſeventy ſix, by the ſaid Honorable Congreſs, and all political connection between them, and the Crown of Great-Britain is in conſequence thereof diſſolved.

WE

Introduction

GOVERNMENT: Who Needs It?

Frank Carson sat at the dining table reading through some business mail. Suddenly he shouted, "I am sick and tired of the government. I wish it would get off my back."

"Hey Dad, quiet down, will ya?" asked his 14-year-old son, Steve. I can't hear the TV.

"Then turn it off," ordered Mr. Carson.

"But I have to watch 'The Lawmakers'–it's a homework assignment," explained Steve.

"Lawmakers!" thundered his father. "You mean politicians. You turn them off right now. I've had it with politicians."

Steve flipped off the TV and slouched into the kitchen. He asked his mother, "What's the matter with him tonight?"

"Well, on top of the court hearing tomorrow, he just received something about a new state regulation on auto parts businesses. He says it's going to cost the company money to comply with it," explained Mrs. Carson.

"Darn right it is," added Mr. Carson coming into the kitchen. "This law is really going to cut into profits. The federal government, the state government, the city government–taxes, regulations! We'd be better off without any government."

Steve went up to bed thinking about his father's words "better off without any government." He thought, "I wonder how much better it would be."

The sound of his father's car woke Steve up. He looked at his alarm clock. Stopped! The power must have gone off! He dressed quickly and hurried downstairs.

"How's Dad this morning?" he asked.

"Much better," replied his mother. "He heard this morning that he doesn't have to appear in court and most likely he won't have to meet that new state regulation. He went off to the warehouse in a good mood."

"That's great," said Steve as he gulped down his breakfast.

"Would you please make a couple of stops on your way home this afternoon? I need a prescription filled and some stamps from the post office," said Mrs. Carson.

"Sure, Mom." Steve grabbed his backpack and hopped on his bike.

A block from his house, Steve was almost knocked off his bike by a car weaving from side to side. "Crazy drunk," thought Steve. Then he noticed how few cars seemed to be observing the 35-mph speed limit.

Suddenly a car and a pickup truck collided at the next intersection.

"What happened?" Steve asked a man standing on the corner. "Did someone run a red light?"

"Light's out," said the bystander. "Been lots of near misses this morning."

"Where's the crossing guard for the elementary school?"

The man laughed, "She didn't have to work today. Haven't you heard? There's no school."

"No school?"

"Certainly, didn't you hear about it?" The man looked surprised. Bewildered, Steve decided to pick up the things his mother wanted before heading home.

He pedalled over to the shopping plaza. Some merchants were boarding up their store windows. One was wearing a pistol on his hip. In front of the drugstore, a man with a shotgun appeared to be standing guard.

"What's going on?" asked Steve.

"Move on kid, before you get hurt," the man ordered.

"But I have to get a prescription for my mother," replied Steve nervously.

The man standing guard let Steve into the drugstore. "Can I get this prescription filled?" he asked.

"Sure," replied the pharmacist. "That is if you've got something to swap."

"Swap?"

"I'll take jewelry, gold, silver, and maybe something else of value, but no money."

"No money! Why?" Steve looked shocked.

"It's worthless now, didn't you hear?" asked the pharmacist.

Steve rode off on his bike. "This is weird," he thought. When he reached the post office, he stopped to read a large sign on the door, "Closed Until Further Notice."

He was thinking, "How can the post office close down?" when a tough-looking guy walked up to him.

"Nice bike, kid. Get off!" he ordered, flicking a knife in Steve's face.

Steve froze in terror. "But, this is my . . . ."

"It *was* yours, now it's mine," said the tough guy as he grabbed Steve by the throat. "The law is what I say it is. Ain't you heard? There ain't no government, no laws, no cops . . . ." He released Steve and rode off on the bike.

Steve ran, not looking back. He headed for his father's warehouse, his heart pounding as he raced through the streets.

Then he saw the smoke. A crowd was standing in front of the warehouse. "Where's my father? Isn't anybody going to help? Call the fire department," he shouted frantically.

"Are you kidding?" said a man staring at the flames. "Even if there was a fire department, there's no water to put it out."

"Dad, Dad!" screamed Steve.

"Steve, Steve. You'd better get up. You'll be late for school." His mother's voice seemed to float up the stairs.

Steve staggered out of bed. He could hear his father talking in the kitchen. Steve mumbled to himself, "No more government, huh? Boy, do I have an argument for you, Dad."

GOVERNMENT AND SOCIETY

What happened when government disappeared in Steve's dream. Disorder and confusion! Suddenly it was "every man for himself." Each person stood alone.

Actually three governments disappeared in Steve's dream: a local government which operated police and fire departments, a state government which provided criminal laws and courts, and the federal government which provided postal and monetary systems.

Why did Steve and his parents need these governments? For help in putting out a fire? For protection against thieves? For water service? Sure, but basically they needed government because they lived with other human beings in a society. A society is a group of people with a common way of life who share a common territory. (If they had lived "on their own" in the wilderness, they would really have had no need for government.)

Without organized direction and control—that is, without government—a society could not survive. There would be disorder and confusion as in Steve's dream. Everyone would have to be "on his own."

WHAT IS GOVERNMENT?

Government consists of people, and it consists of institutions. The people in government are the mayors, governors, legislators, judges, and thousands of other officials who make and carry out the laws. The institutions in government include written constitutions and laws, courts, taxes, legislatures, and law enforcement agencies. They are our established ways of doing things. Government, then, is (1) the people that help direct and control society, and (2) the institutions for carrying out that direction and control.

How much direction and control may a government exercise? In the United States, that's up to the people.

The United States is often called a *democracy* because its government is "of the people, by the people, and for the people." The government is *of* the people because final authority belongs to them. It is *by* the people because they exercise their authority through voting. It is *for* the people because it exists to help them meet their needs.

In chapter 1, you will be introduced to state government, the middle level in the American system of government. You will see that our United States Constitution and Georgia Constitution provide for government *of* and *for* the people. You will also see that powers for directing and controlling different parts of American society are divided between the national and state governments.

Chapter 2 focuses on elections and voting in Georgia: the means for "government *by* the people."

1 Beginning of Government In Georgia

In memory of Tomo-chi-chi
The Mico of the Yamacraws
The Companion of Oglethorpe
And the Friend and Ally of
The Colony of Georgia.
—Monument to Tomo-chi-chi, Savannah

Tomo-chi-chi stood on the high bluff above the Savannah River, watching as the boat pulled onto the shore. James Oglethorpe stepped ashore and climbed the bluff. It was February 12, 1733.

At their meeting, the English leader obtained permission from the Creek Mico, or chief, to bring settlers to the area. With these settlers would come a way of life that would eventually sweep away Tomo-chi-chi's town, his government, and—in time—the Indians themselves.

When Oglethorpe landed at Yamacraw Bluff, the main government of the Indians was the town government. Its main features were a chosen chief and a council which met to make decisions. Tomo-chi-chi was the chief of such a town government. When he gave his permission for the English to settle, he did not speak for all the Indians in Georgia. He spoke only for those living at Yamacraw. But his decision would help a new way of life, including a new kind of government, eventually extend to all of Georgia.

Before Georgia became a state, it had two governments. At first, Georgia was run as a sort of private corporation by the "Trustees for Establishing the Colony of Georgia in America." The English settlers had little say in their own government.

Later, in 1752, after the trustees became discouraged with their colony, they turned it over to the British government. Under royal governors appointed by the king, Georgia grew and prospered. But this form of government, too, would soon give way to government based on some rather new ideas.

IDEAS BEHIND AMERICAN GOVERNMENT

The English settlers who came to Georgia and the other colonies brought several important ideas about government with them.

The first of these ideas is known as "government by consent of the governed." People who believed in this idea argued that a government should rule only as long as the people give their consent (or agreement) to be governed.

James Oglethorpe, one of the 21 trustees who founded Georgia, was the colony's leader until 1743. He is shown here meeting with Tomo-chi-chi, chief of the Yamacraw Indians.

They said, "There is a contract between the people and the government. We, the people, will live up to our end of the agreement (we'll pay taxes and obey the laws, for instance) as long as government lives up to its end of the agreement (provides protection and justice and respects our rights, for instance)."

What if the government doesn't meet its obligations to the people? "Then we may take back our consent to be governed," went the argument.

A second idea the settlers brought with them is called "limited government." They argued, "The government is limited in its power by *natural law*. This law is higher than any government. It says we, the people, have natural rights–life, liberty, and property."

Can the government take away these rights? "No!" said the people who believed in this idea. "Government has no power to take away any of these rights because they come from God."

The third idea was "representative government." Supporters of this idea argued, "We, the people, have the right to elect persons to represent us in government decisionmaking which may affect our lives. Our elected representatives must be able to assemble to make laws, *levy* taxes, and deal with our local affairs."

THE MOVE TOWARD INDEPENDENCE

After the French and Indian War, which ended in 1763, the government in England began to tighten its control over the colonies. It began to require that colonists pay more of the cost of government.

Many colonists resented England's actions. They felt these actions violated their rights as Englishmen. They resisted the new laws and refused to pay new taxes imposed by a government in which they had no voice. The colonists' slogan became "no taxation without representation." By 1776, the colonies had declared their independence.

Of course, they had to win their independence, and the Revolutionary War would drag on for six years.

In 1776, while the fighting raged, the Continental Congress published the Declaration of Independence and a new nation came into being. Each colony was called on to set up a new state government. From then on the thirteen colonies became known as states.

The Declaration of Independence, mainly the work of Thomas Jefferson, set down some of the ideas on which the new state governments would be based.

It included the following ideas:

1. All men are created equal.
2. Everyone is born with certain rights–life, liberty, and the pursuit of happiness.
3. Government gets its power from the people.
4. The people can do away with a government that is unsatisfactory.

The first United States government, called the Second Continental Congress, served during the Revolutionary War. It drew up the *Articles of Confederation* which, after 1781, would be the basis of national government. Still, most people living in the thirteen former colonies thought of themselves, not as Americans, but as Georgians, New Yorkers, Virginians, and so forth. When it came to politics, they cared more about their state governments than any government of united states.

Constitutions

To set up the new state governments, the first thing state leaders did was to write constitutions. A constitution is a plan for the operation of government. It outlines the framework of a government and spells out its powers.

Most importantly, a constitution establishes a government *by law*. This means all laws passed by a government and all actions taken by government officials must be in accord with the constitution, the "supreme law of the land."

The thirteen state constitutions were not all the same, but generally they included the basic principles of government brought here by the colonists. These are the principles of representative, limited, and divided government.

Representative Government

All the state constitutions provided that the people should freely elect their representatives. But not everyone could vote. Laws about who could vote varied from state to state.

Limited Government

The state constitutions reflected the people's fear that government might threaten their rights. Strict limits were placed on what the new governments could and could not do. Most state constitutions included a Bill of Rights which prohibited the state governments from stepping on certain "freedoms." They guaranteed freedom of speech, assembly, the press, religion, and other liberties which the people regarded as natural rights.

Divided Government

To further prevent the growth of power in government, the state constitution writers divided the powers of government. There would be three branches–the legislative, the executive, and the judicial.

The power to make the law was given to the legislative branch. The power to carry out the law went to an executive branch. And, the power to settle disputes involving the law went to a judicial branch.

This feature of government—often called the "separation of powers"—did not mean that the three branches were independent. Rather, their powers were related in a system of checks and balances. No one branch would be able to control the others.

It took time to work out the idea of separation of powers in the state constitutions. At first the executive was a weak branch. Later, however, all state governments began to appear as shown in the diagram below.

THE UNITED STATES CONSTITUTION

THINK ABOUT IT

1. Why was the United States Constitution written to replace the Articles of Confederation?
2. What does the federal Constitution guarantee to the states? to a state's citizens?

For eight years after the Revolution (1781-1789), the national government operated under a constitution called the *Articles of Confederation*. This document did not have much impact. The thirteen independent states remained very independent.

The weak national government under the *Articles* could not prevent squabbling among the states. They continually quarreled over boundaries. They refused to respect each other's laws. They taxed each other's goods.

Many people were not satisfied with the *Articles*. In Philadelphia in 1787 a Constitutional Convention was called to write a new plan of union for the states. Representatives to the convention worked for three months to hammer out a plan. Their goal was to provide national unity and at the same time allow for differences

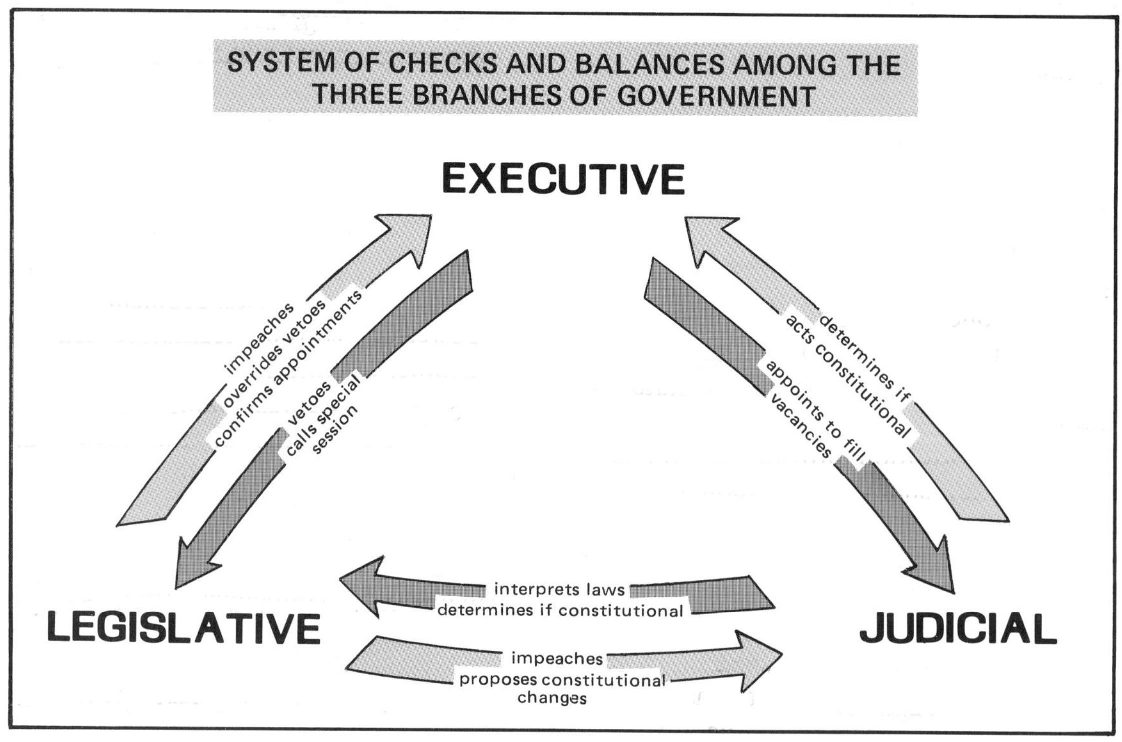

among the states. The result is our present Constitution of the United States.

The new Constitution provided for a federal system of government (see page 10). It included features of the thirteen state constitutions. The most important were representation, limited powers of government, and a separation of powers in three branches.

The new Constitution stated how powers would be divided between the national government and the state governments. It also made certain guarantees to the states and provided for relations between the states.

Guarantees

"The United States shall guarantee to every state in this union a republican form of government. . . ." This means no state can set up a government where the people have no voice. The people are guaranteed a representative democracy.

The Constitution also guarantees that the national government will protect each state from foreign invasion and, if requested, from domestic violence.

State-State Relations

A state's legal records (such as contracts, deeds, and licenses) must be honored in every other state. Further, a citizen cannot be denied any of his rights by moving from one state to another. The Constitution also provides for the extradition (or return) of fugitives from one state to another.

The Constitution provides for the admission of new states to the Union. No new state, however, can be carved out of an existing state (or states) without the agreement of the existing state legislature(s).

When the Constitutional Convention completed its work, the new Constitution was submitted to the states for adoption. On January 2, 1788, Georgia became the fourth state to accept the Constitution. About a year later, the new United States government officially came into being. The new Constitution was flexible enough to endure through 200 years of change.

STATE CONSTITUTIONS

On the other hand, state constitutions have undergone many changes. Generally, they have been more detailed and more easily outdated than the national constitution.

Most have had to be amended (changed) thousands of times and have been replaced in many states several times.*

Georgia Constitutions

Georgia has had nine state constitutions, those of 1777, 1789, 1798, 1861, 1865, 1868, 1877, 1945, and 1976. Only Louisiana, with eleven, has had more.

The earlier Georgia constitutions were rather short and sketchy. They provided for a small state government run completely by the legislature. Later constitutions were much longer and more detailed. They called for a larger state government with a true separation of powers among the three branches.

Georgia's first constitution was written in 1777. In 1789, this was replaced by a constitution more like the new Constitution of the United States. Problems with a too-powerful, corrupt legislature led to still another constitution in 1798.

In 1861 Georgia joined the Confederacy. The events of the Civil War and Reconstruction led to the adoption of four more state constitutions.

The Constitution of 1945 was adopted to replace a constitution which had become a "patchwork," containing over 300

*However, Massachusetts has had the same constitution since 1780, New Hampshire since 1784, and Vermont since 1793.

amendments. The Constitution of 1976, Georgia's present constitution, is largely a rewrite of the 1945 Constitution.

The Constitution of 1976 is in many ways like the United States Constitution (and the other 49 state constitutions).* It has a preamble (introduction) and a Bill of Rights. It has articles which deal with the structure of government, elections, the powers of the three branches, taxation, public education, and local government. And it has an amendment process.

Just as earlier constitutions had to be amended extensively, the Constitution of 1976 is undergoing the amendment process. At almost every general election, amendments proposed by the General Assembly are submitted to the people for a vote.

THE FEDERAL SYSTEM OF GOVERNMENT

Perhaps the most noteworthy feature of the Constitution of the United States is that it places one national government alongside a number of state governments.

THINK ABOUT IT

1. What are some powers that only the national government may exercise?
2. What are some that both the national and state governments may exercise?
3. What are the "reserved" powers of the states? Why is it impossible to list all their reserved powers?
4. How is the power relationship between state and local governments different from that between state and national governments?

Besides having three branches of government—legislative, executive, and judicial—the American system has three main levels of government—national, state, and local. For the citizen, it means an obligation to three governments. He or she may also be obliged to a city government, or a special district such as a school board.

This citizen is obliged to obey laws passed at each level of government and to pay taxes to each level. He or she is obliged to stay informed about politics at each level and to participate in elections at each level. Of course, this citizen receives government services from each level.

Each level of government has lawmaking powers, but those powers are not equal. If there is a conflict between the laws of different levels of government, the higher level prevails.

LEVELS OF LAWS IN GEORGIA
United States Constitution
United States Laws
Georgia Constitution
Georgia Laws
Local Ordinances

Hierarchy

Federalism

With the adoption of the United States Constitution, our present system of government was formally established. It is called a federal system. It consists of one central government—the national government*—and fifty sectional governments—the state governments.

Government powers are divided between Washington, D.C. and the fifty state capitals. In the U.S. Constitution, the people have delegated (or given) certain powers to the national government.

Here are some of the powers that belong only to the national government:

1. Issue coins and paper money

*However, the Georgia Constitution is much longer than the United States Constitution. Including amendments, it runs over 600,000 words.

*The national government is sometimes called the "federal government." National and state governments together make up the "federal system."

2. Declare war and keep an army and navy
3. Set up post offices
4. Regulate business between states
5. Make treaties and deal with other nations

Here are some areas in which both the national government and the state governments exercise power concurrently (at the same time):

1. *Levy* (set) taxes
2. Establish courts
3. Make and enforce laws
4. Take property for public use
5. Provide for the general welfare

The Constitution also gives the United States Congress the power to "make all laws which shall be necessary and proper for carrying into execution the foregoing powers. . . . " This is sometimes called the Constitution's "elastic" clause because it can be stretched to allow Congress to make laws on subjects not specifically listed in the Constitution.

To prevent too much power from being taken by the national government, the Constitution includes this statement:

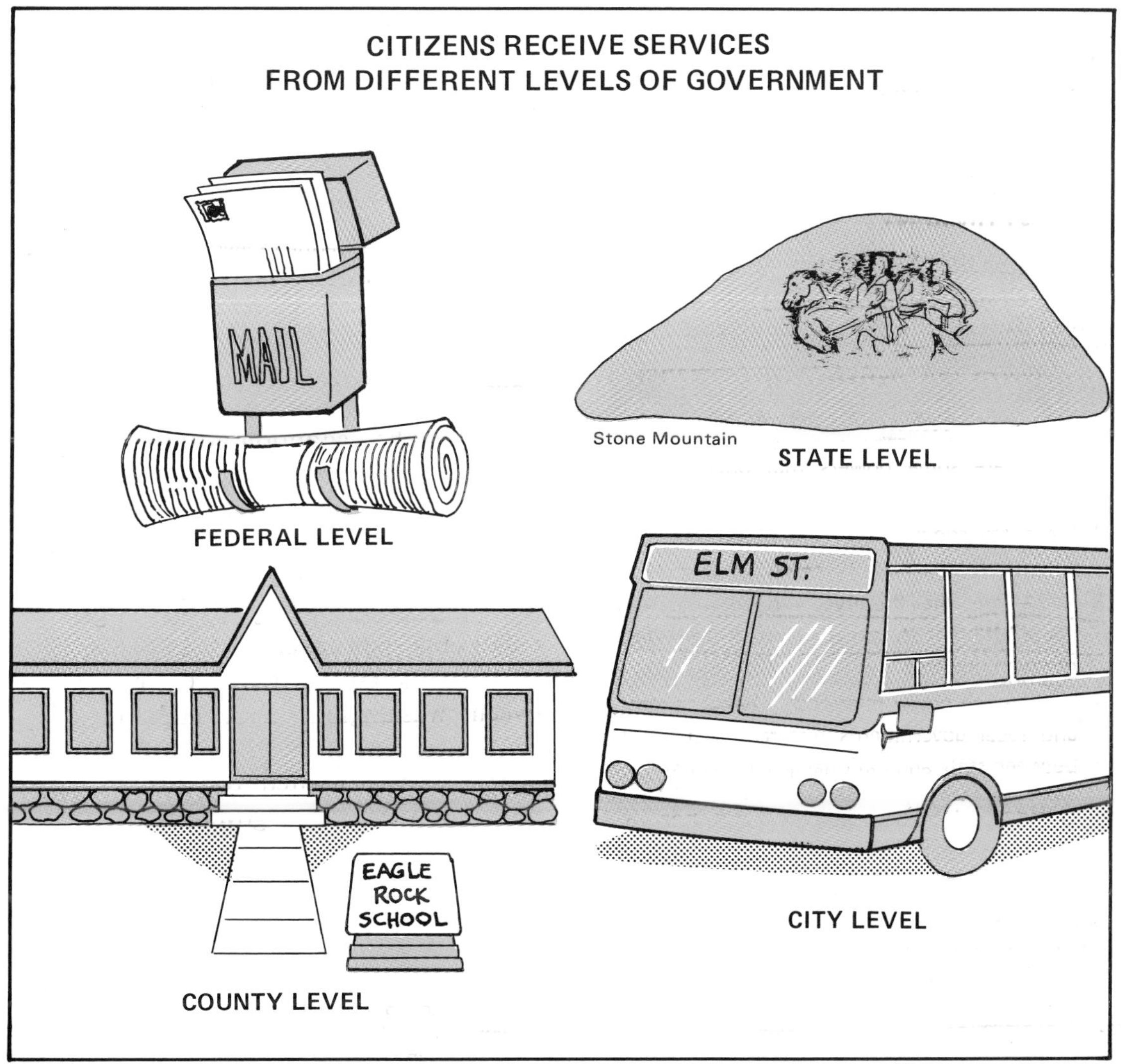

"The powers not delegated to the United States by the Constitution, nor prohibited by it to the States, are reserved to the States respectively, or to the people."

This means that the states have the power to make and enforce laws on just about any subject not mentioned in the Constitution.

Here are some of the things states do under their "reserved" powers:

1. Set up local governments
2. Provide for marriage, divorce, and child custody
3. Operate public schools and colleges
4. Regulate occupations and businesses
5. Conduct elections

Whatever a state government decides is needed to provide for public health, morals, safety, or welfare, it may do as long as it does not violate the Constitution. This power of the state is often referred to as its *police power*. This power, along with the power of *eminent domain* (the power to take private property for public use) and the *power of taxation*, forms the basis for most state actions.

The division of powers between the national government and the state governments is set by the Constitution. The national government alone cannot change it. Neither can the state governments. The division of powers can only be changed if the national government and two-thirds of the states agree to do so.

However, since the Constitution was adopted there has been much debate over the exact division of powers. The fiercest part of this debate resulted in the Civil War.

Federal and state laws have always overlapped. From the beginning of the federal system, two court systems, for example, have operated in each state. Taxes must go to support both.

In the last fifty years, as federal powers

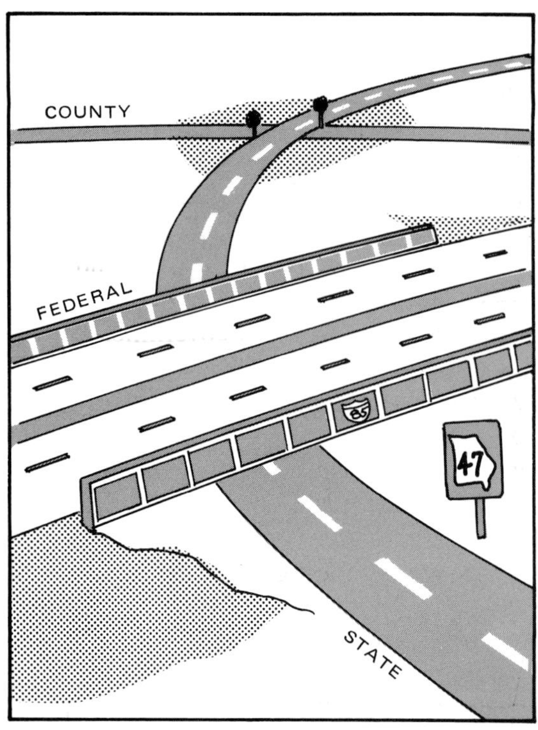

have gradually increased, this overlapping has increased. Many government services are the joint responsibility of national and state governments. Sometimes the two partners disagree on how to carry out and pay for services such as public education, health, and welfare.

Still, the federal system has adapted well to changing conditions. Thirteen states on the Atlantic seaboard have grown to fifty stretching a third of the way around the world. A small agricultural nation has become an industrial giant and a world leader. But the system has required no basic changes. or has it???

THE STATES AND LOCAL GOVERNMENT

Just as the thirteen original states delegated certain powers to the national government in 1787, the states have delegated certain powers to local governments. These local governments—called cities and counties in Georgia—are "creatures of the state." That is, they are created by the state and may be abolished by the state. Of course, a state can act only within the limits set by its state constitution.

The division of power between state governments and local governments is determined by the state alone. This is done through the state constitution and state laws.

In some ways, local governments function as agents of the state and federal governments. For example, county welfare departments carry out state public aid programs for needy persons. The state works through local governments to provide public education. For the most part, it depends on local governments to enforce the law.

In other ways, local governments operate as they see fit to deal with local needs. This is called "home rule." Counties have a certain amount of freedom to provide whatever services they wish. Cities have *charters* which, like constitutions, spell out their powers. Under these charters, some cities provide water and electricity to residents, operate public transportation systems, and build sports stadiums and concert halls.

However, a state government may take away any and all power of a local government, unless that power is protected by the state constitution. National and state governments are equal partners in the federal system, but state and local governments are not equal.

ACTIVITIES FOR CHAPTER 1

Class Discussion

A. Three important features of federal and state constitutions are (1) representative government, (2) limited government, and (3) divided government.

1. How do these features protect the people against too much government power?

2. What might happen if each of these features were not part of government? Give some examples.

B. The founders of the 13 original states and the United States spent a lot of time writing constitutions.

1. What is so important about having a constitution?

2. Would there be any danger in not having a constitution? Explain.

Writing Project

A student from a foreign country is visiting your school. The principal asks you to give the visitor a tour of the building and describe the courses you are taking. One of the questions you get is, "What is the Georgia government? I thought there was only one American government, the one in Washington." You try to think of a quick way to explain the federal system of government.

Assignment: Write out your explanation for the foreign visitor. Tell how the federal system got started and how powers are divided between one national government and 50 state governments.

2 Government By The People

The buzzer sounded at Crandall Manufacturing Company . . . lunchtime! Mary Stein left her workbench and headed for the coffee room. She got her lunch from the refrigerator and sat down at a long table with several other employees. Her friend Vickie sat across from her.

"Hey Mary, can you give me a ride home this afternoon? My car is in the shop," said Vickie.

"Sure," replied Mary. "But, I have to stop at the fire station first."

"Fire station!" Vickie sang out, causing everyone at the table to look up. "Why are you going there?"

"That's where I go to vote," explained Mary.

"Vote? What for?" grumbled Fred Smith who was sitting next to Vickie.

"It's election day today." Mary looked surprised. "Don't you vote, Fred?"

"Me? Naw, I never vote. Never have and never will," continued Fred, munching on his sandwich.

"Why's that?" asked Mary.

"Because I got better things to do than waste my time voting. That's why," said Fred with a sneer.

"But who you have running your government depends on your getting out and. . . ."

"I don't care about the sorry government. No politician ever did anything for me," growled Fred.

"Well, if you don't even bother to vote, you've got no right to gripe about what kind of politicians we have," snapped Mary.

"Wait a minute. . . ." Fred slammed his cola bottle down on the table. "Don't you tell me I can't gripe. This is a free country!"

"Sure, free because some of us vote," Mary replied sweetly.

Fred glared at her. The coffee room got quiet.

"I have never voted either," came a low voice from the far end of the table.

Everyone turned to look at Charlie Tayson, a new employee at Crandall.

"Welcome to the club," mumbled Fred Smith. "The smart club."

"I would vote if I could," continued Charlie, "but I am not allowed to."

"Why not?" asked Vickie.

"I am not an American citizen. . . yet." replied Charlie. "But, I go to class at night to learn to become a citizen. As soon as I am a citizen, I will register to vote. It is very important to me. I never had a chance to vote in Viet Nam. There was the war, and then the communists took over and. . . ." Charlie's voice trailed off.

"Well, two years from now, on election day, we'll both go vote. Right, Charlie?" Mary smiled.

"You know it," Charlie grinned back.

Fred Smith stomped out of the coffee room.

"Poor Fred," thought Mary to herself. "Poor, stupid Fred."

You can have government without voting, but you can't have government by the people without voting by the people. In the story introducing this chapter, Mary Stein understood this. Fred Smith didn't.

In Georgia, there are a lot of Mary Steins, people who see that their own votes are needed if government is to work for them. Unfortunately, there are also a lot of Fred Smiths, people who don't see the connection.

In recent elections, less than one-half of Georgia's voting age population voted. This gives Georgia one of the worst voting records of any of the fifty states.

PERCENTAGE OF VOTING AGE POPULATION CASTING VOTES: 1960-1980 PRESIDENTIAL ELECTION

	1960	1964	1968	1972	1976	1980
U.S.	62.8	61.9	60.9	55.5	54.3	53.3*
Georgia	29.3	43.3	43.9	37.9	43.3	43.1

*Estimate.

What are the reasons for non-voting? Do people not know the importance of voting? Do they think that elections are dishonest or unfair? Are they afraid someone will find out who they voted for? Is it too hard to register or to vote? The readings in this chapter will, perhaps, answer some of these questions.

VOTING RIGHTS

Under the law, all U.S. citizens are equal members in the nation. All deserve equal treatment from their government. However, not all Americans have always received equal treatment from their government. Black Americans were legally denied the right to vote until after the Civil War. Women were not allowed to vote until 1920. American Indians could not vote until 1924. Even after laws were passed to guarantee equal treatment, some Americans were illegally denied equality as citizens. They were treated as "second class citizens." They were required to pay taxes and obey the laws, but they had no voice in setting those taxes or passing those laws.

Some big changes have occurred in the last 30 years, though. As a result of the movement for civil rights—a movement for equal treatment—many more Americans now have full membership in the nation. Although the civil rights movement had many targets, one of its most important goals was voting rights (suffrage)—for all citizens.

CASTING YOUR VOTE

Today the right to vote means the right to cast a secret *ballot* and have that ballot counted the same as any other person's ballot. This was not always so in the United States.

THINK ABOUT IT

1. How has the voting procedure been improved since the first elections in Georgia?
2. How many different kinds of elections may appear on a ballot?
3. How may a voter participate in direct decisionmaking?
4. Who is in charge of running elections in each county? Who supervises elections statewide?

In the colonial period, voting was usually by hand or voice. During the Revolutionary War, Georgia became one of the first states to use a paper ballot. Although the paper ballot was an improvement, it did not insure secrecy. The voter had to write out the name of his choice with election officials and other persons looking on.

Later, ballots printed up by the political parties were handed out at polling places. This ballot, which was often called a "party ticket" because it looked like a railroad ticket, listed the party's candidates. Depending on which party ticket a voter took and placed in the ballot box, onlookers knew how a person voted. Voters could still be pressured to vote one way or another. Votes could be bought and sold.

The ballot used today is a secret one. The system works like this. An official ballot, containing the names of all candi-

Voting Is Easy !

IF YOU ARE

18

(17½ now, but will be 18 by election)

OF GEORGIA AND COUNTY

A CITIZEN OF THE UNITED STATES

YOU ARE ELIGIBLE TO REGISTER TO VOTE

YOU MUST first go to the Board of Registrars' office which is usually in the courthouse of your county, or if you are a student in a private or public high school, or an area vocational school, you may register with the principal, assistant principal, or director of your school.

THERE the Registrar will inform you of the procedure and you will register.

ON PRIMARY OR ELECTION DAY

go to your election district polling place.

NOW YOU ARE ready to vote.

YOU then can vote for the persons you wish to run your government.

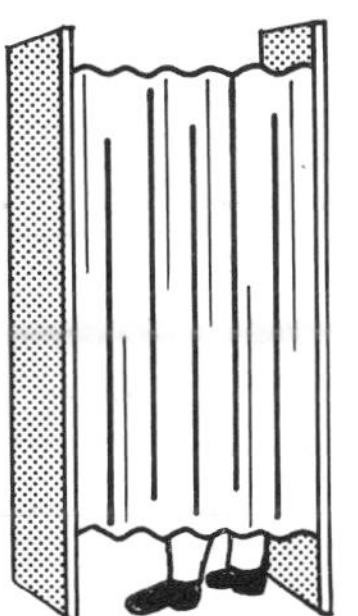

dates, is printed by the government. At the polling place, the voter picks up a ballot and goes into a voting booth to mark it in secret. (Several counties use a punch-card ballot—called a vote recorder.) After leaving the booth, the voter drops the ballot in a locked ballot box.

In larger cities, voting machines have replaced the paper ballot. In the voting machine booth, the voter pulls a lever next to each candidate's name. When the voter leaves the booth, the levers pulled flip up recording the votes. It's all in secret.

Elections in Georgia are conducted under the Georgia Election Code. This set of laws applies to any general and special elections in the state to fill any federal, state, or county office. (It does not apply to city elections.)

The purpose of the Code is to make sure that all elections are conducted fairly and that they follow the same rules throughout the state. Under the Code, the Georgia secretary of state, the State Election Board, and an election superintendent in each county run the elections.

The secretary of state is the chief elections officer. He decides the form of ballots and *certifies* which candidates have qualified to be listed on the ballot. He also furnishes to the counties all materials needed to conduct elections and receives the election results from each county. His office computes the votes and publishes the results.

In most counties, the judge of the probate court serves as the election superintendent. The superintendent advertises upcoming elections and sets up the polling places. He or she also appoints and supervises poll officers and computes and publishes the election results in the county.

How Many Candidates Does a Voter Have to Choose From?

Not all government officials are elected. In fact, there are many more appointed officials than there are elected ones.

However, at each level of government—local, state, and federal—the most important officials are elected. They appoint the other officials and direct them in their work.

What officials may a Georgia citizen vote for? Perhaps the best way to answer the question is to look at a ballot.

The sample ballot on page 19 shows three kinds of elections—federal, state and county—in which a voter may participate.*

At the federal level, the only elected officials are president and vice-president, United States senators (2 for each state), and United States representatives (10 for Georgia).

By far the greatest number of races in which a citizen may vote is at the state level:

Judicial Officers
Supreme Court Justices
Appeals Court Judges
Superior Court Judges
District Attorneys

Executive Officers
Governor
Lieutenant Governor
Secretary of State
Attorney General
Comptroller General
Superintendent of Schools
Commissioner of Agriculture
Commissioner of Labor
Public Service Commissioners

Legislative Officers
State Senators
State Representatives

At the county level, the number of elected officials varies. Some counties have, for example, elected school boards. Others have appointed boards. Also, the number

*City residents may also elect city officials.

(Tear off) (Tear off)

OFFICIAL

BALLOT

NUMBER STRIP

STATE OF GEORGIA

.................................County

.................................Election District

General Election – November 7, 1978

No.

(Tear off before depositing ballot in ballot box) (Tear off before depositing in ballot box)

OFFICIAL

BALLOT

STATE OF GEORGIA

.................................County

.................................Election District

General Election – November 7, 1978

To vote a straight party ticket, place a cross (X) or check (√) mark in the square in the party column opposite the name of the party of your choice.

If you do not desire to vote a straight party ticket, then place a cross (X) or check (√) mark in the square opposite the name of each candidate you choose to vote for.

To vote for a person whose name is not on the ballot, manually write his name, accompanied by the title of the office involved, in the write-in column.

If you spoil your ballot, do not erase, but ask for a new ballot. Use only pen or pencil.

DEMOCRATIC PARTY

☐ To vote a straight Democratic Party ticket, place a cross (X) or check (√) mark in the square to the left.

FOR UNITED STATES SENATE
☐ SAM NUNN

FOR GOVERNOR
☐ GEORGE BUSBEE

FOR LIEUTENANT GOVERNOR
☐ ZELL MILLER

FOR SECRETARY OF STATE
☐ BEN W. FORTSON, JR.

FOR ATTORNEY GENERAL
☐ ARTHUR K. BOLTON

FOR COMMISSIONER OF AGRICULTURE
☐ TOMMY IRVIN

FOR COMPTROLLER GENERAL
☐ JOHNNIE L. CALDWELL

FOR STATE SCHOOL SUPERINTENDENT
☐ CHARLES McDANIEL

FOR COMMISSIONER OF LABOR
☐ SAM CALDWELL

FOR PUBLIC SERVICE COMMISSIONER
(To Succeed Mac Barber)
☐ MAC BARBER

FOR PUBLIC SERVICE COMMISSIONER
(To Succeed Ben T. Wiggins)
☐ BILLY LOVETT

FOR ASSOCIATE JUSTICE, SUPREME COURT OF GEORGIA
(To Succeed Jesse Groover Bowles for the unexpired term of William B. Gunter, resigned, beginning November 7, 1978, expiring December 31, 1980)
☐ JESSE GROOVER BOWLES

FOR ASSOCIATE JUSTICE, SUPREME COURT OF GEORGIA
(To Succeed Robert H. Hall)
☐ ROBERT H. HALL

FOR ASSOCIATE JUSTICE, SUPREME COURT OF GEORGIA
(To Succeed Harold N. Hill, Jr.)
☐ HAROLD N. HILL, JR.

FOR ASSOCIATE JUSTICE, SUPREME COURT OF GEORGIA
(To Succeed Thomas O. Marshall for the unexpired term of G. Conley Ingram, resigned, beginning November 7, 1978, expiring December 31, 1982)
☐ THOMAS O. MARSHALL

FOR JUDGE, COURT OF APPEALS OF GEORGIA
(To Succeed Harold R. Banke for the unexpired term of Irwin W. Stolz, resigned, beginning November 7, 1978, expiring December 31, 1980)
☐ HAROLD R. BANKE

FOR JUDGE, COURT OF APPEALS OF GEORGIA
(To Succeed A. W. Birdsong, Jr. for the unexpired term of Thomas O. Marshall, resigned, beginning November 7, 1978, expiring December 31, 1980)
☐ A. W. BIRDSONG, JR.

FOR JUDGE, COURT OF APPEALS OF GEORGIA
(To Succeed Braswell D. Deen, Jr.)
☐ BRASWELL D. DEEN, JR.

FOR JUDGE, COURT OF APPEALS OF GEORGIA
(To Succeed William LeRoy McMurray, Jr.)
☐ WILLIAM LeROY McMURRAY, JR.

FOR JUDGE, COURT OF APPEALS OF GEORGIA
(To Succeed Arnold Shulman for the unexpired term of H. Sol Clark, resigned, beginning November 7, 1978, expiring December 31, 1978)
☐ ARNOLD SHULMAN

FOR JUDGE, COURT OF APPEALS OF GEORGIA
(For a full six year term beginning January 1, 1979)
☐ ARNOLD SHULMAN

☐ FOR U. S. REPRESENTATIVE IN 96TH CONGRESS FROM THE .... CONGRESSIONAL DISTRICT OF GEORGIA

☐ FOR STATE SENATOR FROM .... DISTRICT

☐ FOR STATE REPRESENTATIVE IN THE GENERAL ASSEMBLY FROM .... DISTRICT, POST NO. ....

☐ FOR JUDGE, SUPERIOR COURT OF THE .... JUDICIAL CIRCUIT

☐ FOR DISTRICT ATTORNEY OF THE .... JUDICIAL CIRCUIT

☐ FOR JUDGE OF STATE COURT OF .... COUNTY

☐ FOR SOLICITOR OF STATE COURT OF .... COUNTY

☐ FOR COUNTY COMMISSIONER OF .... (District or Post when applicable)

☐ FOR COUNTY BOARD OF EDUCATION OF .... (District or Post when applicable)

☐ FOR ANY OTHER COUNTY OR DISTRICT OFFICE

REPUBLICAN PARTY

☐ To vote a straight Republican Party ticket, place a cross (X) or check (√) mark in the square to the left.

FOR UNITED STATES SENATE
☐ JOHN W. STOKES

FOR GOVERNOR
☐ RODNEY M. COOK

FOR LIEUTENANT GOVERNOR
☐ JAMES W. (JIM) WEBB, II

DEMOCRATIC PARTY

☐ To vote a straight Democratic Party ticket, place a cross (X) or check (√) mark in the square to the left.

FOR UNITED STATES SENATE
☐ SAM NUNN

FOR GOVERNOR
☐ GEORGE BUSBEE

FOR LIEUTENANT GOVERNOR
☐ ZELL MILLER

FOR SECRETARY OF STATE
☐ BEN W. FORTSON, JR.

FOR ATTORNEY GENERAL
☐ ARTHUR K. BOLTON

FOR COMMISSIONER OF AGRICULTURE
☐ TOMMY IRVIN

☐ YES
14 ALL COUNTIES
Shall the Constitution be amended so as to change the provisions relating to nonprofit bingo games so as to authorize the General Assembly to legalize, define, and regulate nonprofit bingo games?
☐ NO

☐ FOR U. S. REPRESENTATIVE IN 96TH CONGRESS FROM THE .... CONGRESSIONAL DISTRICT OF GEORGIA

☐ FOR STATE SENATOR FROM .... DISTRICT

☐ FOR STATE REPRESENTATIVE IN THE GENERAL ASSEMBLY FROM .... DISTRICT, POST NO. ....

☐ FOR JUDGE, SUPERIOR COURT OF THE .... JUDICIAL CIRCUIT

☐ FOR JUDGE OF STATE COURT OF .... COUNTY

☐ FOR SOLICITOR OF STATE COURT OF .... COUNTY

☐ FOR COUNTY COMMISSIONER OF .... (District or Post when applicable)

☐ FOR COUNTY BOARD OF EDUCATION OF .... (District or Post when applicable)

☐ FOR ANY OTHER COUNTY OR DISTRICT OFFICE

WRITE-IN CANDIDATES

To vote for a person whose name is not on the ballot, manually write his name, accompanied by the title of the office involved, in this column.

Proposed Constitutional Amendments

If you desire to vote FOR a proposed Amendment, place a cross (X) or check (√) mark in the square opposite the word "Yes". If you desire to vote AGAINST a proposed Amendment, place a cross(X) or check (√) mark in the square opposite the word "No".

1 ☐ YES ☐ NO — ALL COUNTIES
Shall the Constitution be amended so as to completely revise Article II relating to the elective franchise?

2 ☐ YES ☐ NO — ALL COUNTIES
Shall the Constitution be amended so as to completely revise Article X relating to retirement systems and educational scholarships and to change other provisions of the Constitution in connection with such revision?

3 ☐ YES ☐ NO — ALL COUNTIES
Shall the Constitution be amended so as to provide that a special commission shall be authorized to incorporate amendments into the Constitution?

4 ☐ YES ☐ NO — ALL COUNTIES
Shall the Constitution be amended so as to provide for four-year terms for members of the General Assembly effective with those members elected at the general election in 1978 and thereafter?

5 ☐ YES ☐ NO — ALL COUNTIES
Shall the Constitution be amended so as to permit the issuance of general obligation debt of the State for the purpose of constructing, acquiring, improving, extending and enlarging buildings and facilities for public and independent school systems?

6 ☐ YES ☐ NO — ALL COUNTIES
Shall the Constitution be amended so as to authorize the State Board of Education to establish and maintain a curriculum laboratory, to charge reasonable fees, and to retain the revenues produced therefrom for the purposes of such curriculum laboratory?

7 ☐ YES ☐ NO — ALL COUNTIES
Shall the Constitution be amended so as to provide the circumstances under which the authority and obligation of the governing authorities of counties which have wholly or partly within their boundaries a city of not less than 200,000 population to levy a tax for educational purposes not to exceed 1½ mills on all property located within the county, including property located within any independent school district, upon the request of the boards of education of such counties shall be terminated?

8 ☐ YES ☐ NO — ALL COUNTIES
Shall the Constitution be amended so as to provide that any disabled veteran who is a citizen and resident of Georgia shall be granted an exemption from all ad valorem taxes on the vehicle he owns and on which he actually places the free HV motor vehicle license tag he receives from the State of Georgia?

9 ☐ YES ☐ NO — ALL COUNTIES
Shall the Constitution be amended so as to authorize the General Assembly to provide for additional penalty assessments in criminal cases and provide that the proceeds derived therefrom may be used for the purpose of providing training to law enforcement officers and prosecuting officials?

10 ☐ YES ☐ NO — ALL COUNTIES
Shall the Constitution be amended so as to provide that when private property is taken or damaged for any public transportation purposes by the State and the counties and the municipalities of the State, just and adequate compensation therefor may be paid when the same has been finally fixed and determined as provided by law?

11 ☐ YES ☐ NO — ALL COUNTIES
Shall the Constitution be amended so as to authorize the General Assembly to exempt from the return of, or payment of the ad valorem tax on, intangible personal property when the reasonable costs, as specified by law, of receiving, processing, and other administration of an intangible personal property tax return exceeds the liability of the taxpayer for the tax?

12 ☐ YES ☐ NO — ALL COUNTIES
Shall the Constitution be amended so as to authorize the General Assembly to exempt swine, bovines (cattle), and horses from all ad valorem taxation?

13 ☐ YES ☐ NO — ALL COUNTIES
Shall the Constitution be amended so as to authorize the General Assembly to provide by general law for granting additional powers to counties or municipalities, or both, to allow such political subdivisions to establish and maintain more effective redevelopment programs and to provide for other matters relative thereto?

14 ☐ YES ☐ NO — ALL COUNTIES
Shall the Constitution be amended so as to change the provisions relating to nonprofit bingo games so as to authorize the General Assembly to legalize, define, and regulate nonprofit bingo games?

15 ☐ YES ☐ NO — ALL COUNTIES
Shall the Constitution be amended so as to authorize the General Assembly to provide by general law for the recall of public officials who hold elective office?

16 ☐ YES ☐ NO — ALL COUNTIES
Shall the Constitution be amended so as to provide for the effective date of amendments to the Constitution?

17 ☐ YES ☐ NO — ALL COUNTIES
Shall the Constitution be amended so as to provide that certain property located within any county of this State having a population of 600,000 or more according to the United States Decennial Census of 1970 or any future such census which is owned by a nonprofit corporation organized for the primary purpose of encouraging cooperation between parents and teachers to promote the education and welfare of children and youth shall be exempted from all State, county, municipal and school taxation, including such taxation to pay interest on and retire bonded indebtedness?

18 ☐ YES ☐ NO — ALL COUNTIES
Shall the Constitution be amended so as to increase the homestead exemption from $12,500.00 to $25,000.00 for disabled veterans who have been disabled due to loss, or loss of use, of both lower extremities, such as to preclude locomotion without the aid of braces, crutches, canes, or a wheelchair, or blindness in both eyes, having only light perception, plus loss, or loss of use, of one lower extremity, or due to the loss, or loss of use, of one lower extremity together with residuals of organic disease or injury which so affects the functions of balance or propulsion as to preclude locomotion without resort to a wheelchair and to provide for a homestead exemption equal to the homestead exemption received by the veteran during his lifetime for his unremarried widow or minor children so long as his unremarried widow or minor children continue to actually occupy the home as a residence and homestead?

☐ YES — ALL COUNTIES
Shall the Constitution be amended so as to authorize the General Assembly to provide by law for ...

22 ☐ YES ☐ NO — ALL COUNTIES
Shall the Constitution be amended so as to authorize the General Assembly to provide by law for a health insurance plan for retired public school teachers and to further authorize the General Assembly to appropriate funds to finance the administration of the plan and the employer contributions of such retired persons?

23 ☐ YES ☐ NO — ALL COUNTIES
Shall the Constitution be amended so as to provide for funds, insurance or a fund or a combination thereof for the purpose of providing indemnification with respect to the death of any law enforcement officer, fireman or prison guard killed in the line of duty?

24 ☐ YES ☐ NO — ALL COUNTIES
Shall the Constitution be amended so as to require a notice of candidacy of write-in candidates in special elections?

25 ☐ YES ☐ NO — ALL COUNTIES
Shall the Constitution be amended so as to change the methods and procedures for overriding the Governor's veto of bills enacted by the General Assembly?

26 ☐ YES ☐ NO — ALL COUNTIES
Shall the Constitution be amended so as to provide for the transfer of all existing municipally owned or operated sanitary landfills or garbage disposal systems located within the unincorporated area of any county of this State having a population of 600,000 or more according to the United States Decennial Census of 1970 or any future such census, or within any municipality located wholly or partially within any such county, together with the personal property, debts, assets and employees thereof to such county for operation of said sanitary landfills or garbage disposal systems; and to provide that no municipality located wholly or partially within any such county may operate a sanitary landfill or garbage disposal system?

27 ☐ YES ☐ NO — ALL COUNTIES
Shall the Constitution be amended so as to authorize the General Assembly to create a unified municipal/county water and sewer system between any county having a population of 600,000 or more according to the United States Decennial Census of 1970 or any future such census, and the largest municipality lying wholly or partially therein?

28 ☐ YES ☐ NO — ALL COUNTIES
Shall the Constitution be amended so as to authorize the General Assembly to enact general, local or special laws applicable to any county of this State having a population of 600,000 or more according to the United States Decennial Census of 1970 or any future such census, and applicable to any municipality located wholly or partially within such county, so as to provide for the preparation and annual updating, by such county governing authority, of a comprehensive plan for all of the unincorporated county, and to provide for a countywide framework plan which shall consist of the adopted comprehensive plans of each municipality in such county, which has developed a comprehensive plan along with the comprehensive plan for the unincorporated portion of such county?

29 ☐ YES ☐ NO — ALL COUNTIES
Shall the Constitution be amended so as to provide that under certain conditions the General Assembly shall be authorized by law to provide requirements relative to the financing of services by counties of this State having a population of 600,000 or more according to the United States Decennial Census of 1970 or any future such census and for other matters relative thereto?

30 ☐ YES ☐ NO — ALL COUNTIES
Shall the Constitution be amended so as to provide for the transfer of all existing library facilities and services located within any county of this State having a population of 600,000 or more according to the United States Decennial Census of 1970 or any future such census and within any municipality located wholly or partially within any such county, together with the property, with certain exceptions, debts, assets, and employees thereof, to the countywide library service; to designate such facilities and services as, and make them a part of, the countywide library service; to provide that such county shall be the funding government of the countywide library service; and to provide for a library board of trustees who shall administer the countywide library service?

31 ☐ YES ☐ NO — ALL COUNTIES
Shall the Constitution be amended so as to authorize the General Assembly to enact general, local or special laws applicable to any county of this state having a population of 600,000 or more according to the United States Decennial Census of 1970 or any future such census, and applicable to any municipality located wholly or partially within such county, so as to provide for the assessment of property in any such county or municipality by a board of assessors; to establish county boards of equalization within any such county and for other matters relative thereto?

32 ☐ YES ☐ NO — ALL COUNTIES
Shall the Constitution be amended so as to authorize the General Assembly by law to require the tax receiver, tax collector, or tax commissioner of any county of this State having a population of 600,000 or more according to the United States Decennial Census of 1970 or any future such census to receive tax returns of and collect taxes due to the largest municipality located wholly or partially within any such county and to any or all other consenting municipalities located wholly or partially within such county at no charge to said municipalities?

33 ☐ YES ☐ NO — ALL COUNTIES
Shall the Constitution be amended so as to provide that the requirement that 51% of the registered voters in each county school district or independent school system concerned in a proposed merger thereof shall apply only in counties having a population of more than 600,000 according to the United States Decennial Census of 1970?

34 ☐ YES ☐ NO — ALL COUNTIES
Shall the Constitution be amended so as to change the definition of the term 'income' with respect to determining the right to the $10,000.00 homestead exemption for certain disabled persons and persons 65 years of age or older of Fulton County so that the term 'income' shall not include Federal old-age, survivors or disability insurance benefits and benefits under the Federal Railroad Retirement Act?

35 ☐ YES ☐ NO — ALL COUNTIES
Shall the Constitution be amended so as to create the City of Conyers Public Facilities Authority, to provide for the powers, authorities and duties of such Authority, to authorize such Authority to issue its revenue bonds and to provide for the method and manner of such issuance and for the validation thereof, to authorize the Authority to contract with the City of Conyers and other public bodies, and to authorize the City of Conyers to contract with the Authority for the use by said City or its residents of any facilities or services of the Authority?

☐ YES — ALL COUNTIES
Shall the Constitution be amended so as to create the Downtown Americus Authority and to provide for the powers, authority and duties of such Authority, ... the Authority to issue its ...

of commissioners is not the same in all counties. In all Georgia counties, however, county commissioners, sheriffs, judges of the probate court, and clerks of the superior court are elected.

Federal, state, and county elections are regularly held every two years. In addition to regular elections held in November, special elections may be held most anytime. For example, if an official resigns in the middle of a term, a special election may be held to fill the position.

Another kind of special election is known as a "recall." A recall election is used to remove certain officials from office before their term of office ends. If a person is removed from office, then another special election follows to fill the vacant office.

Voting on Questions

Besides voting on persons running for office, voters may also vote on questions and issues. This kind of voting is an example of direct decisionmaking by the people.

Amendments to the Georgia Constitution are regularly placed on the ballot for a "yes" or "no" vote. In special "bond issue" elections, voters can say "yes" or "no" to whether government should borrow money for special projects such as a new high school.

All in all, the average Georgia voter has many chances to use the ballot.

INTERVIEW WITH A GEORGIA SECRETARY OF STATE

Ben Fortson was secretary of state from 1946 until his death in 1979. He was confined to a wheelchair since an auto accident early in life. But he put more energy into his work than many government officials. His office at the state capitol was always open to citizens. Visitors would just as likely find him working on a Saturday as on a weekday.

Mr. Fortson was in charge of Georgia's elections for over 30 years. He worked hard to give the people the kind of elections he felt were needed to have government by the people. Much of the credit for fair, honest elections in Georgia today goes to Mr. Fortson.

This interview took place in the winter of 1978 just a few months before Mr. Fortson died.

THINK ABOUT IT

1. According to Mr. Fortson, why do we have elections?
2. Why don't more people participate in elections?
3. What was Mr. Fortson's attitude toward being secretary of state?

Mr. Fortson, you've been involved in Georgia elections for many years—first as a member of the General Assembly and, since 1946, as secretary of state. Have elections changed much during those years?

Tremendously. The change has been almost total. We had very few laws governing elections in those days. Political parties held the primary. And, we didn't have but one party, the Democratic Party. So, if you were nominated in the primary held by the party officials themselves, why that was as good as being elected. Except when there was a presidential election. Then we would have a good many people voting Republican. Always did.

Then with the federal court decision doing away with the white primary, the polls were open to all people.

Since I came into office in '46, the election laws have been tightened and strengthened. The General Assembly has had a very fine attitude toward correcting anything wrong in the elections to give every person an equal chance.

The purpose in having an election. . . it's not for the parties, not for the candidates. The whole purpose of an election, purely and simply, is to allow a person—a legitimate voter—to come in and vote like he wants to, in secret, and to have that vote counted, to have it tabulated, and to have it added in the final results. And to do that without any attempt by those who run the election to influence or suggest or do anything except give the people the opportunity to vote.

That's my main idea in being secretary of state. Government should not exist unless it gives a service to the people. If it gives no service, it ought to be done away with.

So, with that in mind and with the idea that the success of our type of government rests upon elections, I can say elections are the most important thing we do in this country.

Are there still places in Georgia where it's difficult to insure fair elections?

We have about 140-145 counties in Georgia that do a marvelous job—an honest, decent job in running elections. There may be some errors, but not on purpose. And, it's getting better.

But, we also have some areas in the state that don't care. They do not try to straighten things out. Nobody from the outside—no court or anybody else—can do anything about it until the people in the county themselves take a hold and make the change.

Is there any one part of the election code that is especially hard to enforce?

It used to be that at polling places candidates and their supporters would grab voters by the arm and try to convince them at the last minute. It made some polling places so obnoxious that voters wouldn't go through.

Now, the General Assembly has stopped that. No one can come into a polling area unless he is a voter. No candidate can come in except to vote. He votes and gets out. He can say nothing to anybody. He can't distribute anything within 250 feet of a polling place.

It's a hard law, and it's working to the good of elections. But it's the most difficult part of the election code to enforce.

What about registration? Hasn't that changed a lot since 1946?

There's not but a few requirements now. First, you've got to be a citizen of the United States. Then you've got to be 18 years of age and be a resident, which means, "I'm here, I intend to stay here" . . . provided you're not a criminal who's not been pardoned and you haven't been declared insane or incompetent.

Dead people can't register! Now that sounds foolish, but there was a time when worlds of dead people's names remained on the voter list in certain counties. That led to fraud. Somebody knowing about it would go into a polling place and claim they were so and so. "Ah, yes you're on the list. Go ahead and vote." That's not as common as it used to be.

With it being easier to register and vote today, why don't more voters turn out on election day?

Everybody's going to let George do it. "I want to take a trip. I want to take my children somewhere or my wife out." Today, in the minds of too many people, there's not that keen sense of value to voting.

We are more and more a generation of watching television and going out. People always have something else to do.

What about running for office? There are usually dozens of unopposed candidates on the ballot. Isn't it much easier to run for office today?

Yes, I would say it's easier. And, there are more people running. I hate to use the term "unqualified," but I would say there are more people running today—qualified and unqualified—because it's easier to be a candidate.

But, there are still many who are unopposed.

Mostly, those who are unopposed are ones who already hold office. And there doesn't seem to be anything too much against them. So nobody runs against them because they think it'll cost too much to beat 'em. And it might.

Except for your first campaign, you yourself haven't had serious opposition. Why is that?

Well, I couldn't tell you—except for this reason, I reckon. I run an open office. We do our best to help people. That's the purpose of this office.

I'm not interested in anything except service to the people. When I got hurt I wasn't expected to live but about five years. So life means more to me in giving than in getting. And, I have many friends all over Georgia who know that anybody can come in here, get anything, see anything. We've got nothing to hide. That's how I try to act. That's the only reason.

It seems to me that with your responsibility to see that everyone else's election is fair and square, your own office has to be non-political; has to be above the political battles. Is your office ever really involved in politics?

No sir, it's not. Now I run as a Democrat, always have. But in this office, we don't ask anyone what their religion is or what their politics are. We treat them all alike. I don't support anybody. I don't ever get involved in anybody else's campaign. Never have.

And, when I run, I never allow anybody in this office to put one penny in my campaign. I won't take it. I won't let them do it unknown to me. I tell them if I find it out, I'll fire them.

What's it take to be effective in this office?

Honesty!

POLITICS AND PARTIES

Politics—a part of any political system—is something like a game. The aim is to win and hold control of government and to influence society through government's powers. To achieve these goals, certain tactics and strategies must be used. Those who play the game regularly are called politicians. Some play the game better than others. They gain political power and become leaders in government. Most play fairly, but some cheat.

THINK ABOUT IT

1. What do political parties do?
2. How are parties involved in elections in Georgia?
3. What is the purpose of having a primary? A general election?
4. How does a candidate get on the primary ballot? On the general election ballot?

Signs seen in Georgia at election time.

Political Parties

Political parties formed when people who agreed on certain public issues began to unite into one group. Those with other ideas would also band together.

What is the purpose of having political parties? For one thing, they provide a way for people to combine their efforts to influence politics. Parties may take sides on issues. Parties also work to get laws passed.

Most important, political parties nominate (or select) candidates to run for election to local, state, and federal offices. Parties then work to get their candidates elected.

Political parties are not an official part of government. Still, they must obey certain state and federal laws to prevent unfair tactics.

The United States has a two-party system. The Democratic Party and the Republican Party are the only major parties nationwide. Since the Civil War, only candidates of these two parties have been elected to the presidency. Only a very few candidates from minor parties have been elected to other major offices.

The Parties in Georgia

Georgia, like some other Southern states, is more a one-party than a two-party state. From the 1870s until the 1960s, almost all elected officials were Democrats. This situation stemmed from the reaction of whites to participation by blacks in state government during the Reconstruction period following the Civil War. During Reconstruction, many blacks were elected to the General Assembly and other state offices as Republicans.

By 1900, the Georgia Democratic Party had become a party of whites only. Georgia blacks were not allowed to vote in the party-run primaries to nominate candidates for election. Because the Democratic Party was really the only party in Georgia, the voting rights of black citizens were effectively taken away.

Not until the 1960s, after a series of Supreme Court decisions and the passage of civil rights laws, did black citizens once again have a voice in Georgia politics. Blacks got the vote back and began to be elected to office. The Democratic Party was no longer "white only."

About the same time, the Republican Party began to grow in Georgia. Voters elected Republican congressmen and members of the Georgia General Assembly. In 1980, Georgia voters elected a Republican to the U.S. Senate.

The Democratic Party still dominates state politics. Georgia is still largely a one-party state. But with the continued growth of the Republican Party, it could be a two-party state.

THE ELECTION PROCESS IN GEORGIA

On the Tuesday after the first Monday in November in even-numbered years, voters in Georgia and the rest of the nation go to the polls. This election is called the *general election.* The process of electing persons to state offices begins long before that November day. The process involves the party system.

During the late spring in election years, campaigning begins for the August *primary* elections. These primary races draw many candidates. Voter interest is often higher in August than in November.

A primary is a party election. In the past, the parties conducted their own primaries. Today, however, government conducts the primaries according to the Georgia Election Code.

Primaries give voters a chance to participate in *nominating* the candidates whose names will appear on the general election ballot in November. In the Democratic primary, Democrats run against each other. Democratic voters choose one person for each race in the general election. Meanwhile, in the Republican primary, other voters choose Republican candidates.

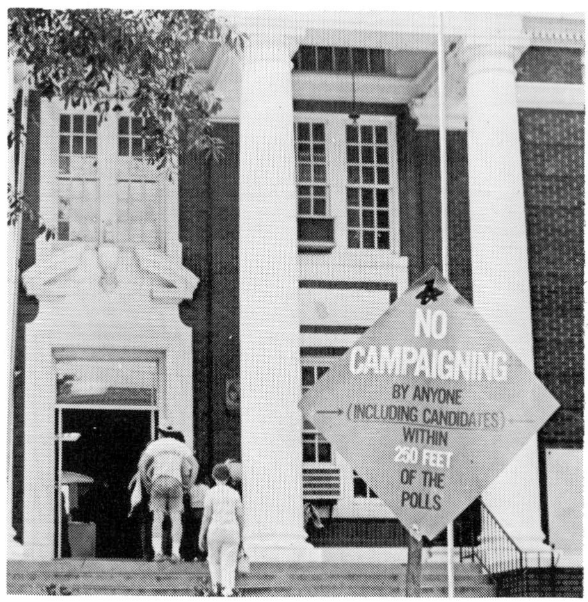

Barrow county citizens go to the courthouse to vote on election day.

What happens if no one runs in the primary of one of the parties? The person chosen in the other primary would be unopposed in the general election. (This is often the case in a one-party state.)

A party may nominate its candidates in other ways. In the past, they were often chosen at state conventions or at a caucus (a meeting of party leaders). Today, the primary system is almost always used.

Georgia's primaries are called "open" primaries. This means that both the Democratic and Republican primaries are open to any registered voter. One does not have to be a member of the party organization to vote in a primary. A voter can switch parties from year to year.

However, if a voter decides to vote in, let's say, the Republican primary in a certain year, that voter cannot also vote in the

Democratic primary. If no candidate wins the majority vote and a *runoff* is necessary, the voter has to stick with the same party.

In the November general election, the names of all candidates for state offices, opposed or unopposed, nominated in primaries or by petition (see page 27) appear on the ballot. (Of course, the names of candidates for local and federal offices will also be on the ballot.)

In this election there are no rules governing party voting. A voter may choose all Democrats or all Republicans, some from each party, any independents on the ballot, or may write in the name of a person not on the ballot.

If no candidate in a race gets a majority, a runoff is held three weeks after the regular general election. A runoff is seldom needed, though, because usually only two names appear on the ballot for each race in the general election.

The winner of the general election takes office the following January.

RUNNING FOR THE GENERAL ASSEMBLY

How do you go about getting elected to public office in Georgia? To find out, let's follow the process as carried out by a young man named Tom Cody (not a real person). Tom learns that a local legislator in his county will not seek re-election to the Georgia Senate. He considers running for the seat himself. He discusses the idea with friends. Should he run as a party candidate or as an independent? A party label almost always helps, and most candidates want one.

To be a party candidate in the general election Cody must first qualify for and then win a party primary election.

Tom decides to enter the Democratic primary. He does not have to be a member of the Democratic party organization. He can choose to run in a Republican primary. But he cannot run in both.

Qualifying. Since Tom wants to have his name placed on a primary ballot–in this case the Democratic ballot–he must first qualify as a candidate. To do this, he must file certain forms. He must show that he meets the requirements set for members of the Georgia Senate. He must also pay a qualifying fee of $400 to the Democratic Party.*

The party then certifies to the Georgia secretary of state that Tom Cody is qualified to seek its nomination for a specific seat in the Georgia Senate. The party also gives the secretary of state 75 percent of the qualifying fee. This helps pay the cost of running the primary election. The other 25 percent goes into the party treasury. It helps pay for general election campaigns and other party expenses.

Winning Nomination. To be nominated in the primary, Tom Cody must receive a majority of the votes. Because more than two candidates

*The amount of the fee depends on which office a candidate is seeking. The $400 fee applies to General Assembly seats. Candidates too poor to pay the fee may qualify to run in a primary by officially declaring themselves to be paupers instead of paying the fee.

TOM CODY RUNS FOR THE GENERAL ASSEMBLY

	**Early in an even-numbered year—**	Tom Cody decides to run as a Democrat for seat in General Assembly.
2	**Between 9 a.m. on 4th Wednesday in May and 12 noon on 2nd Wednesday in June—**	Tom qualifies for Democratic Primary. Pays $400 qualifying fee to party organization. Party keeps 25% and turns over 75% to state election officials.
3	**During June, July, and August—**	Tom campaigns against other Democrats for nomination in Democratic Primary.
4	**On the 2nd Tuesday in August—**	Primary election held. Tom and two other Democrats face each other. Results: Cody, 10,000; Smith, 7,000; Jones, 5,000. No candidate gets required majority of votes to win.
5	**Three weeks later—**	Runoff primary election held because no candidate got majority of votes in primary. Two top vote-getters (Cody and Smith) face each other. Results: Cody, 13,000; Smith, 9,000. Cody wins nomination.
6	**During September, October, and November—**	Tom, now the Democratic nominee, campaigns for votes in the general election. (The Republican nominee is doing the same.)
	**On Tuesday after 1st Monday in November—**	General election held. Tom Cody, the Democratic candidate, faces Republican candidate. Results: Cody, 14,500; Davis, 8,500. Tom Cody receives majority of votes and is elected.

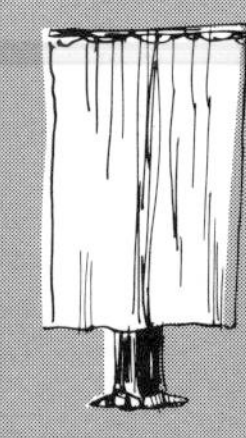

are in the race, it is possible that no one will receive a majority. In this event, a second, or runoff, primary must be held.

Only the top two vote-getters can be in the runoff. One of them will get a clear majority and win. The names of the winners in each party primary will appear on the general election ballot in November.** Cody is one of the top two in the primary and goes on to win the runoff.

Winning Election. To be elected to office, Tom Cody must receive a majority of the votes. Because he has only one opponent, one of the two will get the majority (unless of course there is a tie vote!). Tom wins. After the election, Tom's name is certified to the secretary of state by the election superintendent in his district as the winner.

**A petition method for getting on the general election ballot is also provided for by the Georgia Election Code. Petitions are used by persons who choose not to qualify in a primary, but who wish to run in the general election as either independent or party candidates. The petition must contain the signatures of at least 5 percent of the total number of voters eligible to vote in the last election for the office the candidate is seeking.

ACTIVITIES FOR CHAPTER 2

Class Discussion

A. Ben Fortson said "elections are the most important thing we do in this country." Think about *why* it is important for people to have a voice in matters that affect them.

1. Why is it important for a government to have the people's consent before doing something? How do people react when they are forced to do something for which they haven't given their consent?
2. Why is it important for a government to respond to people's needs? How do people react when their needs are ignored?
3. If there were no elections how could people give their consent? How could a government respond to their needs?

B. In a televised speech, a political candidate warned citizens to "take advantage of your rights."

1. How does a citizen take advantage of his or her rights? Explain.
2. Does a citizen lose out when others take advantage of *their* rights, but he or she doesn't? Explain.

Writing Project

"The voting record in our community is becoming the worst in Georgia," thundered the president of the Middletown Civic Association. "Hardly any of our 18- to 24-year-olds ever go near the polls. If this keeps up, we'll soon have no more government by the people."

Assume you are a member of the association. You've agreed to help in an advertising campaign to get these younger citizens to register and vote.

Assignment: Write up several ideas for the ad campaign. Ideas might include slogans to go on bumper stickers or billboards. You might compose a jingle or announcement for radio and TV spots. Be prepared to explain why your ideas would appeal to young citizens.

II THE LEGISLATIVE BRANCH

Representation in the General Assembly
Organization of the General Assembly
Procedures in the General Assembly
Lobbying at the General Assembly

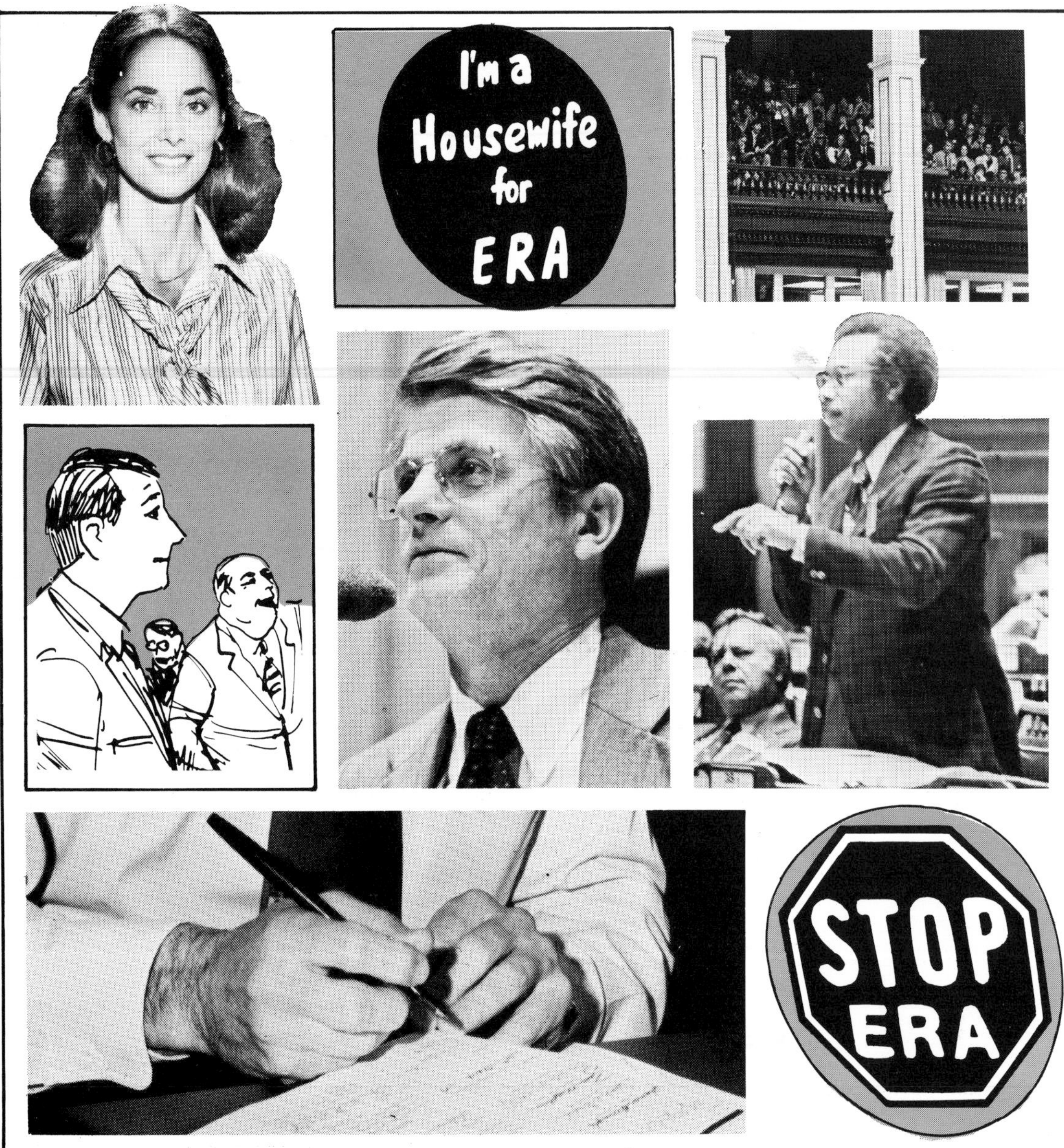

Introduction

The General Assembly makes laws for the state. All actions of state government are based on laws passed by the General Assembly.

Each year, the General Assembly meets in Atlanta for 40 days. During that time, it may pass new laws, abolish old laws, and change existing laws.

What kinds of laws may the General Assembly pass? Within limits set by the United States and Georgia constitutions, the General Assembly of Georgia may pass whatever laws it decides are needed for the well-being of the state's people.

Generally, these laws fall into four groups:

1. *Laws which provide for state services.* Examples are laws which set up state parks, hospitals, schools, and the state highway system. Under these kinds of laws, social workers, state troopers, health inspectors, and other state employees provide services to the public.
2. *Laws which regulate a person's conduct.* Examples are laws against drunk driving, robbery, and other criminal acts. Persons breaking these kinds of laws may be fined or put in prison.
3. *Laws which allow the state to raise and spend money.* Examples are laws which set up the 3 percent sales tax and the taxes on alcohol and tobacco. These laws allow the state to collect money from the people. Other laws tell how much the state can spend on road construction, teacher salaries, conservation programs, and so forth.
4. *Laws which provide for local government.* Examples are laws which enable school boards to operate public schools, cities to set up fire and police departments, and counties to collect property taxes. Local governments get their power to act from the General Assembly.

In its 40-day session, the General Assembly considers hundreds of *bills*—proposals for laws.

Of course, not everyone agrees on just what laws should be passed. Society is made up of groups of people having different problems, interests, and needs. The rich, the poor, property owners, apartment renters, farmers, union members, government employees, taxpayers, church members—each group may see a proposed law in a different light.

The job of the General Assembly is to see that the laws it makes are in the best interests of all people. No one group should be favored over others.

This is not an easy task. Different interest groups work to get laws passed or abolished. Some have more power than others. They work to get candidates for the General Assembly elected or defeated. They put pressure on members of the General Assembly to pass or kill certain bills.

Then, too, the members of the General Assembly are themselves members of groups. They are elected from different parts of the state. Their own views often reflect the interests of different groups or different parts of the state.

Even different parts of government work to influence lawmaking. Officials of city, county, and state governments have their own special interests in seeing certain laws passed. Sometimes these officials work with each other, sometimes against each other.

You can see that lawmaking is not simple. Laws are often the result of tough bargaining and noisy debate. Many different viewpoints are expressed in the political battles within the General Assembly. There are always some winners, always some losers.

Part II of GEORGIA STATE GOVERNMENT examines the lawmaking process. It begins in Chapter 3 with a look at the lawmakers themselves. Chapters 4 and 5 show how the General Assembly is organized and how it makes laws. Finally, Chapter 6 looks at the ways interest groups can influence lawmaking.

3 Representation in the General Assembly

When Tom Cody ran for the Georgia Senate only the voters living in his *election district* could vote for him. On the same day that he was elected, voters in over 200 other districts were electing local residents to seats in the Georgia House and Senate.

Who decides how many members there will be in the Georgia Senate and House of Representatives? Who draws up the election districts?

The Georgia Constitution gives the General Assembly the power to decide how many members it will have and how the election districts will be arranged. The make-up of the two houses differs slightly.

Senate

- Not less than 54 and not more than 56 members
- Each senator elected from and represents one senatorial district
- General Assembly may create, rearrange, and change senatorial districts
- *Apportionment* (distribution of seats) of Senate to be changed by General Assembly, if necessary, after each United States *decennial census**

House of Representatives

- Representatives apportioned among representative districts of the state
- General Assembly may create, rearrange, and change representative districts
- Apportionment of the House to be changed by the General Assembly, if necessary, after each United States decennial census

THE REAPPORTIONMENT PROBLEM

The seats in the General Assembly each represent an equal portion of Georgia's population. Seats in the General Assembly represent people, not land area.

For the purpose of electing persons to these seats, the General Assembly must draw up Senate and House election districts. It is supposed to make sure that people living in all parts of the state will have an equal voice in the lawmaking process. However, fair apportionment of legislative seats has been a problem. Some of the reasons for this are explained in the following reading.

**Decennial Census.* Every 10 years the federal government makes an official count of the number of people living in the United States.

THINK ABOUT IT

1. What was the argument of the people favoring apportionment based on counties? of those favoring apportionment based only on population?
2. How was the controversy decided?
3. Why are some districts in each house larger or smaller in geographic area than others? In what parts of the state are the larger districts located?
4. How do House districts compare to Senate districts in geographic size? in population size?
5. In which Senate district do you live? In which House district? Do some students in your class live in different districts? How can this happen?

Populations change. The number of people living in each section of the state does not stay the same from year to year. Some communities grow steadily over many years. Some get smaller. Some grow and then decrease.

The population figures for four selected counties show these kinds of changes.

POPULATION CHANGES (1940-1970)

County Name	1940	1950	1960	1970
Bulloch	26,010	24,740	24,263	31,585
Chattooga	18,532	21,197	19,954	20,541
Houston	11,303	20,964	39,154	62,924
Randolph	16,609	13,804	11,078	8,734

Which county had the steadiest growth? Which lost population at some time or another?

Since populations are always changing, the General Assembly must reapportion (or redistribute) its members after each census. Members should fairly represent the number of people living in each area of the state. This means redrawing the boundaries of election districts.

However, the methods used in the past to draw up districts were not always fair to all citizens. Some wanted the methods changed. *Reapportionment* became a legal and political issue lasting many years.

Until fairly recently, the Georgia General Assembly, as well as other state legislatures, did not organize its election districts on the basis of population alone. Districts for both houses of the General Assembly were based on counties or combinations of counties.

As long as Georgia's population was mostly rural and rather evenly distributed around the state, few people disagreed with this way of setting up districts. However, in the 1940s and 1950s Georgia's population shifted more and more from the farms and small towns to the larger cities.

People began to complain that representation based on counties was unfair. Those who wanted a change to apportionment based entirely on population claimed that under the county method the legislature passed laws favoring the rural areas. People living in cities suffered as a result.

On the other hand, supporters of the county method argued against apportioning seats on the basis of population alone. They said that it would cause rural citizens to suffer from control by city dwellers. Representatives of cities could easily pass laws favoring city residents.

Because state legislators in Georgia and other states couldn't resolve the issue themselves, the battle moved to the courts.

In the 1960s, in a series of rulings, the U.S. Supreme Court said that elections must be based on the idea, "one person, one vote." This idea affected legislative elections as well as other elections. It meant that, no matter where he or she lives in a state, a person's vote counts no more, no less than any other person's vote.

In 1972, for the first time, the General Assembly created districts that were not drawn up strictly according to county lines. Today, districts are based on population alone.

Did this change have any effect on the General Assembly? Yes, power in the legislature has shifted somewhat from rural to urban areas. Also, partly as a result of reapportionment, there are now a number of black and women members. Almost all of them are from urban districts.

The two maps that follow show the 1974 apportionment of the Georgia Senate and the Georgia House of Representatives.

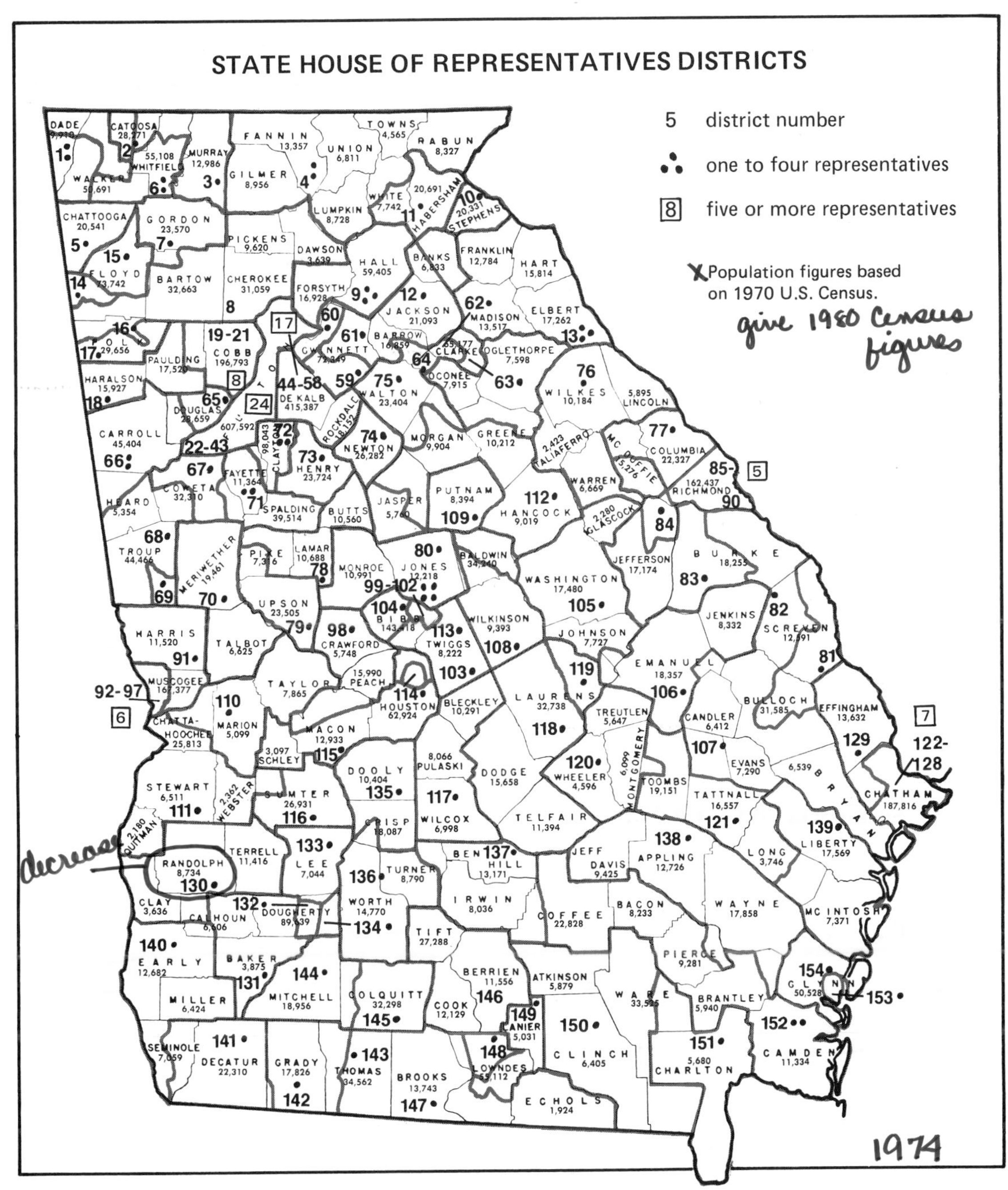

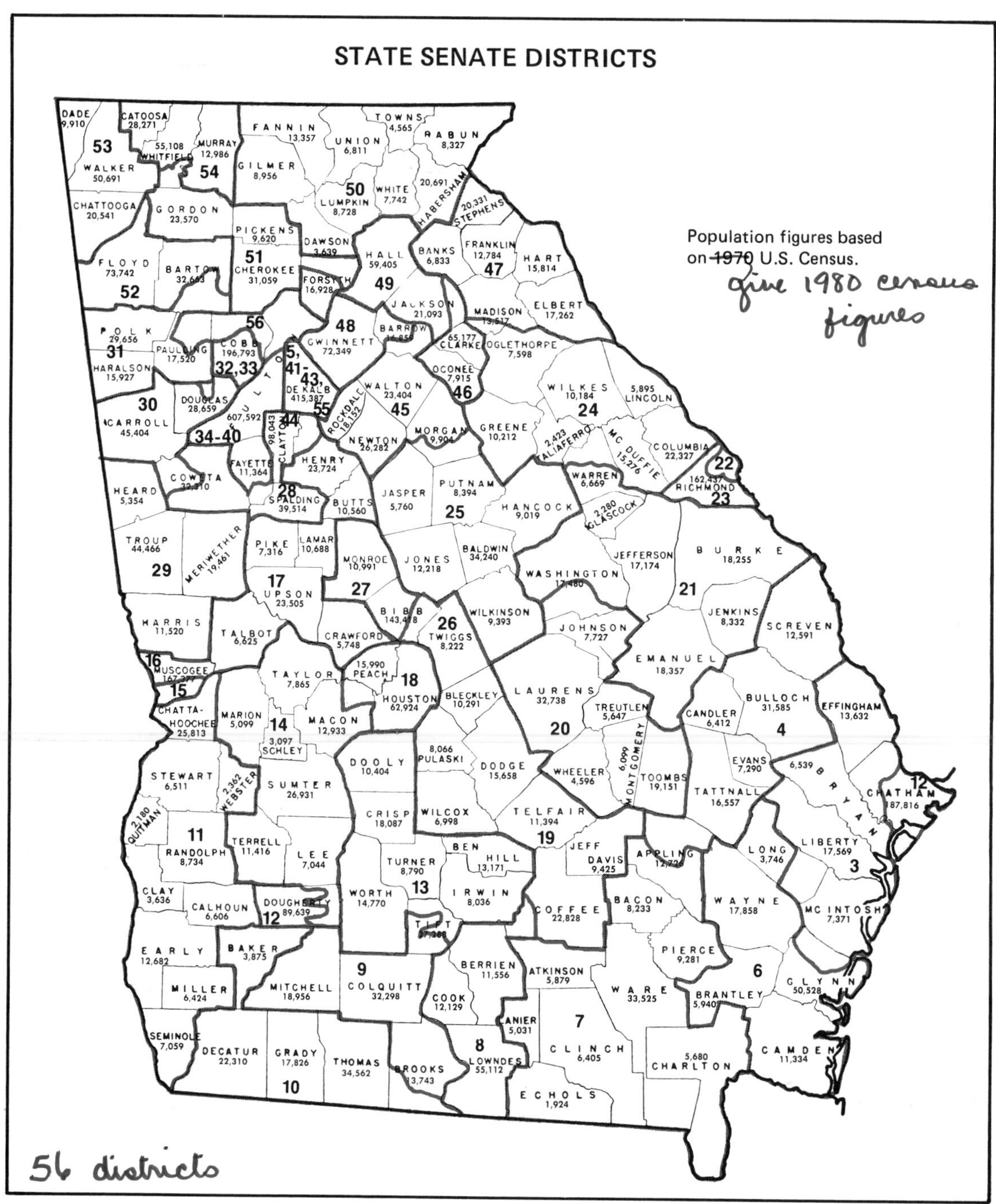

In the Senate, one member is elected from each of the 56 senatorial districts. In the House, there is usually one representative for each district. The larger districts have two or more representatives. There are 180 representatives from 154 House districts.

Now that the 1980 U.S. Census is complete, the General Assembly will begin drawing up new districts. Much of the work will be done by computer to make sure that all districts have as close to an equal number of people as possible.

WHO GETS ELECTED TO THE GEORGIA GENERAL ASSEMBLY?

Do voters usually elect a representative who is a lot like themselves? Would a rural district be likely to send to Atlanta a legislator who fully understands rural problems? Would a big-city district normally elect a person who knows the needs of urban residents?

Voters usually want to know how the candidates stand on certain issues. They also want to know something about the candidates' backgrounds, experiences, and lifestyles. Why? Because many voters feel that these characteristics can influence how a legislator will vote on issues.

Most legislators are part-time "citizen-lawmakers." Except during the 40-day session of the General Assembly, their workdays are spent at regular jobs.

For the most part, they are ordinary people elected to make decisions on behalf of other citizens. But, just as the populations of election districts across the state are made up of different sorts of individuals, so is the General Assembly.

STATISTICAL PROFILE OF THE GENERAL ASSEMBLY

Who gets elected to the General Assembly? One way to answer this question is to look at data about the members.

The following graphs are based on information supplied by members of a recent session of the General Assembly. Of course, the information would change slightly from one General Assembly to the next.

Five Basic Characteristics

Figure 1 presents data in five bar graphs. Each member of the General Assembly falls into one of two categories on the basis of sex, race, party, education, and military service.

THINK ABOUT IT

1. Taking the statistics from only these five graphs, what "picture" of the membership emerges?
2. Which characteristic is probably most like that of the population of Georgia? Which characteristic is least like that of the pop-

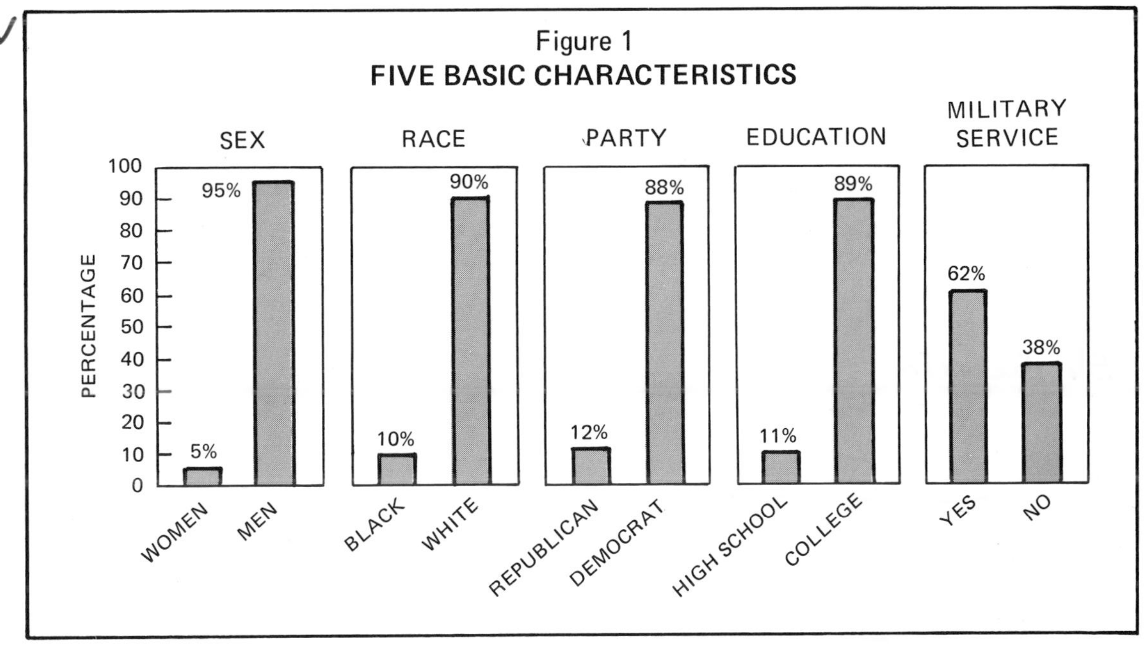

ulation? Explain your answers. Check with your teacher for more information.

3. Could any of these characteristics influence how legislators vote on issues? What kinds of issues?

Age

Being "too young" or "too old" in the eyes of the voters may influence whether a candidate wins or loses an election. Figure 2 shows the percentage of members in four age groups.

THINK ABOUT IT

1. Which age group has the most members in the General Assembly? What could be some reasons for this?
2. Does the membership seem balanced in terms of age groups in Georgia's population?
3. How could a legislator's age influence his or her viewpoint?

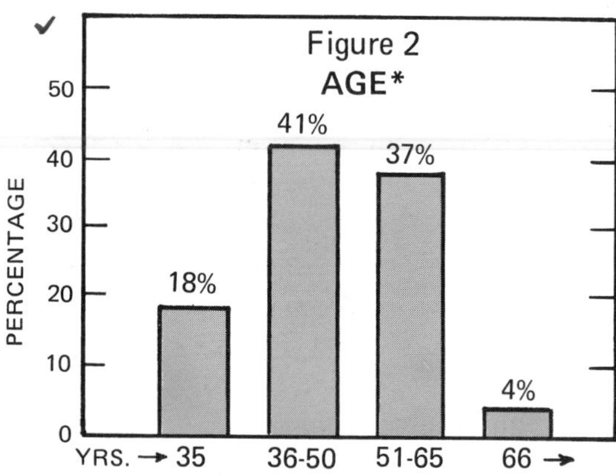

*Remember, a state senator has to be at least 25, a representative at least 21. There is no upper limit on age.
Age computed as of Jan. 15, 1980

Occupation

Lawmaking in Georgia is a part-time job. The General Assembly meets in session for only 40 days each year. Most General Assembly members continue in their regular jobs after their election.

Figure 3, a pie graph, shows what percentages of Georgia legislators fall into several job categories. Occupations have been grouped into general categories. For example, merchant, wholesaler, manufacturer, and sales representative are grouped in a business-industry category.

THINK ABOUT IT

1. What occupation groups are most represented in the General Assembly? Are these high, middle, or low income occupations?
2. What could explain the large number in the business-industry category? The law category?
3. Would a pie graph showing the job categories for all Georgians look like this one?
4. What influence might a person's occupation have on his or her view of certain legislative issues? Give some examples.

Figure 3
OCCUPATION

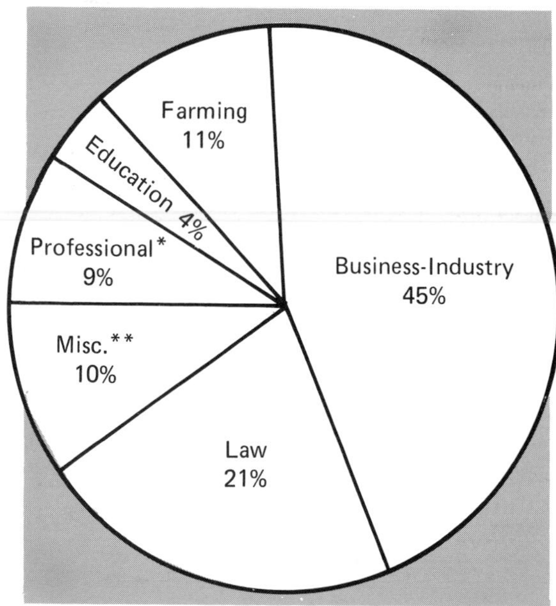

*Includes accountant, dentist, engineer, physician, pharmacist, etc.

**Includes homemaker, secretary, lecturer, minister, retired persons, etc.

Religion

Some citizens believe that religion is an important influence on a legislator's decisionmaking. Figure 4 shows the percentages of Georgia legislators who belong to various religious groups.

THINK ABOUT IT

1. What types of legislation might be influenced by religious beliefs?

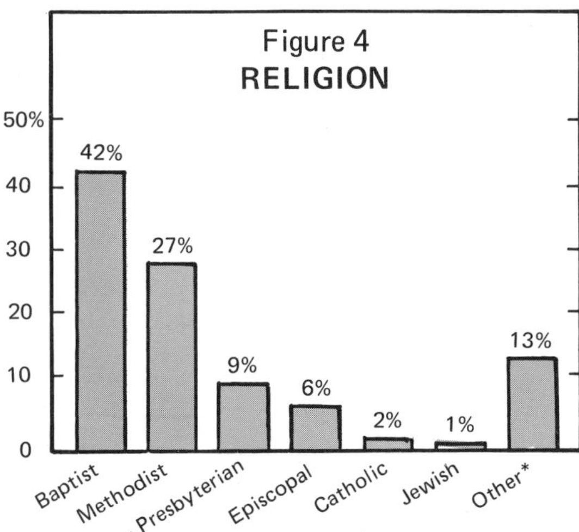

*Includes other Protestant denominations, non-denominational, unlisted.

AN INTERVIEW WITH A MEMBER OF THE GENERAL ASSEMBLY

In the following interview, one member of the General Assembly provides more clues for answering the question, "Who gets elected to the General Assembly?" Representative Herbert Jones, Jr. is from Savannah. He represents the 126th House District, which is made up of a portion of Chatham County. During the 1977 session, he was chosen by his Republican colleagues to be their leader in the House.

THINK ABOUT IT

1. How does Representative Jones get information on legislative issues?
2. What happens if Representative Jones feels differently about an issue than the citizens in his district do? How does he vote?
3. How does he vote on an issue if his constituents (voters from the district of an elected official) disagree among themselves on the issue?

Mr. Jones, what first made you want to seek a seat in the Georgia General Assembly?

In Chatham County where I live, we had a very bad educational problem. Our schools were on double session. My child was getting only a half an education. I was very critical of the school system. I felt like it was only fair to give some alternatives. In working with the Board of Education, I was asked by numerous friends to offer for the Georgia General Assembly. So, I guess what prompted me were friends, neighbors, concerned citizens.

What kind of a person runs for the legislature?

I suspect I'm a lot like my neighbors. I work for a bank. I participate in community and church activities. I cut my own grass and do my own painting. I'm just the normal guy.

What is your district like?

My district covers from the most influential wealthy to some of the poorest people of the county. Generally speaking, they are middle-class citizens who work in a different area from where they live. It is primarily a residential district. We have a large mall and lots of retail merchants, but it's not an industrial area.

What are the big concerns your constituents have?

A primary concern of the people is taxes. Most of them would prefer that government leave them alone. They don't care for all the government requirements. They're concerned, of course, about their schools. But especially about *ad valorem* or property taxes.

What happens if you feel differently about an issue than the people in your district do? This is a situation legislators often face.

In deciding how to vote on an issue, I have to assess what I think is best for the total. I do this based on the information that I have. Also, I have to recognize that sometimes I have more information than is available to the constituent. At the same time, I do participate adequately in the district so people pretty well know my personality and general philosophy.

How do you vote on an issue if your constituents don't agree with each other?

Very frequently you find yourself caught in the middle of a conflict. Then you have to take information from both groups and make up your mind. We have one right now in our district involving a highway. It has an environmental impact, an economic impact, and a long-range financial impact. People are outspoken about this issue. It's seldom that you will have some type of progress that doesn't hurt somebody. And, if that somebody happens to be one of your best friends, you have to forget personality and, based on the information, do what's best for the total.

Today, state government has to act on so many complex problems. Can a part-time citizen legislature still do the job? Wouldn't a full-time lawmaking body be better able to handle the problems?

You have more of the peoples' choice when you have a part-time citizen legislature. If you have absentee representation, which is what a full-time legislature would be, the legislator would miss the emotional concern and the contribution of individuals because he would never be at home enough.

But what do you do if you're faced with a highly technical question? You can't be an expert in all areas, can you?

On complex legislation, I rely on advice from professionals in the field. For example, in education I have to rely on state and local educators. But, as some citizens might not agree with education as the professional sees it, I have to have citizen input, too. On environmental issues, I have to get technical information from environmentalists. But, again, I have to have citizen input, because the environmentalist might want to restrict some project which those citizens want. On highways, the engineer's position may be to build and not to protect the environment. I must recognize that sometimes, based on his profession, he is prejudiced. So, while I have to have the expert advice of a professional, I have to look at the whole situation.

When you're at the capitol, away from your district, who else can you go to for information on a bill?

Lobbyists also are very important. They're not the bad guys that they are sometimes made out to be. A professional lobbyist who is at the capitol has a mass of information on the subject he's interested in.

Finally, I have to rely on the other members of the General Assembly. We have here persons who are experts in one area or another—lawyers, educators, sociologists, physicians. In our committee system we each serve on only three standing committees. But because we have to vote on all bills, we have to rely on others in the General Assembly.

What about the legislator's regular responsibilities back home? Who takes care of the business or the farm? Can the legislator turn his back on his home and family life and devote himself 100 percent to the General Assembly?

I don't believe a day has ever passed that I haven't been on the phone to the office at home. You have to check in because there are a thousand little things that come up. You don't leave all your responsibilities at home when you come to the capitol. Sometimes you have to go home. Your family has to carry on. And there are the normal illnesses and so forth that may drag you away sometimes. You're still the father or mother, the husband or wife, the son or daughter.

ACTIVITIES FOR CHAPTER 3

Class Discussion

A. It has been said that "in a legislature there is strength in diversity."

1. What is the meaning of this statement?
2. What evidence is there that the General Assembly has diversity in its membership? Is there also evidence of conformity?

B. In terms of the characteristics presented in the graphs, how representative is the General Assembly?

1. Do any parts of Georgia's population seem underrepresented in the legislature? If so, which ones?
2. Are any parts overrepresented? Which ones?
3. What might explain these differences in representation?

C. There are many views on what it takes to be a good representative. Here are two:

(1) "You have to be a lot like your constituents in such things as age, income group, political party, and so forth in order to represent their interests."

(2) "You have to be well-informed and consider the best interests of all your constituents to be a good representative."

1. Which view do you think Representative Jones would agree with? Explain why you think so.
2. Which view do you agree with? Why?

Writing Project

Assume that you are a writer for a Georgia newspaper. You are given the assignment to write an article entitled "Who Gets Elected to the Georgia General Assembly?" Your editor suggests, "Come up with a picture of the typical legislator."

a. Write the article presenting a profile of the typical legislator, or

b. Write the article describing how much diversity there is among the members of the General Assembly.

4 Organization of the General Assembly

It was 9:15 a.m., Monday, January 10, the first day of the new session of the General Assembly.

Tom Cody pulled into the parking lot across from the state capitol. "My name's Tom Cody," he said to the guard. "I'm a new legislator."

"Let's see, Cody, huh," said the guard as he looked at Tom's I.D. "Your parking space is on the back row, down at the end."

Tom parked, locked his car, and hurried across the lot. He noticed the license tags on other legislators' cars, "Fannin, Telfair, Muscogee, Early, Pulaski . . . from all over Georgia," he thought.

In the capitol, the halls were filled with legislators, other officials, families, friends, clerks, and secretaries.

"The first day sure brings everybody and his brother," Tom said to himself.

Glancing around, Tom saw several representatives talking excitedly as they swirled in little clusters toward the House chamber. The lieutenant governor, trailed by 10 or 12 people, swept by toward the other side of the capitol.

Tom moved along toward the Senate chamber. A lot was going on and it was noisy.

Senators were moving about, shaking hands and slapping backs. Aides were busy putting papers on each desk. A couple of technicians were testing the microphones. Some newspaper photographers were snapping pictures.

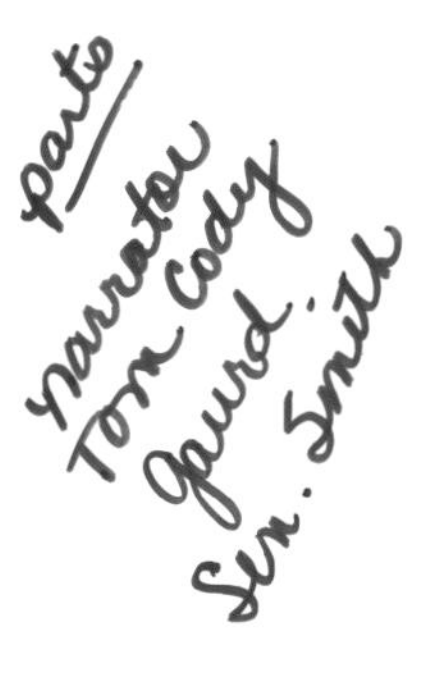

Tom found his desk and looked at his watch–9:45. He leaned over and introduced himself to the white-haired senator at the next desk.

"Senator Smith, do you think we'll start at ten o'clock?" asked Tom.

"The laws says ten and ten it'll be. If you think this is mass confusion, you should see the House chamber. There's 180 of 'em over there."

"That's what bothers me," Tom came back. "I can't see how, with all this confusion and the pile of bills facing us, we'll ever finish in 40 days."

"You can accomplish a lot in 40 days." Senator Smith grinned and puffed on his cigar. "The secret is organization. Most of the work gets done in committees, anyhow. And the leaders do a pretty good job of keeping us on track."

"You mean the lieutenant governor and the. . ." interrupted Tom.

". . .and the floor leaders and the committee chairmen," continued Senator Smith. "They know how to push things along–or slow'em down, if they want to."

"They sure would have to be good to get this crowd organized," said Tom, looking around at the seeming confusion.

"Well, you may be surpised. . . . You see," the senator nodded toward the podium, "it's ten o'clock and here comes the gavel."

The legislator's term of office begins on the second Monday in January after the general election. State law says that the first meeting of the new General Assembly shall start that day at 10:00 a.m. at the state capitol.

Before taking their seats, the new senators and representatives must take the following oath:

Oath of Office
Members of Georgia General Assembly

I do hereby solemnly swear or affirm that I will support the Constitution of this State and of the United States, and on all questions and measures which may come before me, I will so conduct myself, as will, in my judgment, be most conducive to the interests and prosperity of this State.

I further swear or affirm that I am not the holder of any public money due this State, unaccounted for, that I am not the holder of any office of trust under the government of the United States, nor of any one of the several States, nor of any foreign state, that I am otherwise qualified to hold said office according to the Constitution and laws of Georgia and that I am not a member of the Communist Party.

THE GENERAL ASSEMBLY LEADERSHIP

One of the first tasks of the sworn-in legislators is to elect persons to some of the leadership positions. These positions are shown in the chart on the next page and described in the reading that follows.

THINK ABOUT IT

1. Which leaders are chosen from among the members of the House and Senate? Who does the choosing?
2. Who are the most powerful leaders in the House and Senate?
3. In addition to the voters, whom does a floor leader "represent?"
4. What role do party leaders play?

Handout chart with this.

LEADERSHIP IN THE GEORGIA GENERAL ASSEMBLY				
	Senate		House	
	Title	*Filled by—*	*Title*	*Filled by—*
Officers specified in the Constitution of Georgia	✓President of the Senate Zell Miller	the lieutenant governor	Speaker of the House Tom Murphey	a member elected by the House
	✓President pro tempore Al Holloway	a member elected by the Senate	Speaker pro tempore Jack Connell	a member elected by the House
	Secretary of Senate	a nonmember elected by Senate	Clerk of the House	a nonmember elected by the House
Leaders of Democratic and Republican members of General Assembly	Majority leader	a member elected by majority party	Majority leader	a member elected by majority party
	Minority leader	a member elected by minority party	Minority leader	a member elected by minority party
The governor's legislative leaders	Administration floor leader	a member appointed by governor	Administration floor leader	a member appointed by governor
Committee leaders	Committee chairman	a member appointed by a committee	Committee chairman	a member appointed by the Speaker

5. How do the Clerk and the Secretary help the General Assembly conduct its "business?"

The Presiding Officers

Each house of the General Assembly has a presiding officer who guides its actions. In the House of Representatives this person is called the Speaker of the House. According to the Georgia Constitution, the Speaker must be elected from the House membership. The representatives choose the Speaker when the session opens in January.

In this century, the Democrats have always been the majority in the Georgia House. Therefore, the Speaker has always been a Democrat.

In the Senate, the presiding officer is officially called the president of the Senate. Under the Georgia Constitution, the lieutenant governor of Georgia serves as the president of the Senate. It is possible for the lieutenant governor to be of a different party than the majority of the senators. However, this has never happened.

The chief duty of these two officers is to preside over (or conduct) meetings of the House and Senate. To do this, they have special powers set forth in the *House Rules* and the *Senate Rules*. These rules, which govern the operation of the House and Senate, are made up by the legislators themselves.

★ Most important are the presiding officers' powers to—

1. decide which member has the right to the floor, (to speak, when)

2. stop members from debate that is off the subject and command silence,
3. rule out amendments that are off the subject of a bill,
4. call to order any member violating the chamber's rules,
5. order visitors' galleries and lobbies cleared of disorderly persons,
6. compel members to be in attendance in order to have a *quorum* (the number of members that must be present to conduct business),
7. decide on the order of business to be taken up,
8. order a roll call vote on any matter, and
9. refer bills and resolutions to committee.

The Speaker has several powers that the lieutenant governor doesn't have. For example, the Speaker assigns new representatives to committees and appoints committee officers. Unlike the lieutenant governor, who cannot vote in the Senate, the Speaker can vote to break a tie.

The Speaker of the House and the lieutenant governor are usually considered to be the two most powerful state leaders after the governor. Their actions can often make or break a piece of legislation.

Speaker Pro Tempore and President Pro Tempore

Each house elects one of its own members to preside in the absence of the Speaker or president. This officer is called the Speaker pro tempore (or pro tem) in the House and the president pro tempore (or pro tem) in the Senate. When presiding, they have the same powers and duties as the regular Speaker and president.

Majority and Minority Leaders

In the Senate and in the House, the Democrats and Republicans each have their own informal party organizations. This type of organization is usually called a *caucus*. It is set up to keep party members together on legislative issues.

Each caucus chooses a party leader, a party whip (so-called because this legislator's job is to "whip" party members into line), and other officers.

The leader and whip of the party in

Speaker of the House Thomas B. Murphy presiding over the Georgia House of Representatives.

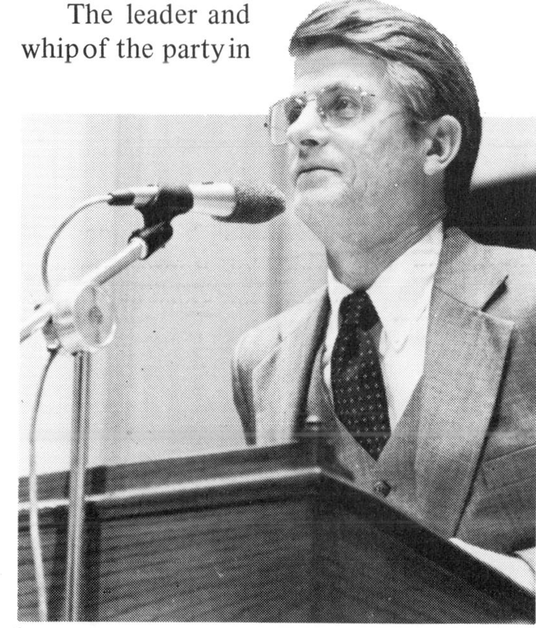

Lieutenant governor Zell Miller presiding over the Georgia Senate.

the majority are known as the *majority leader* and the majority whip. Likewise, the officers of the other party are known as the *minority leader* and the minority whip.

Administration Floor Leaders

Only members of the General Assembly can introduce legislation. Even the governor cannot do so. Therefore, if the governor would like to have a bill introduced, he must select a legislator to do it. In both the House and the Senate, this legislator is called the *administration floor leader.* The governor appoints these two leaders and their assistants to introduce bills the governor wants passed. They also work to convince other legislators to pass these bills. Sometimes they work to defeat bills the governor does not want passed.

Committee Chairmen

Committee chairmen conduct the meetings of the committees, which do most of the work of the General Assembly. They decide when committees will meet, when bills will be taken up, and when committee votes will be taken. Thus, committee chairmen have a powerful voice in determining whether a bill will pass or fail.

In the House, committee chairmen are appointed by the Speaker. In the Senate, they are appointed by the Committee on Committees, made up of the lieutenant governor, the president pro tem, and the majority leader.

The Clerk and the Secretary

The Clerk of the House and the Secretary of the Senate are not legislators. But they are elected by the members of each house to serve as full-time officers. They and their assistants help to make sure the General Assembly is run smoothly and efficiently.

These are some of the major duties of the Clerk and Secretary:

1. Receive and file all bills and resolutions to be introduced.
2. Print and distribute copies of bills to all legislators and, upon request, to the public.
3. Have all bills read aloud three times at House and Senate sessions.
4. Tally all votes and retain copies of all recorded votes.
5. Advise presiding officers on questions of parliamentary procedure.
6. Compile the *House Journal* and the *Senate Journal,* the official records of the General Assembly.

OTHER PERSONNEL IN THE GENERAL ASSEMBLY

A number of government workers help the elected members of the General Assembly during the 40-day sessions.

For example, any member of the General Assembly who wants assistance in writing a bill may ask one of the attorneys in the *Office of Legislative Counsel.* These attorneys help make sure bills are written in the proper form and if passed would not conflict with existing laws.

Legislative interns are students who, as part of their college work, assist legislators in researching bills and issues. Secretarial and clerical help is also available to legislators during the session.

A visitor to a General Assembly session may observe other workers. *Doorkeepers* prevent unauthorized persons from coming onto the floors of the House and Senate. *Messengers* aid in enforcing orders of the presiding officers. The *sergeant-at-arms* helps maintain order in the House chamber and galleries. Several young people working as pages (see ad, page 45) may be seen on the floors of both houses.

HELP WANTED

Pages needed in the Georgia General Assembly. Male or Female. Minimum Age: 12. No experience required. Must be neat, well-groomed, and fast on feet. No salary. Excused absence from school. Contact: Local state senator or representative.

What's a *Page*? In the Middle Ages, a page was a youth who served as an attendant of a high-ranking person. Today, pages carry messages, distribute documents, and perform other similar services for legislators during House and Senate sessions. Pages may go onto the floor of the General Assembly chambers whenever a legislator needs their services. The messengers in the House and Senate supervise the work of the pages.

The Page Program was set up to provide young people with an educational experience in government. Students who wish to participate should first talk to a teacher or principal. Then they should get in touch with a member of the General Assembly representing the district in which they live.

During each 40-day session, thousands of bills and resolutions are introduced. To divide up this workload, the members of the House and the Senate are organized into a committee system. The committees are set up to cover the major subject areas of legislation. For example, there are committees on agriculture, education, industry, and transportation. These committees are called *standing committees* because they are more or less permanent—they "stand" from one session to the next.

THINK ABOUT IT

1. What are some advantages in having a committee system?
2. What is the job of a standing committee? of a sub-committee?

THE COMMITTEE SYSTEM

The Standing Committees

The committee system saves time. If the full House or Senate had to examine every bill as carefully as each committee does, very little legislation could be acted upon in the 40-day session. The General Assembly can do a lot in a short time by—

1. distributing the work among legislators grouped in committees, and

2. relying on the committees' recommendations on whether to pass legislation.

The standing committees meet during the 40-day session whenever they need to consider bills referred to them by the presiding officer.

Each senator and representative is a member of two or three committees. A legislator may ask to serve on a particular committee, but may not get his or her first choice.

Committee members are expected to study all bills which the presiding officer sends to the committee. In committee meetings they discuss and vote on them.

The committee system helps to make sure that all legislative proposals get careful attention. Although a legislator cannot be an expert on every subject, he or she can become a specialist in some areas. A senator or representative does this by continuing over several terms to serve on particular committees. For example, a legislator serving on the transportation committee soon learns a lot about highway matters. Other legislators then come to respect this member's recommendations on highway bills.

The House and Senate each decide

STANDING COMMITTEES OF THE GENERAL ASSEMBLY, 1980

House Standing Committees	Number of Members
Agriculture and Consumer Affairs	22
Appropriations	46
Banks and Banking	27
Defense and Veterans' Affairs	10
Education	33
Game, Fish and Recreation	22
Health and Ecology	21
Highways	27
Human Relations and Aging	11
Industrial Relations	13
Industry	20
Insurance	18
Interstate Cooperation	5
Journals	6
Judiciary	20
Legislative and Congressional Reapportionment	11
Motor Vehicles	14
Natural Resources	16
Public Safety	12
Retirement	13
Rules	28
Special Judiciary	17
State Institutions and Property	30
State Planning and Community Affairs	18
State of Republic	10
Temperance	11
University System of Georgia	26
Ways and Means	26

Senate Standing Committees	Number of Members
Agriculture	7
Appropriations	20
Banking, Finance and Insurance	15
Community Affairs	7
Consumer Affairs	5
Defense and Veterans' Affairs	5
Education	11
Governmental Operations	12
Higher Education	8
Human Resources	11
Industry, Labor and Tourism	7
Judiciary	8
National Resources and Environmental Quality	9
Offender Rehabilitation	5
Public Utilities	5
Retirement	7
Rules	13
Special Judiciary	7
Transportation	7

how many and what kinds of committees there will be. Over the years, committees may be abolished and new ones created. Sometimes this is done because of changed conditions in the state. For example, after environmental problems arose, both houses set up committees on natural resources and the environment.

There are usually many more bills in some subject areas than in others. For example, in each session there will be a lot of bills on criminal law and the courts. There won't be so many on alcoholic beverages. So, while the House Judiciary Committee may study over 200 bills in a session, the House Temperance Committee may receive only a dozen to consider.

Because of the differences in their workload and their importance, the standing committees differ in size. Most of the larger committees are divided into subcommittees to handle special kinds of legislation. For example, the House Ways and Means Committee, which handles bills about taxes, has four subcommittees. These subcommittees give special attention to income taxes, taxes on public utilities, real estate taxes, and sales taxes.

Although the number of committees may change slightly from year to year, the list on page 46 shows how the two houses set up their committees in recent years.

Other Committees

The Speaker of the House and the Senate Committee on Committees regularly set up other kinds of committees for special purposes.

Interim Committees do their work between sessions of the General Assembly. They investigate and make reports on matters which require special study. For example, for several years there was a committee which studied ways to improve the Georgia court system. After finishing its special assignment, an interim committee is dissolved.

Conference Committees are sometimes set up when the House and Senate pass different versions of the same bill. This committee, made up of both senators and representatives, works out the differences in the two versions. (See page 55).

Committees of the Whole are made up of the entire House or Senate. These committees are used when the members want to have an informal discussion on an important measure.

ACTIVITIES FOR CHAPTER 4

Class Discussion

A. Over the years, the presiding officers in the Georgia House and Senate have sometimes been criticized for exercising too much control over lawmaking and other lawmakers. Examine the presiding officers' powers on pages 42 and 43.

1. Which of these powers merely help the presiding officers have a smooth-running meeting or cut down on wasted time?
2. Which of the powers could help them influence the passage or defeat of legislation? Give examples of how lawmaking could be affected.

B. The passage or defeat of a bill usually depends on the recommendation of the committee which studies it.

1. Why would a legislator tend to rely on a committee recommendation in deciding how to vote on a bill?
2. If there were no committee system, how might the legislature's operation be changed?

5 Procedures in the General Assembly

Linda Jackson swung her car into the left lane to pass a slow-moving truck, but there was another car ahead in the left lane traveling just as slowly as the truck. Linda waited awhile for the car to pull over.

"Darn!" exclaimed Linda to her friend Bobbie. "Why doesn't that guy pull over so I can pass?"

"Honk your horn," suggested Bobbie.

Linda blew the horn several times, but the car ahead didn't move over.

"Here we are on a four-lane highway with a 55-mph limit, having to creep along at 25. Boy, does it make me mad!" Linda glared at the car ahead.

"Isn't there some law that says you have to get over to the right to let people pass?" asked Bobbie.

"Slower traffic is supposed to keep to the right," answered Linda. "But, I don't know if there's any law to require it."

"Well, if there isn't such a law, there ought to be one," said Bobbie firmly.

"Great idea," agreed Linda. "But, how do we go about getting a new law?"

"I'll call Mr. Cody, my mother's law partner," answered Bobbie. "He just got elected to the General Assembly."

The lawmaking process begins with an idea. Many ideas come from legislators. Others come from private citizens, lobbyists, government officials, and business organizations.

Turning an idea into a *bill*—a proposal

to enact (pass), amend (change), or repeal (abolish) a law—is the next step. The actual drafting (or writing) of a bill does not have to be done by a legislator. Any citizen who has an idea for a new law may draft a bill. However, regardless of who drafts a bill, a member of the General Assembly must agree to introduce or present it.

Before he or she agrees to introduce it, the legislator has to ask certain questions:

1. Is this an important proposal?
2. What is the basic issue?
3. Who would benefit if such a law is passed?
4. Would anyone be disadvantaged by the law?
5. Would it conflict with existing laws or other proposed legislation?
6. What controversies might the proposal raise?

HOW TO WRITE A BILL

To be considered by the General Assembly, a bill must be on an appropriate subject, and it must follow a certain form.

The following reading discusses the subject-matter and form for bills.

THINK ABOUT IT

1. What kinds of subject-matter may General Assembly bills have?
2. What's the difference between general and local bills?

Subject Matter

The General Assembly passes two basic kinds of bills: *general* and *local.* General bills, if enacted, become laws applied throughout the state. For example, the law requiring annual auto inspections is a general law. It applies to all car owners all over the state.

Local bills, if enacted, become laws which apply only to certain cities and counties. For example, the law setting the number of members on the Cherokee County Commission is a local act. It applies only to that county.

The Georgia General Assembly is a *state* legislature. It can consider only bills which fall within the area of state powers (look back to pages 11-13 in Chapter 1). It cannot, for instance, pass legislation for declaring war or printing money. Only Congress can pass laws covering these matters.

There are dozens of areas subject to state legislation. They include the following: advertising • agriculture • alcoholic beverages • business practices • child custody • civil law • consumer protection • credit and loans • criminal law • divorce • drugs • education • elections • highways • hunting and fishing • law enforcement • marriage • obscenity • prisons • professions and trades • public safety • public utilities • taxes • traffic • welfare • health care

The following summaries of laws show the subjects of a few bills:

ACTS PASSED BY THE GEORGIA GENERAL ASSEMBLY

846 (1953)—Provides that a motel shall not be operated without first obtaining a permit from the State Board of Health . . .

500 (1975)—Provides that it shall be unlawful for any person knowingly to tamper with, adjust, alter, change, set back, disconnect, or fail to connect an odometer of a motor vehicle, or to cause any of the foregoing, so as to reflect a lower mileage than the motor vehicle has actually been driven.

1101 (1976)—Provides that any peace officer may assume temporary custody, during school hours, of any child subject to compulsory attendance who is found away from home and who is absent from school without lawful authority or valid written excuse.

714 (1953)—Provides that election managers shall not begin to count the votes in any election until the polls are closed.

Source: *Summary of General Statutes of the General Assembly of Georgia.*

Form

Each bill introduced in the General Assembly must follow a certain form. The proper form is spelled out in the *House* and *Senate Rules.*

Each bill is given a number when introduced. Bills are numbered separately in the House and Senate. For example, H.B. 563 would be a House bill, and S.B. 229 a Senate bill. This number helps legislators keep track of the hundreds of bills they have to consider in each session.

Each bill has to have a *title.* The title sets out the subject-matter of the bill. In Georgia, no bill can be passed which contains several unrelated subjects. For example, a bill requiring the licensing of dogs and also regulating the hunting of deer would be prohibited.

The *body* of a bill may contain several *provisions.* The types of provisions a bill contains differ according to the purpose and subject-matter of the bill.

For example, a provision may just define important words used in the bill, or it may state how such a law would be enforced. Provisions also may set penalties for breaking the law. They may repeal prior laws that might conflict with the new law.

A new law may set a specific date to go into effect, but if none is provided its effective date is July 1.

THE BILL'S JOURNEY

The following reading should help you become familiar with the General Assembly's lawmaking procedure. The chart on pages 52 and 53 outlines the steps which must be followed. What happens at each step is described in the text.

THINK ABOUT IT

1. At what steps in the legislative procedure are decisions made whether or not a bill passes?
2. At what steps could the average citizen have some influence on whether or not it passes?

The General Assembly deliberately made difficult the procedure for getting a bill passed. This is because it is just as important for the legislature not to pass bad bills as it is to pass good ones.

A bill may be introduced in either house of the General Assembly. Bills to raise money or spend money are the exceptions. By law, they must be introduced in the House of Representatives. No matter where a bill begins its journey, it must follow certain steps in both houses of the legislature.

Some of these steps are more important than others. At *decisive steps* (shaded on the chart), legislators make decisions on a bill. Lobbyists, executive branch officials, and interested citizens may attempt to influence those decisions. At *routine steps* (not shaded on the chart), clerical or ceremonial activities are carried out.

Reading of Bills

All bills are read aloud three times in each chamber. This ceremonial practice, required by the Georgia Constitution, goes back to the state's early years. Reading aloud was important then because many citizens, including some legislators, could not read. Also, bills were written by hand, so not everyone could have a copy.

The first and second readings are by title only. In the third reading, the bill is read section-by-section, word-by-word, before the full house.

Referral to Committee

One way the Speaker of the House and the president of the Senate can influence the passage of a bill is through their power to refer it to committee.

H. B. No. 1260

By: Messrs. Morgan of the 70th, Smith of the 74th and Adams of the 36th

A BILL TO BE ENTITLED
AN ACT

To amend an Act making it unlawful to alter the suspension system of any private passenger motor vehicle, approved April 13, 1973 (Ga. Laws 1973, p. 458), so as to provide that it shall be unlawful to operate any private passenger motor vehicle upon which the suspension system has been altered more than two inches above or below the factory recommendation for any such vehicle; to provide an effective date; to repeal conflicting laws; and for other purposes.

Title

BE IT ENACTED BY THE GENERAL ASSEMBLY OF GEORGIA:

Section 1. An Act making it unlawful to alter the suspension system of any private passenger motor vehicle, approved April 13, 1973 (Ga. Laws 1973, p. 458), is hereby amended by striking Section 1 in its entirety and inserting in lieu thereof a new Section 1, to read as follows:

"Section 1. It shall be unlawful to alter the suspension system of any private passenger motor vehicle more than two inches above or below the factory recommendation for any such vehicle or to operate any vehicle upon which the suspension system has been altered more than two inches above or below the factory recommendation for any such vehicle on any public street or highway located in this State."

Body

Section 2. This Act shall become effective upon its approval by the Governor or upon its becoming law without his approval.

H. B. No. 1260

Most of the time, the presiding officers refer bills to committee according to the bill's subject matter. However, if the presiding officer strongly favors a bill, he may send it to a committee that he thinks will give it a "do pass" recommendation. Likewise, if the presiding officer wants to stop a bill, he may refer it to a committee he thinks will kill it.

Committee Work

The standing committee does the real work on a bill. It considers the bill and recommends to the full house what should be done with it.

Although many bills are disposed of quickly, some require days or even weeks of committee work. If there is much controversy over a bill, a committee may decide to hold a *public hearing* on it. This gives interested citizens a chance to state their opinions on the bill. While it has the bill, a committee may also call on government officials, professional experts, lobbyists, and other persons to supply information.

While a bill is "in committee," lobbyists may meet informally with committee members. They may suggest *amend-*

How A Bill Becomes A Law

HOUSE OF REPRESENTATIVES

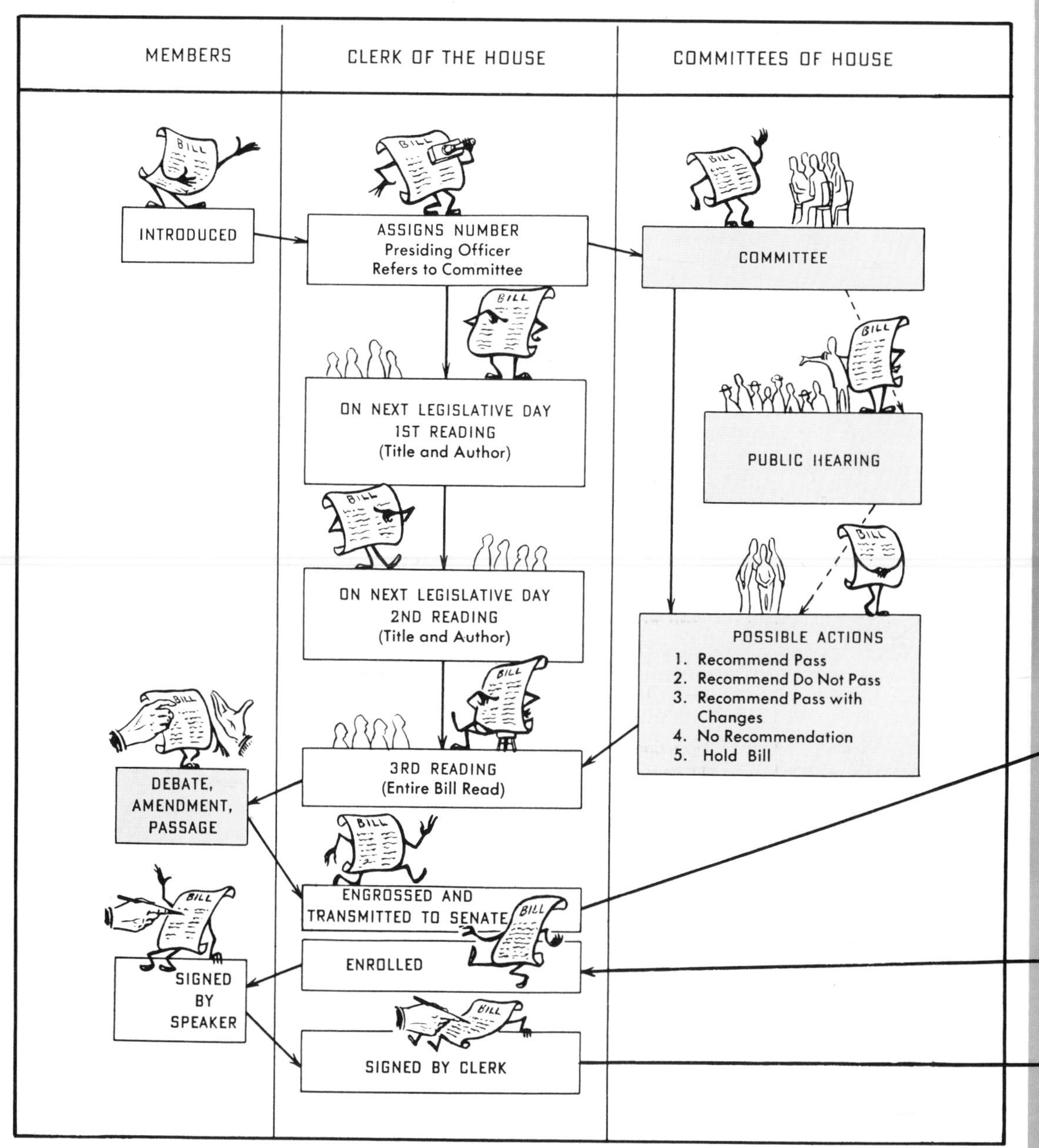

CONFERENCE COMMITTEE

If the two houses have difficulty reaching agreement on a measure, a Conference Committee may be established with representatives of both houses. To complete passage both houses must agree.

This chart is based on a bill introduced in the House. Bills may also originate in the Senate.

SENATE

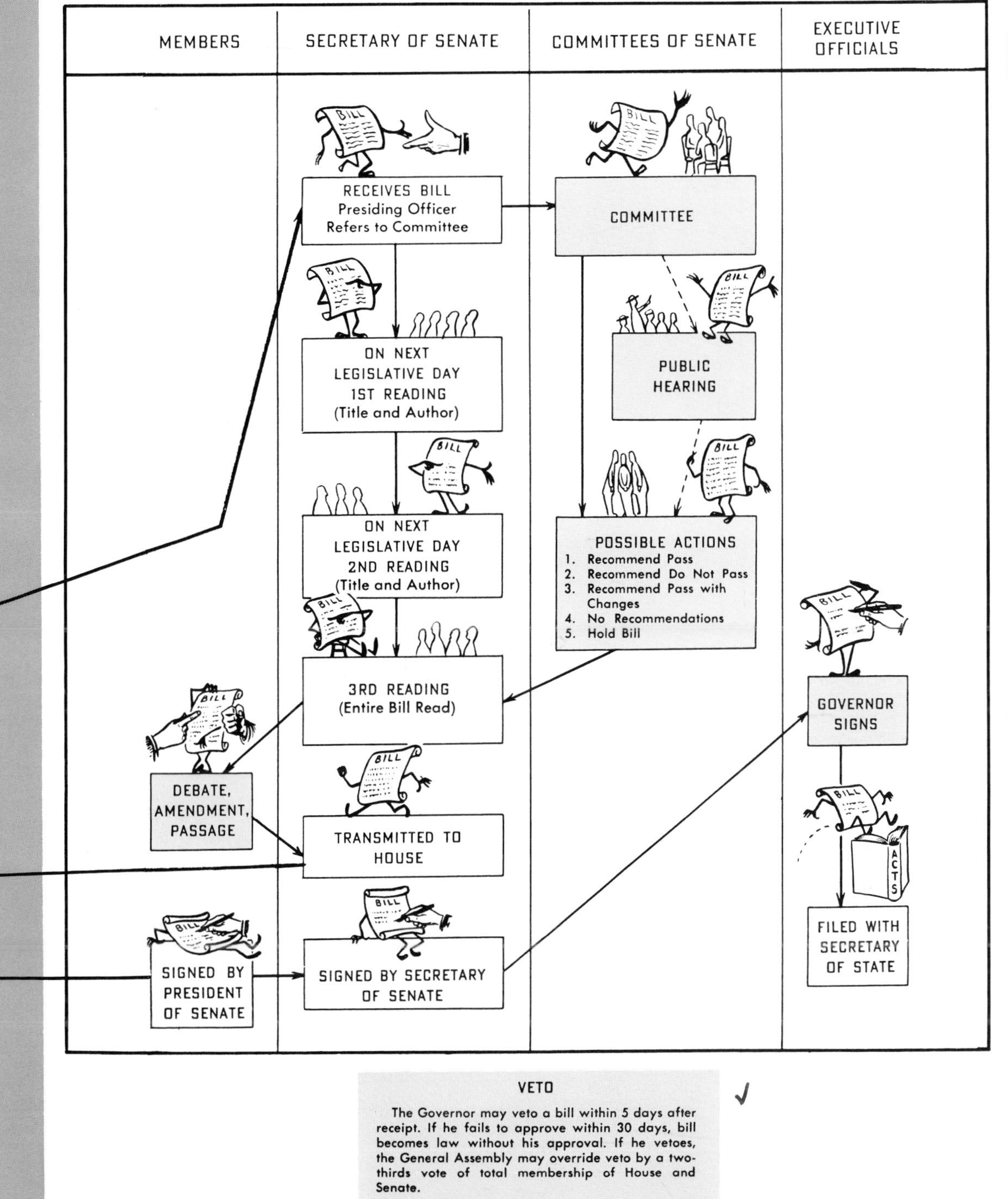

VETO

The Governor may veto a bill within 5 days after receipt. If he fails to approve within 30 days, bill becomes law without his approval. If he vetoes, the General Assembly may override veto by a two-thirds vote of total membership of House and Senate.

Reprinted courtesy of the Georgia Business and Industry Association.

ments (or changes) to strengthen or weaken a bill. Sometimes they try to get the committee members to recommend that the full house pass or reject a bill. Lobbying groups, such as business organizations, unions, and professional associations, regularly use telephone campaigns and mass mailings to influence committee members.

Government officials, including mayors, county commissioners, sheriffs, and the governor, may tell the committee their feelings about a bill. Sometimes, the state's newspapers will carry editorials supporting or opposing a bill.

Finally, the committee has to make a decision.

Possible Committee Actions

When they have finished studying and discussing a bill, the committee can dispose of it in several ways.

1. The committee may report the bill back to the house favorably without any changes. It recommends "do pass."
2. It may report the bill back to the body favorably with amendments (which may be so many as to make up, in effect, a substitute bill). It recommends "do pass with changes."
3. It may report the bill back unfavorably. It recommends "do not pass."
4. It may report the bill back without recommendation (in the House only).
5. It may hold the bill (not reporting it at all).

If the committee report is unfavorable, the bill is most likely dead for that session of the General Assembly.

If the bill is favorably reported by the committee—with or without amendments—it can then be placed on the *calendar* for action by the full Senate or House.

Calendar

To come before the House or Senate for debate, a bill must first be placed on the calendar and then called up by the presiding officer. The calendar is a daily listing of bills and resolutions that are ready for consideration. Although it is the presiding officers' duty to call up each bill for floor action, they could delay or speed up doing this, depending on how they feel about the bill.

Floor Action

After a bill has been called up for a third reading, all the members of a house may debate it. And, they may offer amendments from the *floor*.

On the floor of the chamber, members try to convince each other to support or oppose the bill. The author, the floor leader, and the majority leader may work to line up the vote they wish on the bill. The presiding officer, too, often uses his position of power to gain passage or defeat of the bill.

Off the floor, lobbyists continue to meet informally with legislators. They may ask individual members to amend the bill. They may try to convince them to pass or defeat it.

Voting is the final part of floor action. Each legislator has one vote. In order to pass, a bill must receive the approval of a majority of the membership of each house. In the House a majority is 91 and in the Senate, 29. In special cases, such as voting on proposed constitutional amendments, a two-thirds majority is required—120 in the House, 37 in the Senate.

On most important matters, a roll call vote—a count of the "yeas and nays"—is taken. This means that how each legislator voted on a bill is recorded. The public is then able to know who voted for and who voted against a bill.

Sometimes, however, there is only a voice vote or a show of hands. In these cases, no individual legislator's vote is recorded.

When a bill is passed by the House or Senate, it is *engrossed*—proofread and approved. Then the bill, including any amendments, is sent over to the other house.

Action by the Other House

In the second house, the bill goes through the same stages as in the first house. A committee studies the bill and reports back to the full house. Lobbyists continue to work for or against the bill. Amendments may be made in committee or on the floor.

A bill is just as likely to die in the second house as in the first house it journeyed through.

Citizens packed the visitors' gallery when the House debated a bill to raise the drinking age to 19. Some were allowed to address the session.

Conference Committee

Often the second house will pass a slightly different version of a bill. However, for a bill to become a law, it must pass both houses of the General Assembly in exactly the same form.

If neither house agrees to the version passed by the other, a *conference committee* is appointed by the two presiding officers. It is made up of three senators and three representatives. They try to work out a bill that both houses will accept. Their report must be approved by both houses for the bill to pass the General Assembly.

After both houses pass exactly the same version of a bill, it is *enrolled.* This means that an official final copy of a bill is prepared. This enrolled copy is sent to the governor.

Action by the Governor

Sending the bill to the governor is the last step in a bill's journey. People who are still opposed to it may urge the governor to *veto* the bill. Others may urge the governor to sign it into law.

If the governor approves the bill and signs it, the bill becomes law. If the governor doesn't fully support the bill, he may choose not to sign it. In this instance, it becomes law without his approval.

If the governor decides to veto the bill, it returns to the house in which it was introduced. The bill is dead unless the General Assembly votes to override the veto. This takes a two-thirds vote of the total membership of each house. If a veto is overriden, the bill becomes law without the governor's approval.

Once a bill becomes law, the enrolled copy is kept in the office of the Georgia secretary of state. This is the official text of the new law. The secretary of state prints copies of all laws enacted in a session. They are then distributed throughout the state.

LEGISLATORS' PANEL

Hugh M. Gillis, Sr., Senator District 20, Soperton

How important is compromise—the give and take of politics—in getting a bill passed in the General Assembly?

Gillis — Compromise is very important. In the first place, your bill may need amending so that it will apply fairly to all the people in Georgia. Second, you must be able to accept some changes to pick up the votes needed for passage. Often, the "give and take" necessary to pass a bill results in a better bill after all.

Holmes — It's crucial. Any bill that would make a real change in what people are used to is likely to cause disagreement. Usually such a bill must be amended to make it acceptable to enough legislators.

Robinson — Often the difference between a "do pass" and a "do not pass" recommendation depends on how willingly the author allows changes in the bill. The author must be careful, though, to make sure the bill is not "watered down" so that it is no longer a good bill.

Steinberg — It is often necessary to make changes in a bill in order to gain enough support for its passage. However, compromise should not occur just for the sake of getting a bill passed. One must often decide between what seems "right or best" and what has the best chance of passing.

With so many bills being introduced, it's easy for a bill to get lost in the shuffle. How do you avoid this?

Gillis — It's important to introduce the bill early in the session. The author must follow the daily progress of the bill. He must also inform his fellow legislators of its merits.

Holmes — The author must keep in contact with the subcommittee considering the bill. He should also be in touch with the presiding officer so that the bill can be considered at the time the author desires.

Robinson — The Secretary of the Senate keeps a record of all legislation introduced. This can be used by interns and staff members to follow a bill's progress and keep a senator informed as to when it will come before the standing committee. The senator can make timely remarks and contacts as the bill moves through the process.

Steinberg — First one must gain support from members of the committee to which the bill is assigned. Then one must work with legislators in the House and Senate to get the bill passed. It also helps to work with "advocacy groups"—people who are interested in particular legislation. By showing support for a bill, they increase its chances of passing.

Bob Holmes, Representative, District 39, Atlanta

W. Lee Robinson, Senator, District 27, Macon

Cathey M. Steinberg, Representative, District 46, Atlanta

In addition to its merits, what else influences whether a bill is passed?

Gillis — You must show that the bill is an improvement in the present law. You must show why it needs to be passed in the current session. You must also cooperate with your fellow legislators and make sure your facts are correct.

Holmes — To pass any important bills, you must have the support of the party leadership and often the governor's office as well. Without this kind of political support, the bill may not even come to the floor for a vote.

Robinson — Personality often enters into the process. The fact that the author of a bill supported other bills by his fellow senators could easily win some votes. The phrase "you owe me one" means just that, although "pay backs" are usually limited to minor bills. Also, public opinion normally helps determine the vote on controversial legislation.

Steinberg — I try to inform as many legislators as possible about the legislation I'm working on. I ask some of them to co-sponsor this legislation and assist me by talking to other legislators and speaking in favor of it on the floor. The support of the leadership and influential members is very important, as is "grassroots" support from the citizens of Georgia.

What one or two things do you feel would do most to improve the lawmaking process in the General Assembly?

Gillis — The session should be lengthened a few days to handle the large number of bills and resolutions that are introduced. The last two days should be reserved to consider committee reports to resolve differences between House and Senate versions of bills.

Holmes — Extend the session. Forty days is not adequate to consider 1,500 or more bills. Also, legislators should receive higher salaries. That way persons other than independently wealthy people, lawyers, and businessmen can serve in the General Assembly without great personal sacrifice.

Robinson — The legislative staff should be expanded. Much of a legislator's time is spent providing services to constituents, such as help in dealing with government agencies, even in getting a driver's license renewed. More staff are needed to help with these services, and also to aid the more active Senate committees.

Steinberg — With more staff, legislators could do more research, be more informed and more prepared for issues on which they must vote. Also, some type of pre-filing of bills before a session begins would give legislators more time to study legislation.

OTHER ACTIVITIES OF THE GENERAL ASSEMBLY

Lawmaking is the main function of the legislature. However, the legislature does other things besides making laws.

Resolutions are regularly passed by either house or both houses. These are formal actions used to express the feelings or opinion of the legislature. They may request or authorize actions by state officials (such as the selling of state land), or set up special committees to investigate state problems.

Most important, resolutions are used to propose constitutional amendments for the people to vote on.

A resolution is similar to a bill in that it is introduced and voted on. But, in most cases, a resolution is not a law.

Appointments are made and confirmed by the General Assembly. Certain officials, such as members of the State Transportation Board, are chosen by the legislature. Also, many of the appointments made by the governor must be confirmed (approved) by the Georgia Senate.

Impeachments are trial-like proceedings conducted by the General Assembly. They can be used to remove public officials from office for misconduct. The legislature rarely uses this power.

ACTIVITIES FOR CHAPTER 5

Class Discussion

A. The lawmaking procedure is like an obstacle course. Only the stronger bills make it to the finish line. In fact, more bills fail than pass in each session. However, the lawmaking procedure is often criticized in the news media, especially when popular bills get bottled up in committee or killed by some action of the leadership.

1. How could the procedure be revised to make it speedier?
2. What advantages would there be in making it easier to pass bills? Are there any disadvantages?

B. To be an effective lawmaker, a member of the the General Assembly has to know all the details of the formal steps shown in the chart on pages 52-53. He or she also has to understand and be skilled in the "politics" of lawmaking discussed by the panel of legislators.

1. Make a list of all the things you, as a legislator, might do to get one of your own bills passed.
2. Make a list of some things another legislator might think about in deciding whether or not to support your bill.

Writing Project

Assume that you are a member of the General Assembly. One day you get a phone call at home from a constituent. She is upset because a certain bill hasn't been passed. She asks, "Could you quickly tell me how this lawmaking business works?"

Referring to the chart on pages 52-53, write out your description of the bill's journey as you'd give it over the phone. Be sure to mention which steps are the most important and why.

6 Lobbying at the General Assembly

The word *lobby* has two meanings. It can mean "a hall, corridor, or waiting room." Or, it can refer to "activities aimed at influencing legislators." These two definitions seem very different, but they are related.

In our political system, citizens may try to influence public officials through letters, written petitions, and phone calls. Sometimes, they talk to the legislators in the halls—or lobbies—of their legislative chambers. This is where the term "to lobby" began.

Our society is made up of many groups of people. These groups have their own special interests. For example, businessmen are interested in profits, parents are interested in better schools, and minorities are interested in equal rights. Naturally, each of these groups is concerned about legislation that affects them as a group—that affects their special interest.

Special interest groups can influence the lawmaking process. Many spend a lot of money to organize lobbying activities. Some hire persons skilled at lobbying to work for their interests.

THE LOBBYIST

Persons who lobby can be divided into several groups. First, there are private individuals who give their own views to their legislators. Any citizen may write, phone, or meet in person with members of the General Assembly to give his or her views on legislative matters.

Citizens often "lobby" in the capitol lobby, where they can meet legislators on their way in and out of meetings.

Second, there are persons who represent the interests of some other person, a business, or organized group. Some of the persons in this second group are professional lobbyists. They are paid to represent one or several clients. Their clients include corporations, business associations, labor unions, and organizations of doctors and lawyers. Other lobbyists are unpaid. They may be members of professional organizations or volunteers representing neighborhood citizens' associations.

Several hundred lobbies, or interest groups, are active at each session of the General Assembly. Their concerns vary from tax issues to mental illness to gun control.

Whether paid or unpaid, lobbyists who represent some special interest are required by law to register with the Georgia secretary of state. They must pay a small registration fee and give the name of their client. While lobbying at the state capitol, they must wear an identification badge. These lobbyists are officially called *registered agents.*

Interview with Lobbyist Jim Parkman

Jim Parkman is a lobbyist representing the Georgia Business and Industry Association. He is a registered agent at the General Assembly and has his office across the street from the state capitol.

THINK ABOUT IT

1. What is the lobbyist's role in the legislative process?
2. According to Mr. Parkman, what does it take to be an effective lobbyist?
3. How is the lobbyist's job similar to that of the legislator?

Mr. Parkman, how does the lobbyist help in the lawmaking process?

The lobbyist helps in the lawmaking process by serving as an extension of the legislative staff. In Georgia, members of

the General Assembly have very limited assistance available to them. For researching bills, help is usually limited to student interns. An intern works with a legislator on a particular assignment. There are never enough interns to handle all the research needed.

Do lobbyists actually help write proposals to be introduced by legislators?

Often they do. A piece of legislation that's needed may affect only a certain group. It's natural for legislators to call on an association that represents the particular group for help in drafting legislation. Sometimes the association may help with writing the bill. Sometimes it just provides ideas and information.

A legislator has a constituency in a geographic area that he or she has to listen to and to answer to. Does a lobbyist have a constituency too?

Yes, the lobbyist represents the number of people who have a special interest. A business or city government or even a labor union would be the constituency of the lobbyist.

What is your own constituency?

My constituency is the business and industry of Georgia. My association hopes to have an effect on the atmosphere in which business operates. We want to make sure the businessman has a healthy climate so he can be competitive within Georgia and with business from outside the state.

In what specific kinds of legislation are your constituents most interested?

My constituents are interested in issues in two categories. Of primary concern are issues affecting business directly. They include taxation, environmental laws, workers' and unemployment compensation, safety and industrial health legislation, and employer/employee relations legislation. The second category includes any changes in laws affecting Georgia citizens and their rights. These include such things as education and health.

Is lobbying a part-time job or a full-time one?

It's definitely a full-time job in January, February, and March when the General Assembly is in session. It also remains a part-time job the balance of the year. Interim committees are meeting. Preparations are going on for the actual 40-day session. Administrative agencies which have an effect in your area are operating. Conditions are constantly changing. Legislative activity in some degree goes on 12 months of the year. So, lobbying is a blend of full-time and part-time. You can't be really effective if you lobby only part of the year. You must continually be involved and maintain contacts.

What are the characteristics you feel a lobbyist has to have to be good at his or her job?

A good lobbyist certainly has to be honest. He must have knowledge in the areas he wishes to influence. He must be persuasive. That is, he has to be able to express in words his knowledge, opinions, and attitudes about legislation. To be successful, a lobbyist needs to have legislators believe him and feel they can rely on him. So, the information he supplies must be based on facts.

What do you do if a legislator asks for information and you don't have it?

If you don't have the answers, you must readily admit you don't. However, if you are asked for information you don't have, you must seek it out and provide it. To be really effective, you must know both sides of an issue. You have to know what arguments there will be against legislation that you are for in order to present counter arguments.

LOBBYING: TWO VIEWS

Sometimes, the activities of lobbyists raise questions about fairness and honesty in government. As long as lobbying involves appealing to a legislator's reason, there is no problem. However, lobbying has included other tactics, such as providing legislators with favors, gifts, and loans. Legislators influenced by these tactics leave themselves open to charges of corruption.

Because lobbying often included such tactics, the writers of the Georgia Constitution felt the need to include this statement:

> Lobbying is declared to be a crime, and the General Assembly shall enforce this provision by suitable penalties.

However, to protect the right of all citizens to have some say in lawmaking, Georgia law allows lobbying activities "intended to reach the reason of the legislators."

There are several different views about what lobbying is and what it should be.

Two such views are presented in excerpts from newspaper articles. While one critically examines the influence of "corporate lobbyists," the other looks at the new breed of "grass-roots lobbyists."

LOBBYISTS' POWER MOUNTING

Adapted from the Atlanta Journal and Constitution, *December 26, 1976*

In 1974, then-Gov. Jimmy Carter became so exasperated over the influence that special interests had over the legislature that he toyed with the idea of seeking an injunction to ban them from the capitol.

"The influence of lobbyists is too great in our state government," Carter thundered in his 1974 state-of-the-state address before the General Assembly.

Judging from the information gathered in interviews with dozens of politicians, lobbyists, and capitol observers over the past few weeks, what some call "the fourth branch of government" is possibly even more powerful now than during the Carter years at the capitol.

And, the great source of that power is the untold and some insiders say "tremendous" financial resources that special interest groups, primarily the pro-business lobbyists, spend shaping Georgia's laws.

No one knows how much money is spent for this purpose by the nearly 400 registered lobbyists and the corporations and organizations they represent. Georgia is one of 27 states that do not require lobbyists to report their expenditures. Several attempts to pass a law requiring this have failed. . . .

According to informed sources, the methods special interest groups use to perpetuate a legislature "run lock, stock and barrel by big business"—to use the phrase of two of them—are subtle, complex and often ethically questionable.

It's pretty well agreed that a lobbyist cannot corrupt a legislator for the price of dinner and drinks.

But frequent invitations to lunch, evenings out on the town, occasional hunting trips, invitations to conventions in resort cities and giving gifts which include dearly sought football tickets are subtle but effective ways of establishing the very personal relationship lobbyists consider vital. . . .

. . . Special interest groups know if you can convert a legislator into your lobbyist, he'll do you a lot more good than any 10 guys loitering around the halls of the capitol.

This means campaign support and continuing support of the legislator during his term to insure that his constituents feel he is ably representing them. . . .

Do special interest groups actually offer bribes that are accepted?

"That depends on what you mean by bribery," one politician said. "And, hardly anybody knows what bribery means. You'd have to prove that such and such an action resulted directly from such and such a payment. . . ."

Is cash ever given and received for favors?

"You hear talk, rumors, sometimes," one legislator with a reputation for being honest replied. "I don't know of any senator that's ever gone to the extent of putting out a press release saying he'd taken so much money. I've never seen it. But then, I don't suppose you would even if it was going on all around you."

A senator said on one occasion he had the strong impression a lobbyist was "in so many words" dangling the prospect of financial reward before him. "I just had that feeling, but he was so slick he could see I wouldn't be taking even before he let his cat out of the bag."

Most of those interviewed flatly said they did not believe cash changes hands in the General Assembly.

One thing is certain. Few legislators would welcome taking the witness stand in open court to testify against one of their own colleagues.

"That," one said, "would be an unpleasant subject."

1. According to the author of *Lobbyists' Power Mounting*, what are some ways that special interest groups can influence legislation?

2. What does it mean to have a conflict of interest? How could a legislator avoid having a conflict of interest?

Grass-roots lobbying is somewhat different from the kind of lobbying discussed in the previous newspaper article. In "Grass-Roots Lobbying: What is It?" a professional lobbyist who specializes in organizing people discusses "how to do it."

GRASS-ROOTS LOBBYING: WHAT IS IT?

Adapted from the Atlanta Journal and Constitution Magazine, *February 5, 1978*

. . . Grass-roots lobbying has come of age, and Tom Graf, executive director of The Atlanta Association for Retarded Citizens, is considered an authority in the field.

Basically it's mobilizing people who believe in a cause—volunteers for the most part—to influence their fellow citizens and public officials to take their side. The process involves a lot of telephoning, letter-writing and person-to-person contact, holding meetings and rallies, testifying before legislative committees, speaking to civic groups and in general arousing the populace and politicians.

Graf knows some business lobbyists whose fees run as high as $450 per day simply because of their contacts—that is, the officials they know in government. At the grass roots, it's people power that counts.

"For the first time in years, there's more balance in the types of groups that influence government," Graf says. "In the past lobbyists for corporations have had all the clout, but beginning with the civil rights movement in the 60s, some changes started taking place. . . ."

The Georgia Constitution gives every citizen the right "to apply to those vested with the powers of government for redress of grievances by petition or remonstrance."

If the "redress" involves making or changing a state law or the appropriation of state funds, an act of the General Assembly may be required. It takes some doing, but a citizen or citizen's group just may be able to get something done, even as business and labor interests do.

Here are 10 tips for grass-roots lobbying based on techniques developed by Tom Graf:

1. Know exactly what you want. Narrow the issues. Don't reach for the moon in one grab.
2. Get your facts straight. Don't give out less-than-accurate information just to make your cause look better. This can turn legislators off fast, because it can make them look bad if they rely on data that goes sour on them.
3. Stick to your own cause. Beware of alliances with other groups supporting other causes. You may turn off some of your legislative support this way.
4. Start with the legislators from your own district, both senators and representatives, and work out from there. Even if they are not with you and you must look elsewhere for support, don't try to pull off something behind their backs.
5. Letters and telegrams to individual legislators are better than petitions. They should not all sound alike, and they should be written by real people.
6. Get people you know, both average citizens and persons or officials of some importance to contact their legislators.
7. Contact House and Senate leaders and chairmen of the committees which will be handling the legislation you are interested in.
8. Keep track of the legislation. Be sure you know when it will be coming up in committee. Ask to testify, and get others to testify, including experts, if possible.
9. Hold your temper, but be persistent. Do not let temporary setbacks get you down. Pick yourself up, regroup and go on.
10. Follow through. If you promise information, supply it. If you get messages to call, call. And if your bill passes, thank your legislators and then be sure the governor signs the measure.

1. How are grass-roots lobbyists different from corporate lobbyists?
2. How are their tactics similar? How are they different?

Women for and against the Equal Rights Amendment exchange views outside the House chambers.

ACTIVITIES FOR CHAPTER 6

Class Discussion

A. Lobbies have so much influence in lawmaking that they are sometimes referred to as the legislature's "third house."

1. At what points in the legislative process may lobbyists influence that process?
2. How might the legislature's work be made more difficult if there were no lobbying of any kind?

B. Some state legislatures in other states have enacted laws to control lobbying strictly. These laws not only require the lobbyist to register (as in Georgia) but also to report money received for lobbying, money spent for lobbying activities, what specific legislation the lobbyist is trying to influence, and the names of all legislators contacted.

1. What effect might such a law have on the legislative process?
2. If such a law were passed, who should have to meet its requirements? Lobbyists for business and industry? Grassroots lobbyists? All persons appearing at the capitol to influence legislators? Explain your answer.

Writing Project

As a reporter for an Atlanta television station you've been assigned to do a feature story describing the variety of interest groups that lobby at the General Assembly. First, you make a list of groups whose registered agents you spot at the capitol. (Actually these are only a few of the hundreds who register.)

American Civil Liberties Union
Assn. County Commissioners of Georgia
Brotherhood of Locomotive Engineers
Coastal States Life Insurance Company
Coca-Cola Company
Common Cause
Fraternal Order of Police

General Motors Corporation
Georgia Assn. of Educators
Georgia Business & Industry Assn.
Georgia Catholic Conference
Georgia Chamber of Commerce
Georgia Forestry Assn.
Georgia Poverty Rights Organization
Georgia Wildlife Federation
Georgia Nurses Assn.
Georgia Hotel-Motel Assn.
Georgia Automobile Dealers Assn.
Georgia Motor Trucking Assn.
Georgia Power Company
Georgia Farm Bureau
Georgia Sport Shooting Assn.
Georgia Press Assn.
Georgia Assn. of Realtors
Georgia Funeral Directors Assn.
Independent Bankers Assn.
League of Women Voters of Georgia
Metropolitan Atlanta Mental Health Assn.
National Organization for Women
North Fulton County PTA
Seaboard Coast Line Railroad
Sierra Club
Standard Oil Company
State Bar of Georgia
Stop ERA Committee
United Auto Workers
United States Brewers Assn.
Young Democrats of Georgia

Next, you decide to classify the groups on your list according to the general area of interest with which you think they are associated. You decide to have four categories: (1) political/legal issues, (b) economic/financial issues, (c) social/human issues, and (d) environmental/scientific issues. Classify the group as best you can based on clues in their names or what you may know about them. Your teacher may have more information about them.

Start your report with "The most common area of interest of Georgia lobbies is. . ." Complete your report for a five-minute spot on the six-o'clock news. Be sure to include example of lobbies in each of the four categories.

III THE EXECUTIVE BRANCH

The Governor of Georgia
Executive Organization
Education
Human Development
Resources and Roads
State Government and Private Enterprise
Financing State Government

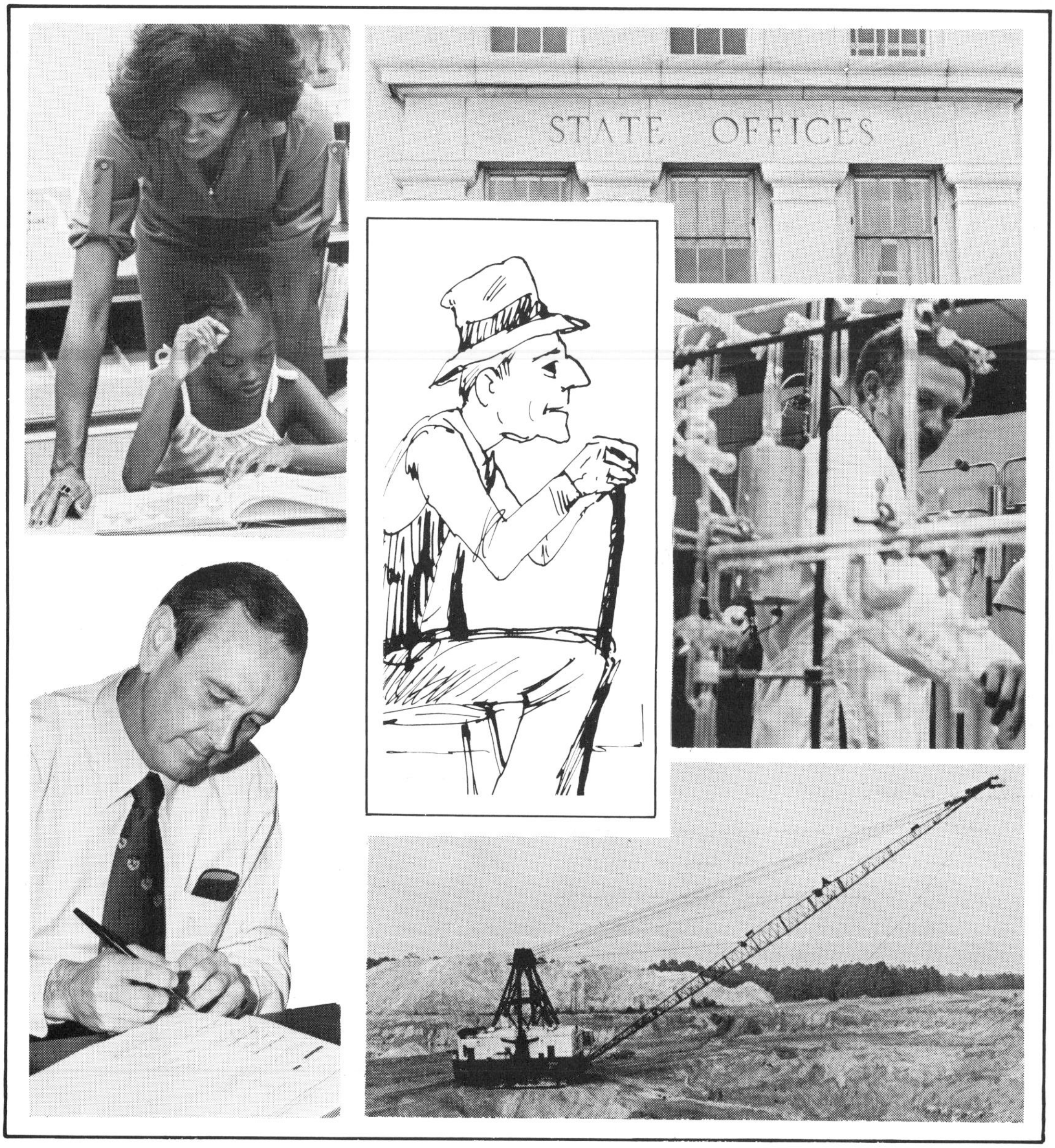

STATE OFFICES

unit 3

Introduction

What happens after a bill becomes a law? How are a law's words turned into actions which actually affect the people?

The responsibility for acting—for carrying out laws—belongs to the executive branch of government. It's a big job. While it takes only a few hundred persons to make state laws, it takes over 70,000 persons to carry out the laws. It's a lot simpler to say in a law "roads shall be built" than it is to build them.

Because it's such a big job, Georgia's executive branch is divided up into dozens of agencies. An agency may be a department, bureau, commission, or other division of government.

Each agency has its own special concern. Often an agency's name tells you what that concern is: Department of Agriculture, Georgia Bureau of Investigation, State Forestry Commission are examples.

While many Georgians may never meet a member of the General Assembly, most come into regular, perhaps daily, contact with persons who work in the executive branch. Unlike legislators, who do most of their work at the state capitol in Atlanta, persons in the executive branch work in agencies scattered all over the state. The social worker helping a poor family, the college professor teaching students, the state trooper stopping a speeder—all are government workers.

The executive branch, then, is the action branch of government. This unit of *State Government in Georgia* looks at those actions. Keep in mind, though, that no government agency, no government worker, may carry out any action—from writing a speeding ticket to teaching a college class—without the legislative branch first passing a law providing for that action.

Unit III has seven chapters. Chapter 7 focuses on the governor, Georgia's chief elected official. Chapter 8 looks at how the executive branch of state government is divided into agencies. The next four chapters describe some of the activities of state government: chapter 9, Education; chapter 10, Human Development; chapter 11, Natural Resources; chapter 12, Regulation. Who pays for all this government activity? Chapter 13 discusses how state government budgets are made and taxes are paid.

Later, in Unit IV, some executive agencies that work closely with Georgia's courts will be presented.

7 The Governor of Georgia

The Augusta Chronicle—June 18, 1975
BUSBEE RECALLS ASSEMBLY TO TRIM GEORGIA BUDGET

Athens Banner-Herald—January 17, 1961
VANDIVER TO GIVE SPECIAL ADDRESS

The Macon Telegraph—February 28, 1958
GRIFFIN DENIES FUNDS TO SENATE FACT-FINDING BODY

The Macon Telegraph—December 14, 1966
ALTO INVESTIGATION CALLED BY SANDERS

What do these headlines have in common? The names—Griffin, Vandiver, Sanders, Busbee—all are names of Georgia governors. At the times these headlines appeared, each of the names was instantly recognized by Georgia citizens as "the governor."

As head of the executive branch, the governor is the chief officer of state government. The governor has more power and more influence in state affairs than any other state official. When he speaks or acts, it's news and people take notice. This is because what the governor says or does can affect the lives of many individuals.

The governor is elected statewide, by all the voters of the state. His powers reach into all areas of government. He is the one state official whom most citizens recognize by name.

THE OFFICE OF GOVERNOR

The Georgia Constitution of 1976 spells out the term of office, qualifications, and election procedure for the governor.

The governor has a term of four years. As long as one term of office does not immediately follow another, no limit is set on the number of times a governor may be reelected. But once a governor serves two terms in a row, he or she may never again be elected governor.

To be eligible for the office of governor, a man or woman must be a U.S. citizen for 15 years and a citizen of Georgia for the 6 years before the election, and be at least 30 years old.

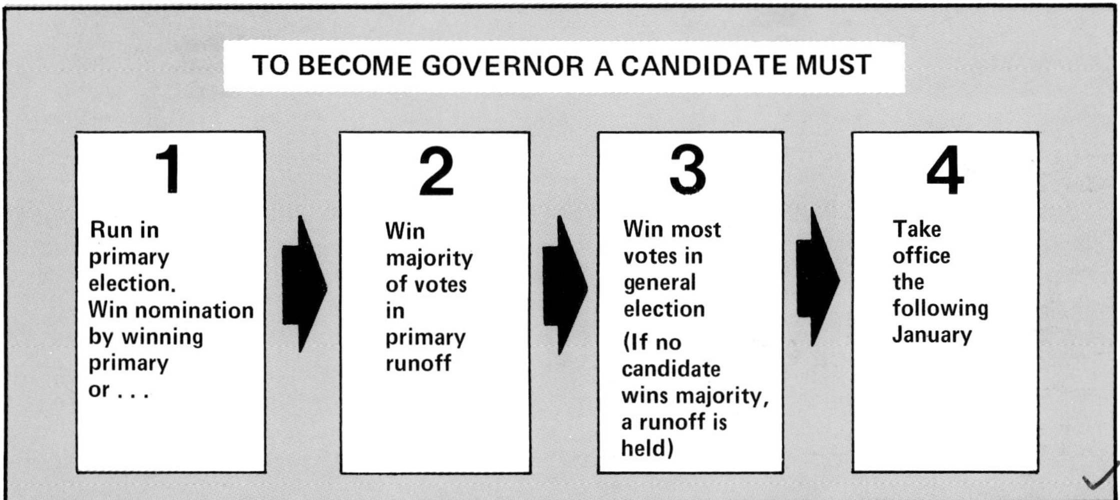

The election for governor is held every four years at the regular general election in November.

The governor-elect takes office the following January.

The Georgia Constitution also provides for a lieutenant governor. The term of office, qualifications, and election procedure are the same as those for the office of governor. The lieutenant governor serves as president of the Georgia Senate. In case of the death, resignation, or disability of the governor, the lieutenant governor acts as governor.

Before assuming office, the governor must take the following oath:

> I do solemly swear (or affirm) that I will faithfully execute the office of Governor of the State of Georgia, and will, to the best of my ability, preserve, protect and defend the Constitution thereof, and the Constitution of the United States of America.

Recent Georgia Governors

What kind of person gets elected governor of Georgia? Since 1930, only white, male, Protestant Democrats have been elected.

However, as the times change, the issues in political campaigns change. And Georgians' preferences in governors change. In fact, most ex-governors who tried to regain office did not get re-elected.

The chart on page 70 shows some characteristics of recent Georgia governors.

Note that until 1943, the governor's term of office was two years.

THINK ABOUT IT

1. What kinds of political offices did the governors hold immediately before becoming governor?
2. What is the most common occupational background of the governors?

Powers of the Governor

The governor is sometimes said to wear "different hats." For example, in one day he may act as chief executive, chief legislator, and commander-in-chief. Some of the governor's powers—the formal powers—are set down in the Georgia Constitution and in statutory law. Other powers—the informal powers—stem from customs and traditions that have grown up around the office.

How a governor uses these powers depends upon his or her own political skill and how he or she views the office. Does

As governor, Jimmy Carter meets with visitors at the capitol.

RECENT GEORGIA GOVERNORS

Governor	Term in Office	Age at Election	Occupation	Political Office Prior to Election
Richard B. Russell, Jr.	1931-1933	33	Attorney	Speaker, Georgia House of Representatives
Eugene Talmadge	1933-1937 1941-1943	48	Attorney Farmer	Georgia Commissioner of Agriculture
Eurith D. Rivers	1937-1941	41	Attorney	Speaker, Georgia House of Representatives
Ellis G. Arnall	1943-1947	35	Attorney	Attorney General of Georgia
M. E. Thompson	1947-1948*	43	Educator	State Revenue Commissioner
Herman Talmadge	1948-1955*	35	Attorney	None
S. Marvin Griffin	1955-1959	47	Newspaper Editor	Lt. Governor
S. Ernest Vandiver, Jr.	1959-1963	40	Attorney	Lt. Governor
Carl E. Sanders	1963-1967	37	Attorney	President Pro Tem, Georgia Senate
Lester G. Maddox	1967-1971	51	Businessman	None
Jimmy Carter	1971-1975	46	Navy Officer Farmer Businessman	Member, Georgia Senate
George Busbee	1975-	47	Attorney	Majority Leader, Ga. House of Representatives

**In the election of 1946, Eugene Talmadge was elected to a fourth term as governor but died before taking office. The Georgia Supreme Court ruled that Thompson, elected as lieutenant governor, would be acting governor until the next general election, which Herman Talmadge, son of Eugene Talmadge, won in 1948.*

the governor see himself as a protector of the people's rights? A fighter for progress? Or as a manager of the state's business? Such differences in views influence how a governor uses power.

THINK ABOUT IT

1. How are formal powers different from informal powers?
2. Examine the newspaper items. Which of the governor's powers are illustrated in each of the newspaper items?

POWERS OF THE GOVERNOR

FORMAL

Chief Executive

1. Insures that all laws are carried out.
2. Appoints persons to many executive offices and boards and to elected judicial offices when vacancies arise.
3. Manages the state's budget. Receives money requests from agencies and oversees state spending.
4. Directs officials to carry out state laws, to conduct investigations, and to submit reports.
5. Orders extradition of criminals to other states and asks other states to return suspects to Georgia. Suspends death sentences temporarily. Directs attorney general to represent state in court cases.

Chief Legislator

1. Develops administration's legislative program. Proposes laws. Prepares budget bill.
2. Signs or vetoes legislation.
3. Addresses General Assembly with "State of the State" and budget messages each year.
4. Calls special sessions of the General Assembly to take up subjects determined by the governor.
5. Adjourns sessions when two houses cannot agree on time to adjourn.

Commander-In-Chief

1. Calls out Georgia National Guard when riots, disasters, or other emergencies threaten state.
2. Sends state troopers and GBI agents into communities when needed.
3. Heads state's civil defense.

INFORMAL

Chief of State

1. Speaks officially for state government and unofficially for the people.
2. Represents Georgia to federal government. Meets with president and other officials. Consults with Georgia's congressional delegation.
3. Meets with foreign government and business leaders to develop trade relations.
4. Represents Georgia to governments of other states.
5. Issues proclamations on holidays, to commemorate events and to honor people.
6. Speaks at ceremonies and other special events. Dedicates public and private facilities.
7. Lends support to charities, fund drives, and other projects.

Chief Politician

1. Honorary leader of state political party. Heads state party delegation to national convention. Appears at major party gatherings.
2. Meets with leaders of interest groups and of legislative and executive branches to develop policies.
3. Pushes administration proposals in General Assembly. Negotiates compromises among legislators. Publicly endorses or opposes bills.
4. Consults with interest groups and local government officials on appointments to positions.
5. Speaks out on important issues and problems affecting the state.
6. Holds press conferences and issues press releases.

GOVERNORS IN ACTION . . .

MADDOX BLASTS BUSING PROPOSAL

Adapted from the Columbus Ledger, *May 9, 1969.*

Atlanta—Gov. Lester Maddox has taken a strong stand against consolidation and closing of schools and busing of school children.

Maddox Thursday called federal policies on busing of school children "cruel, criminal and unconstitutional" and declared that the best interests of Georgia children, education, teachers and parents have been ignored.

Maddox said he realized he has no authority in matters relating to policy and regulations governing schools, but thought that as an elected official he could not stand idly by and ignore the situation.

SANDERS WARNS CITIZENS NOT TO MOLEST MARCHERS

Adapted from the Albany Herald, *August 5, 1965.*

Atlanta (AP)—Gov. Carl E. Sanders says state troopers in Americus have orders to make arrests anytime they see civil rights demonstrators manhandled by spectators.

"When we have an incident, we will step in and stop it," he told a news conference Wednesday. "We have afforded what I call adequate protection to the demonstrators."

"Whenever they have notified us that a demonstration is going to take place, we have patrolmen to make sure that it is done peacefully."

Sanders said the troopers in Americus have full authority to make arrests if demonstrators are molested and, "They will do just that."

CARTER TO TELL LATINS OF STATE

Adapted from the Savannah News Press, *April 9, 1972.*

Marietta, Ga. (AP)—Gov. Jimmy Carter boarded a Lockheed business jet Saturday and flew off to Latin America on a 10-day promotion and goodwill tour.

The governor will boost Georgia products—including Lockheed airplanes—on his visit to Mexico, Costa Rica, Colombia, Brazil and Argentina.

Carter said Georgia was a natural Latin American trade partner because of its location.

"Our port facilities. . . and our close geographical proximity to Central and South America make this area of the world a natural focus for the future development of new markets," he said.

BUSBEE SEEKS THREE NEW PRISONS, HOSPITAL

Adapted from the Atlanta Constitution, *November 15, 1977.*

Dublin— Gov. George Busbee proposed Monday that the state build three new prisons, a prison hospital. . . .

Busbee said he will ask the 1978 General Assembly session to approve design funds for the new institutions to relieve the prison overcrowding crisis.

"While I would prefer to be using the tax money spent for new prisons for public schools or to improve health care, it is impossible to ignore the prison needs," Busbee said.

Busbee also proposed a hospital to be operated by the Medical College of Georgia in Augusta "to serve inmates from throughout the Georgia prison system."

A DAY IN THE LIFE OF THE GOVERNOR

What's it like to be governor of Georgia? One way to answer this question is to look at a typical day in the life of a governor.

Actually, the governor has so many different roles, powers, and responsibilities, that there is no such thing as a typical day. On one day, he may have to spend most of his time on legislative matters. On the next, he may be tied up with public appearances. On the third, the governor may take most of the day to make executive decisions.

But one aspect is typical from day to day: there's never enough time to do all the things a governor is asked to do. Because of this, a governor must carefully budget his time. Otherwise, important matters might be left unattended.

The governor's staff plans his day's schedule in advance. Major activities, such as speeches and meetings away from his capitol office, are planned several months in advance. There are many decisions to be made. For example, on a certain day should the governor attend a fund-raising dinner in Savannah or speak at a labor union convention in Atlanta?

Once the governor's day begins, his schedule may be changed. Emergency situations requiring his attention crop up almost every day. Important phone calls can take a lot of time from the planned schedule. High officials may suddenly decide they need "five or ten minutes" of the governor's time. As a result, scheduled activities–such as a press conference or attendance at a ceremony–sometimes have to be cancelled.

The following "day in the life of the governor" shows how Gov. George Busbee might have kept busy during the legislative session in 1979.

A Day in the Life of the Governor during a Legislative Session

Time	Place	Activity
8:00 a.m.	Peachtree Plaza Hotel.	Breakfast speech. Association of County Commissioners of Georgia
9:15 —	Office.	Meet with floor leaders to discuss progress of bills in each house.
10:15 —	Office.	Swearing-in ceremony. New members of Board of Industry and Trade. Also photographs.
10:45 —	Office.	Meet with Macon business delegation.
11:15 —	Office.	PHOTOGRAPH. With group of high school honor students.
12:00 —	World Congress Center.	Luncheon. International Trade Association.
1:30 p.m.	Capitol Steps.	PROCLAMATION of state holiday.
2:00 —	Office.	Press briefing with press secretary.
2:30 —	Office.	Press conference.
3:15 —	Office.	Meet with Clarke County legislative delegation.
3:30 —	Office.	Courtesy call. Ambassador of Japan.
4:00 —	Office.	Budget briefing with director of Office of Planning and Budget.
8:00 —	Governor's Mansion.	Dinner honoring freshman legislators.

Written-in activities are added to the schedule after the day begins. During the day, there are dozens of other phone calls to the governor and requests to meet with him. These are handled by his executive assistant or other staff members. Members of the staff are almost constantly in and out of his office with papers to be signed, questions to be answered, and decisions to be made.

In the schedule on page 73, you saw how a governor carries out his various powers during a typical day. Which activities show him in his role as chief executive? as chief legislator? Which are public relations activities? ceremonial activities?

INTERVIEW WITH THE GOVERNOR

George Busbee became governor of Georgia in January 1975. During Busbee's term in office, the Georgia Constitution was amended to allow a governor to succeed himself in office. In 1978, Governor Busbee was reelected. He thus became the first Georgia governor to be elected to successive four-year terms.

THINK ABOUT IT

1. In the area of policymaking, what are Governor Busbee's top priorities? Why has he chosen these two areas?
2. According to Governor Busbee, why does a governor have to be a good manager?
3. How does Governor Busbee's experience as a member of the General Assembly seem to influence his view of the office of governor?

Has the job of being governor turned out to be what you expected when you assumed the office in 1975? Were there any surprises?

After 18 years as a member of the Georgia House of Representatives, during which time I observed the operations of five governors, I had pretty solid grounding in the responsibilities of the governor. The biggest surprise was the realization that the demands on the governor's time leave little opportunity for family life or even dinner at home in the evening. I recently noted that my calendar contained nighttime events on 22 consecutive evenings.

What experiences did you have before assuming office that particularly helped you take on the duties of governor?

My experience as majority leader and on appropriations committees gave me a valuable understanding of budget preparation and how the budget works in practically every state agency. This was the most useful preparation for being governor. The budget is the tool with which a governor accomplishes his programs and shapes state government.

What aspects of being governor do you most enjoy?

The most enjoyable aspect of being governor is meeting Georgians from all walks of life and finding out how state government can help them.

Is there some part of the job you'd just as soon not have?

I knew when I assumed office that the ceremonial aspects of service as governor are important and meaningful to certain groups of Georgians. I'm not interested in eliminating any of the functions of the office. But, I do have to balance my schedule so that there is enough time to deal with the issues and problems facing state government.

On what kinds of problems do you find yourself spending the most time?

There is a great variety of problems which may crop up in state government. It is impossible to identify any particular types of problems which occur more regu-

larly than others. I spend the largest block of time in preparing and writing the annual budget. This process begins in October and runs through December.

What kinds of decisions are the most difficult for you to make?

Making appointments to judgeships, boards, bureaus, and commissions is my most difficult task. I try to locate the most qualified individual for each and every vacancy. When there is more than one qualified prospect, the task is even more difficult. The job of talking busy and successful men and women into accepting time-consuming responsibilities in state government is not easy.

How do you determine what's best for all the people of the state? How do you keep in touch with the people?

I am keenly aware that our people still lag behind the national average in such things as income, education, and housing. In choosing education and economic development as my top priorities, I am doing my best to bring Georgia up to national standards. If Georgians have opportunities for a quality education from kindergarten to the college level and have skilled well-paying jobs waiting for them when they leave school, many of our problems with prisons and welfare will diminish.

I keep a strict schedule of weekly news conferences. I also make myself available for call-in radio and television shows on which the people ask questions. I keep up with my mail. On my travels throughout the state, I make a point of talking with average Georgians about their state government.

As a member of the General Assembly and now as governor you have been on both sides of the governor-legislature relationship. How much power can the governor exert in legislative matters without damaging our traditional separation of powers?

There was a time in Georgia when the governor exerted too much power over the legislature. The budget was rubber-stamped with little or no discussion. The governor really chose the House Speaker and important committee chairmen in both the House and Senate. While I was in the House, I was pleased that the legislature achieved independence.

In working with an independent legislature, the power the governor exerts in behalf of his own programs is pretty much measured by how much public opinion is on the governor's side, the rightness of his position, and his personal power of persuasion.

Although he has a wide array of powers—budgetary, veto, appointment—the governor of Georgia shares the executive authority with several other elected officials. Does the governor of Georgia have enough power to get the job done?

Georgia does have an unusual number of elective department heads. As director of the budget, the governor must look at the budget requests of elected constitutional officers in the same manner as the budget requests of appointed department heads. The governor's Office of Planning and Budget watches over expenditures in all agencies, including those with elected heads.

The Constitution and laws of Georgia give the governor adequate authority to see that the functions of all agencies are carried out in the best interests of the people.

To be an effective governor, is it more important to be a good manager or a good politician? Why is that?

It takes a politician to get elected, but once in office a governor must have strong management and administrative skills. Otherwise, he will be made ineffective by persons capable of pulling the wool over his eyes. A governor should be knowledgeable about everything from the current price of asphalt to computer programming. Any politician who expects to gloss over the details of a $3 billion a year service industry would not remain a politician for long. I think the people today look behind mere talk and examine the real credentials of candidates for public office.

Of course, in order to be effective, the governor must keep a strong political base.

ACTIVITIES FOR CHAPTER 7

Class Discussion

A. The governor is responsible for making decisions which ultimately affect the lives of all Georgians. Much of the governor's power rests on this responsibility.

1. How is the governor's decisionmaking responsibility different from the General Assembly's decisionmaking responsibility?
2. On what kinds of questions does the governor make decisions? From what persons or groups does the governor get information on which to base those decisions?

B. In addition to decisionmaking responsibility, the governor has several other sources of power. How might each of the following contribute to the governor's power?

1. personality and political skill
2. public opinion
3. budget-making authority

Writing Project

Assume that you are the governor's press secretary. The governor has received a letter from an eighth grader—in a Georgia history and government class—who asks, "What kinds of things can the governor order people to do? What kinds of things must the governor persuade people to do?"

After discussing his answers with you, the governor asks you to draft a reply to the eighth grader. Write the letter. Be sure to include what you feel are the most important of the governor's powers.

8 Executive Organization

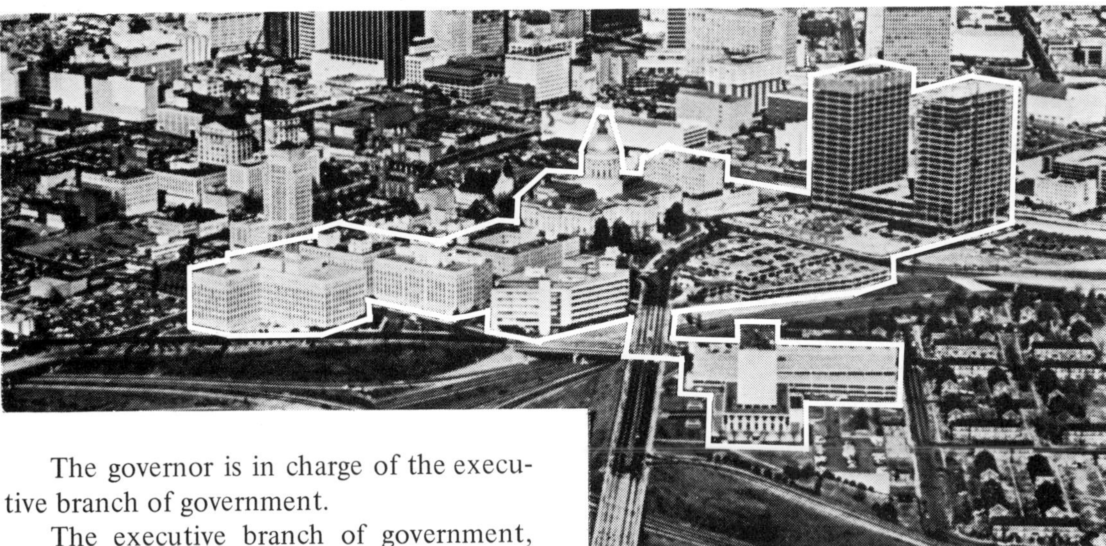

Capitol complex in downtown Atlanta. While the Office of the Governor and the General Assembly are in the capitol, the offices of most state agencies are in other buildings.

The governor is in charge of the executive branch of government.

The executive branch of government, sometimes called the *administration*, sees that the laws passed by the legislative branch are carried out. Some parts of the executive branch deliver services, others enforce regulations, and a few parts make sure the other parts are functioning according to law.

The executive branch can do a good job if it has the following three things going for it: (1) personnel, (2) organization, and (3) finances.

Personnel

In Georgia, over 70,000 people work in the executive branch. It is certainly the largest and most complex branch of government. (The judicial and legislative branches combined had fewer than 1,000 personnel in 1980.) The officials and employees of the executive branch greatly affect the quality of government. State troopers, college professors, highway maintenance crews, forest rangers, and social workers are all employees of the executive branch.

Finances

Money available to government and how it is spent also affects the quality of government services. The bulk of the state's revenue goes to pay for the activities of the executive branch. Each year, approximately 90 percent of the state's budget is allocated to the executive branch.

This chapter focuses on the executive branch's work force—its personnel—and how that work force is organized to carry out government functions. A later chapter will discuss state finances.

The executive branch is organized to divide up the task of carrying out the laws passed by the General Assembly. Each part of the executive branch has certain areas of responsibility and enforces laws that fall into those areas.

Organization

The way that state government carries out the law depends on organization. Even though a government might have good personnel and enough finances, poor organization may prevent it from providing quality services.

CHARTING THE EXECUTIVE BRANCH

The chart on page 79 shows how thousands of public officials and employees are organized into divisions within the executive, judicial, and legislative branches. It also shows how these divisions are related to one another. (Only larger agencies are shown. Small agencies, like the Office of Consumer Affairs, are not shown.)

Some executive agencies are headed by elected officials. Most agencies, however, are headed by appointed officials. Some, such as the Commissioner of Revenue, are appointed by the governor. In other cases, the governor appoints a policy-making board which in turn appoints the agency head. The Commissioner of Human Resources, for example, is appointed this way.

On the chart, elected officials appear *at the same level* as the governor while appointed officials are placed *under* the governor. Why? Also, why would the Georgia electorate—the voters—be put at the top, not the bottom, of the chart?

This chart shows the structure of state government in 1980. If you compared it with charts of state government in 1920 or 1950, you would find many differences. Government organization does not stay the same over a long period of time. It changes. The following reading describes some of those changes.

REORGANIZING THE ADMINISTRATIVE MACHINERY

THINK ABOUT IT

1. What changes in Georgia contributed to the growth of government?
2. What is the difference between constitutional agencies and statutory agencies?
3. What did both Governor Russell and Governor Carter try to do to improve government? Why was there opposition to their efforts?

A government's form of organization is like a factory's machinery. Just as factory workers need machinery to help them produce goods, government personnel need machinery to help them administer government services. This administrative machinery has no nuts and bolts. In a way, its invisible. It is the way that personnel are organized for work. And it is the procedure they follow on the job.

Machinery in a factory has to be changed from time to time to make a factory more efficient. So does administrative machinery. It sometimes has to be

-Xerox-

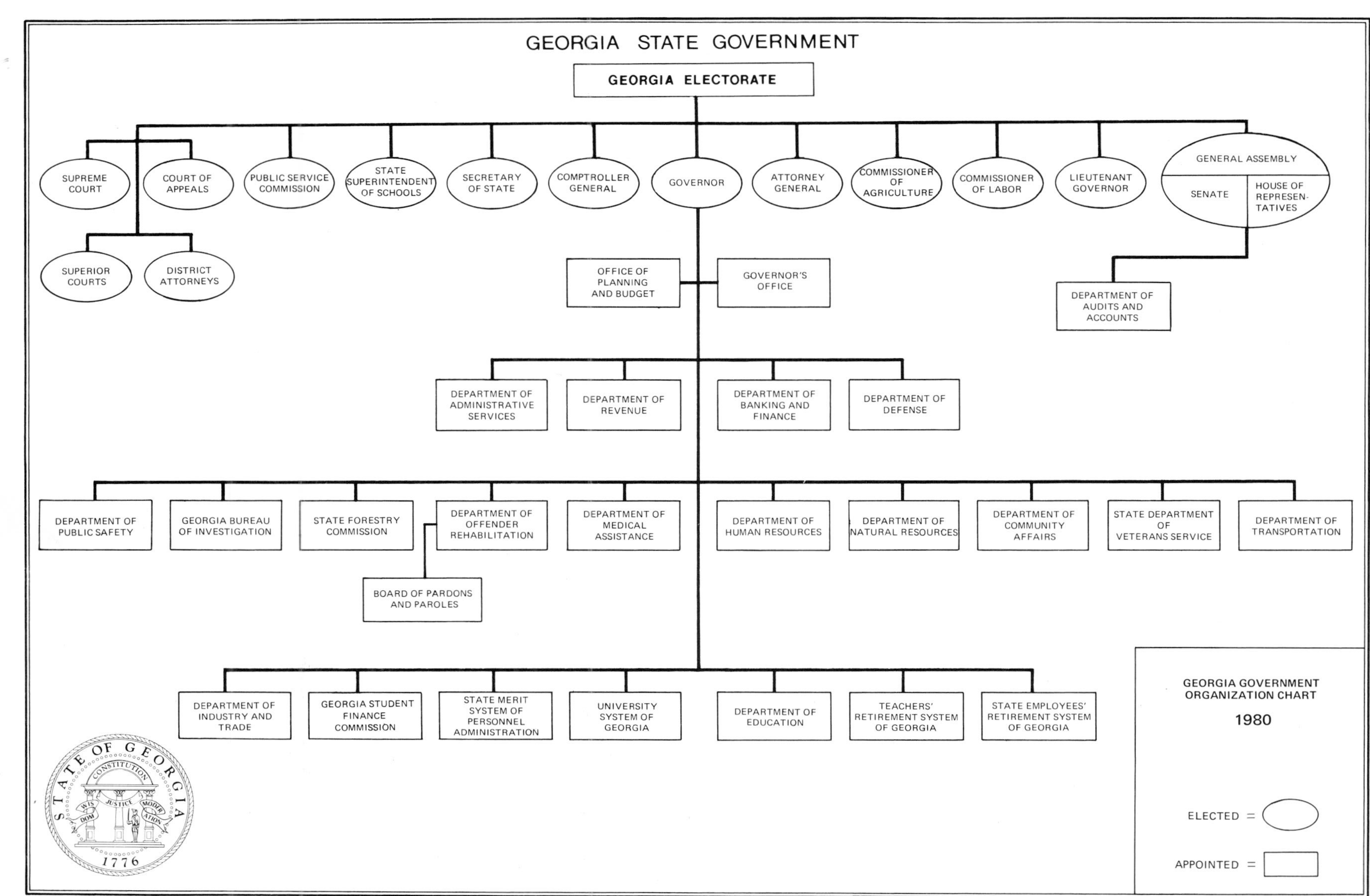
GEORGIA STATE GOVERNMENT
GEORGIA ELECTORATE
SUPREME COURT
COURT OF APPEALS
SUPERIOR COURTS
DISTRICT ATTORNEYS
PUBLIC SERVICE COMMISSION
STATE SUPERINTENDENT OF SCHOOLS
SECRETARY OF STATE
COMPTROLLER GENERAL
GOVERNOR
ATTORNEY GENERAL
COMMISSIONER OF AGRICULTURE
COMMISSIONER OF LABOR
LIEUTENANT GOVERNOR
GENERAL ASSEMBLY
SENATE
HOUSE OF REPRESEN-TATIVES
DEPARTMENT OF AUDITS AND ACCOUNTS
OFFICE OF PLANNING AND BUDGET
GOVERNOR'S OFFICE
DEPARTMENT OF ADMINISTRATIVE SERVICES
DEPARTMENT OF REVENUE
DEPARTMENT OF BANKING AND FINANCE
DEPARTMENT OF DEFENSE
DEPARTMENT OF PUBLIC SAFETY
GEORGIA BUREAU OF INVESTIGATION
STATE FORESTRY COMMISSION
DEPARTMENT OF OFFENDER REHABILITATION
BOARD OF PARDONS AND PAROLES
DEPARTMENT OF MEDICAL ASSISTANCE
DEPARTMENT OF HUMAN RESOURCES
DEPARTMENT OF NATURAL RESOURCES
DEPARTMENT OF COMMUNITY AFFAIRS
STATE DEPARTMENT OF VETERANS SERVICE
DEPARTMENT OF TRANSPORTATION
DEPARTMENT OF INDUSTRY AND TRADE
GEORGIA STUDENT FINANCE COMMISSION
STATE MERIT SYSTEM OF PERSONNEL ADMINISTRATION
UNIVERSITY SYSTEM OF GEORGIA
DEPARTMENT OF EDUCATION
TEACHERS' RETIREMENT SYSTEM OF GEORGIA
STATE EMPLOYEES' RETIREMENT SYSTEM OF GEORGIA
STATE OF GEORGIA
CONSTITUTION
WISDOM
JUSTICE
MODERATION
1776
GEORGIA GOVERNMENT ORGANIZATION CHART
1980
ELECTED =
APPOINTED =

reorganized to make a government more efficient.

New factory machinery might enable a manufacturer to turn out more products at a lower cost. But a factory owner has to decide whether installing new machinery is a wise move.

Government also has to carefully consider such a change. What will it cost? Will it provide more services at lower cost? How will government employees be affected? Will it make a difference?

Georgia's first state governments were very simple. Early state constitutions provided for several officials to be in charge of government services. The General Assembly authorized these officials to hire personnel to help carry out the few activities of state government. As long as government was small, organization wasn't too important. Good government depended mostly on the abilities and honesty of its personnel.

Later, as conditions in Georgia changed, state government took on more functions. The number of people employed to administer these functions grew. And, the administrative machinery grew.

For example, after the Civil War, Georgia needed a public school system to provide education for the newly freed blacks as well as the poorer whites of Georgia. The future of the state depended on a tax-supported school system to educate its youth. So the State Department of Education was organized to carry out the state's educational activities.

Another example: The arrival of mass-produced automobiles created the need for a state network of highways. In response to that need, the General Assembly in 1916 established a State Highway Commission. This new agency eventually grew into one of the largest agencies, the Department of Transportation. It had to grow to meet the needs of an ever-increasing number of motorists using the highways.

Generally the growth of the executive branch was unplanned. Agencies were added to meet demands for new state services.

Sometimes these new departments, bureaus, and commissions were *constitutional agencies.* That is, they were created by amendments to the state's constitution. More often, they were *statutory agencies.* That is, they were established merely by acts of the General Assembly and became part of statutory law.

There is a major difference between constitutional agencies and statutory agencies. The General Assembly may at will create or abolish a statutory agency. A constitutional agency can only be created or abolished by amendment voted upon by the people.

Statutory agencies could appear and disappear more easily than constitutional ones. However, once an agency appeared it tended not to disappear. The result was that by the early twentieth century, there were almost 100 separate state agencies.

Often the activities of one agency overlapped or conflicted with the activities of another. Sometimes services were needlessly duplicated. Sometimes they were neglected. The effect was inefficiency and wasted tax money.

To do something about this, over the years several Georgia governors tried to reorganize the executive branch. They tried to combine into a smaller number of agencies all activities and services that were similar in nature.

In 1931, Governor Richard B. Russell, Jr. asked the General Assembly for a total *reorganization* of the state's administrative machinery. He called for "a complete and thorough overhauling and rebuilding of our present structure of State Government."

WHAT'S A BUREAU?

An elderly woman in Mississippi read in the newspaper about Governor Russell's reorganization plan. She was interested in the news that he was getting rid of a number of bureaus. She wrote the governor that she would like to buy one of them if the price were low enough. Governor Russell wrote back that the bureaus he was doing away with were not the kind she needed and, anyway, they weren't worth even a small amount of money.

If you look up "bureau" in a dictionary, you'll find several different definitions of the word. Could Governor Russell's definition and that of the old woman in Mississippi have the same origin?

People often complain about "bureaucrats" and "the bureaucracy." To whom or what are they referring?

The General Assembly passed Governor Russell's reorganization plan. The number of executive agencies was reduced from over 90 to just 19. The effect was greater economy and efficiency.

Later, new social conditions created the need for more changes in government. The Great Depression of the 1930s, World War II, population growth, increased industrialization, the migration of Georgians from the farm to the city, and the civil rights movement forced state government to assume additional functions.

New agencies were established. Services and activities were shuffled from one department to another. Piecemeal reorganization went on almost constantly. Governors in the 1950s and 1960s pointed out the need for another total reorganization. But opposition to this was strong. Few agency heads were willing to turn over any of their programs to another unit.

In 1971, Governor Jimmy Carter addressed the General Assembly saying:

> Georgia has a long and distinguished history, and our state government has evolved to meet the changing needs of each succeeding year. But it has been almost 40 years since a major reorganization of state government was completed by [Governor] Richard B. Russell. . . .During my campaign I stated that there were 140 agencies in our government. Now I find that in the executive branch alone, we have more than 200 agencies which share the responsibility for conducting the affairs of our people. *It has gotten so that every time I open the closet door in my office, I fear that a new state agency will fall out.*

Governor Carter offered a reorganization plan. Some state officials supported it, but others opposed it. Certain administrators fought any reduction in their agencys' budgets or personnel. Some were determined not to give up any of their power. Still other agency heads argued that lower- not higher-quality services would result from reorganization.

After a long and bitter legislative battle, the General Assembly finally passed

"...WHERE Y'FIGURE ON STARTIN', JIMMY?"

a reorganization plan. Government activities were merged under two dozen major agencies. (Basically those shown on the "Georgia State Government" chart on page 79.) Dozens of small boards and commissions were abolished. Their functions were transferred to larger agencies.

Did reorganization, as Governor Carter had claimed, result in more efficient government performance? Did it make government more responsive to the needs of Georgians? Were there any savings of tax money? These questions continued to be debated long after reorganization went into effect.

Some critics said that the new larger agencies had just as many employees and spent just as much money as the more numerous small agencies had done before.

But Governor Carter could point to the new Department of Administrative Services. It supported other agencies by:

- providing a central payroll system for employees,
- purchasing motor vehicles, equipment, and certain supplies for other agencies, and
- centralizing communication systems, computer services, printing shops turning out reports and other documents, and the supervision of state property.

But change in government is a continuing story. In the 1970s, after Governor Carter's reorganization, each General Assembly faced the task of making some changes in the administrative machinery. Change was necessary to make government meet the changing needs of the people.

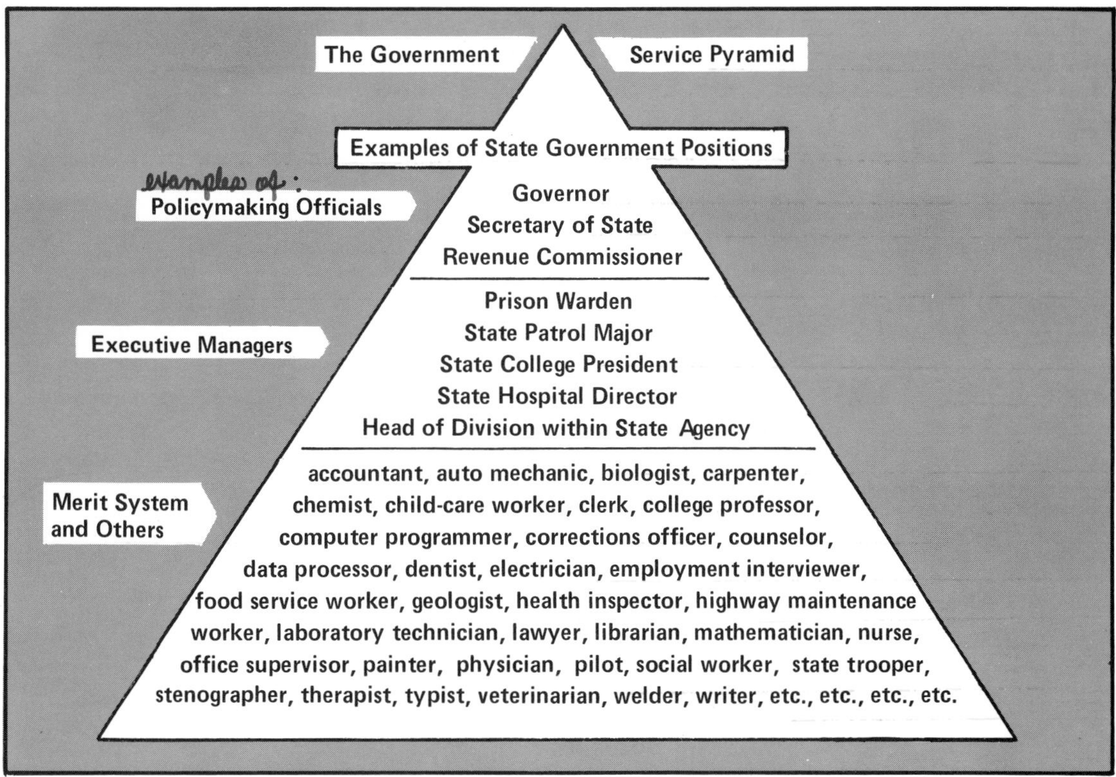

PEOPLE IN GOVERNMENT SERVICE

Good government rests not only on good organization but also on having the right persons in the right jobs.

The reading which follows describes the different categories of government personnel. It also presents the work of a state agency reponsible for seeing that the state hires and promotes people because of what they know, not who they know.

THINK ABOUT IT

1. What is a policymaking official? How are constitutional officers a special group of policymaking officials?
2. What kinds of work would a middle level manager do?
3. What are the functions of the Merit System? How have employment procedures changed under the Merit System?

There are many kinds of jobs in government. The persons who fill those jobs are generally referred to as either government *officials* or government *employees.* Both officials and employees work for the people and both are paid for their work. What's the difference?

The term "official" is usually reserved for someone who makes decisions affecting large-scale operations of government. Officials also organize and direct the work of many other government personnel. They make up only a small part of the total government work force.

On the other hand, the term "employee" usually refers to someone who is hired to work at a specific task. The vast majority of government workers are employees.

Actually, there is no definite dividing line between officials and employees. The "Government Service Pyramid" diagram above shows a different kind of division. A few government workers are at the top where major decisions are made. Most are at the base, delivering services.

Policymaking Officials

A *policy* is a plan of action selected to meet a goal, such as improving the schools or highways or state prison system. Policymaking officials decide, in a general way, what state agencies should do. Of course, they can only act if the General Assembly passes laws allowing them to carry out their programs.

Top policymaking officials may also make specific rules and regulations to carry out laws passed by the legislature. For example, the comptroller general may set fire safety standards for hotels, schools, apartments, department stores, nursing homes, prisons, and other such places.

Most top policymaking officials in Georgia are appointed, either directly by the governor or by boards whose members are appointed by the governor. But some are elected. They are known as *constitutional officers* because they are provided for in the Georgia Constitution. See chart, page 79 . Constitutional offices cannot be created or abolished except by constitutional amendment voted upon by the people.

Executive Managers

Look at the executive managers positions listed in the pyramid. Persons in middle level government jobs are mainly executive managers who are appointed to their positions. They may help to decide some policies, but they have less authority then higher officials.

This level includes personnel who run complex state services. For example, the director of a state hospital is appointed, or hired, to run that hospital. But he or she must follow the policy set by the Board and the Commissioner of Human Resources.

Merit System and Other Employees

Government employees at the base of the government service pyramid deliver the bulk of everyday government services to the people.

Some government employees have more authority than others. They may manage smaller units of government, such as offices scattered around the state.

The examples of jobs government employees perform that are listed in the pyramid are only a fraction of the thousands that actually exist. Practically as many kinds of jobs are performed inside government as outside government.

Each year hundreds of Georgians enter or leave government employment. How does state government get the persons it needs to handle these jobs? That's the responsibility of the Merit System.

ACTIVITIES FOR CHAPTER 8

Class Discussion

At one time almost all state employees were middle-class white males. Women were limited to typing and clerical positions. Now merit system laws prohibit discrimination in personnel matters because of political views, religion, race, sex, age, national origin, or physical handicap.

Yet, there is some criticism of the merit system. Said one official, "I'd like to hire this man I know real well. I know he could step right into this position in my department and do a great job. But, I have to go through the merit system to fill the position. I have to take somebody I don't even know."

1. What advantages might there be in having an official hire friends for government jobs? What disadvantages might there be?
2. Should all citizens have an equal opportunity to get a government job? Why? Why not?

What's a Merit System?

In 1980, over 40,000 state government employees* were covered by the regulations of the State Merit System of Personnel Administration.

The Merit System is a state agency set up to help insure efficiency in the rest of the executive branch. Its job is to see that merit, fitness, and efficiency are the bases for hiring, firing, promotion, and pay raises. And it classifies personnel so that someone doing a particular job in one agency gets the same pay as someone doing the same kind of job in another agency.

Why is there a state agency just to handle employment of personnel?

Before the Merit System was established, each state agency controlled its own hiring, promotions, and dismissals. Often a person's politics or friendships, not his or her abilities, determined whether or not that person got a state job. Usually getting a state job depended more on "who you knew" than on "what you knew." This was a big problem after elections. Each new administration would put its own people in state jobs. The turnover often caused whole departments to come to a dead stop while new employees learned their jobs.

Today, under the Merit System, no one should be employed who is not well-qualified for the job. No one should be promoted except on the basis of merit. And, no employee of any agency covered by merit system regulations may be fired except for good cause.

**Generally excluded from the Merit System regulations are: (1) elected officials, members of boards and commissions, agency heads, and other policymaking officials; (2) employees of the legislative and judicial branches, employees of the governor's office and the university system, and part-time or temporary employees.*

Writing Project

The editorial page of a daily newspaper usually contains not only written editorials, but also editorial cartoons. Such cartoons are used to give an opinion or a point of view. They often comment on an event, a public issue or problem, or the actions and ideas of a public figure. To get their message across, cartoons may exaggerate and poke fun. Sometimes they are deadly serious. A good cartoon might make the reader chuckle. More importantly, it should make him or her think.

Assume you are the cartoonist for a big city daily. To get an idea for tomorrow's cartoon, you read through today's paper. There's a big feature on state government. You jot down a few ideas which stick in your mind as possible subjects for cartoons:

1. "The executive branch is organized to divide up the task of carrying out laws passed by the legislative branch."
2. "As state government took on more functions, its administrative machinery grew."
3. "A few big agencies will spend just as much money and hire just as many employees as many little agencies."
4. "At one time, getting a state job depended on who you knew, not what you knew."
5. "After the elections, whole departments would come to a dead stop while new employees learned their jobs."

Assignment: Draw a political cartoon on one of these five ideas or another idea you get from this chapter. Be prepared to explain your cartoon.

Unit 4

9

Education

> The provision of an adequate education for the citizens shall be a primary obligation of the state of Georgia, the expense of which shall be provided by taxation.—*Georgia Constitution of 1976*

Providing education for all children at public expense is not a new idea in the United States. The founders of this country knew that the success of a democratic form of government depended upon education. How could a people govern themselves if they were not educated and informed?

Thomas Jefferson, who fought long and hard for public education, said, "If a (civilized) nation expects to be ignorant and free, . . . it expects what never was and never will be."

The writers of the United States Constitution decided to leave education to the states. Georgia's early constitutions provided that schools be set up in each county. However, the years before the Civil War saw very little public education in Georgia. Those who could afford it sent their children to private academies.

In 1870, Georgia's public schools got their real start when the General Assembly created a State Board of Education and an office of State School Commissioner. The next year about 31,000 children were enrolled. One hundred years later, there would be over 1,000,000 enrolled. During that hundred years, state government gradually increased its support of education. But for a long time, local *property taxes* furnished practically all the funds for the schools. This meant that if a certain county didn't have much income, it couldn't have very good schools.

Since the 1930s, state government has paid the largest share of the cost of public education in Georgia. It now pays over 50 percent of the cost, mainly from the general *sales tax* and the *income tax*. Local property taxes account for over a third of the cost. Federal funds provide for the rest.

As the state's share of the cost of education grew, so did the state's authority over the public schools.

For most of the hundred years between 1870 and 1970, public education in Georgia was racially segregated. Under the so-called "separate but equal" idea, there was a dual education system: one for whites, one for blacks. State law required segregation. Tax money supported both systems, but more was spent to educate each white child than each black child.

Then in 1954, the United States Supreme Court, in the case of *Brown v.*

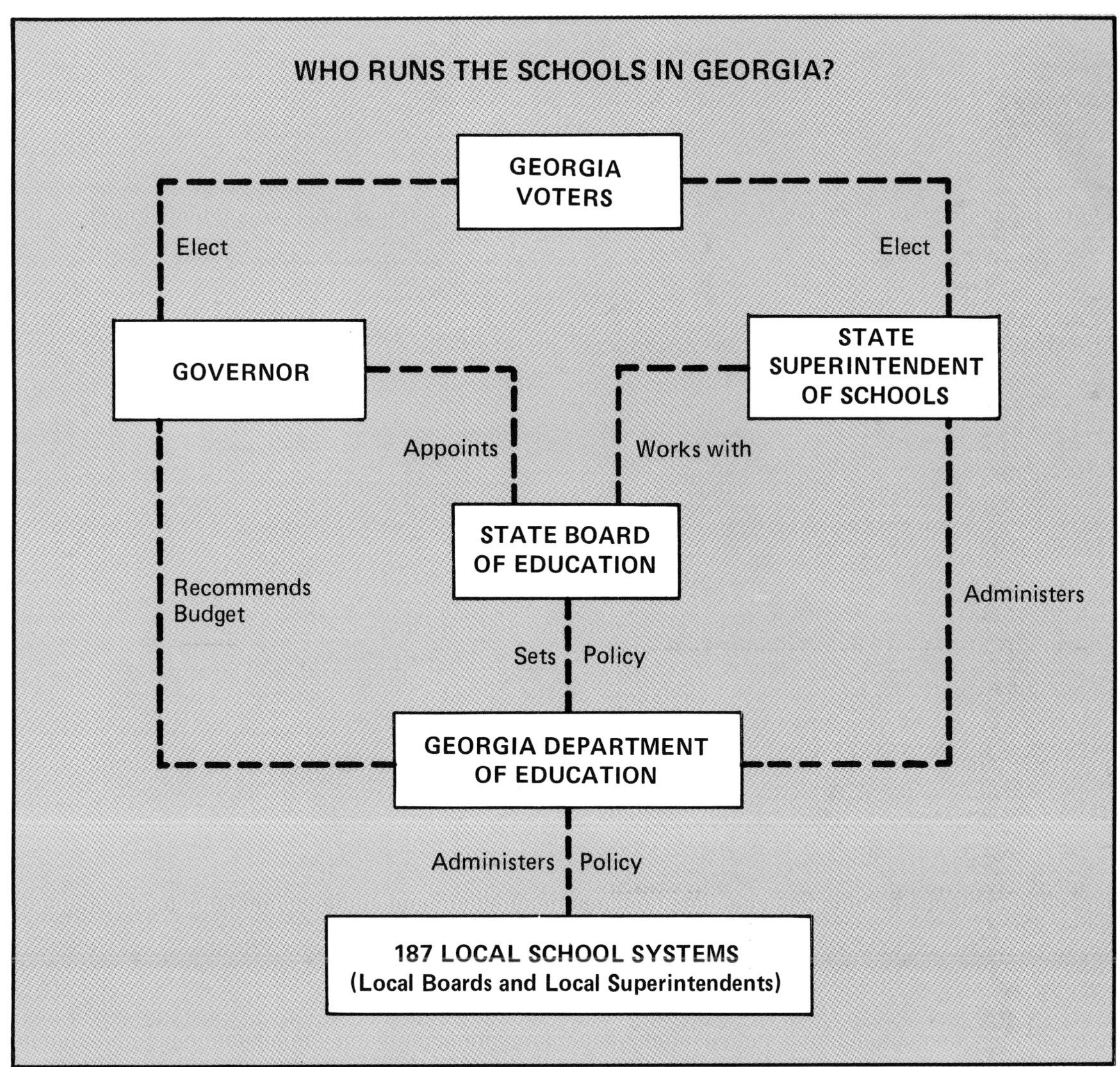

Board of Education, ruled against segregated public schools in another state. This ruling had the effect of wiping out the legal base for Georgia's dual system of schools. However, it took another 20 years to eliminate the segregated system in Georgia.

Today, Georgia operates one public school system under the Adequate Program for Education Act (often referred to as APEG), passed by the General Assembly in 1975. This act guarantees an adequate education to all children, black and white, in the state.

ADMINISTERING THE PUBLIC SCHOOLS

Education is the main responsibility of the state. Over 50 percent of the state budget goes to public schools and colleges each year. Running the public schools involves a sharing of responsibilities by state and local agencies and officials. The relationships among these agencies and officials is shown above. What they do is described in the following reading.

THINK ABOUT IT

1. How are the responsibilities of the State

Board different from those of the State Department of Education?

2. What are some specific ways in which the Department of Education helps local school systems provide education?
3. What is the state superintendent's relationship to the State Board and the Department of Education?

Board of Education

The State Board of Education makes *regulations* and policies for carrying out public education under the laws of the state. Its 10 members, one from each congressional district, are appointed to seven-year terms by the governor.

Here are some of the specific functions of the state board:

1. Establish high school graduation requirements
2. Establish minimum standards for school facilities
3. Establish minimum standards for curriculum and instruction
4. Set qualifications for teachers and principals
5. Adopt textbooks for purchase with state funds
6. Prepare the annual state budget for public schools
7. Supervise the Georgia Department of Education
8. Hear appeals in cases involving local board decisions

Local boards of education and local superintendents must operate county and city school systems within the framework of state board policies.

Department of Education

The Georgia Department of Education is the state agency that carries out the laws, regulations, and policies for the state's public schools. It manages and distributes state education funds (as well as most federal funds provided Georgia) to 187 local school systems. It enforces state

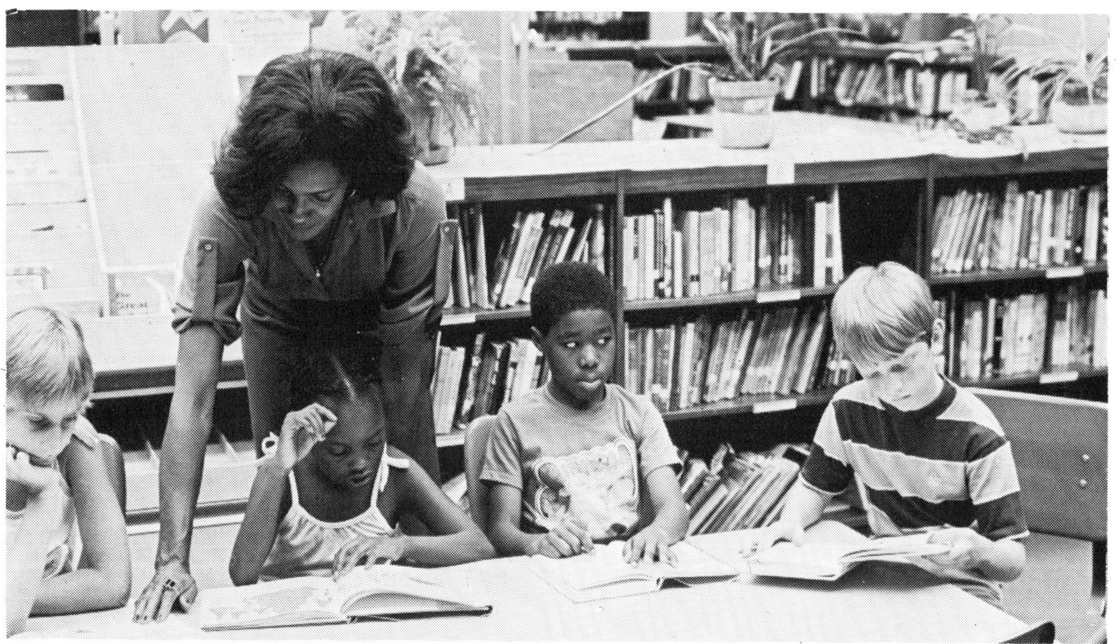

State funds help pay for books and equipment in school libraries like this one in Clarke County.

board standards and assists local systems with their education programs.

The Department of Education helps local schools by providing these services:

- Guidance and advice to teachers, principals, and local superintendents to help them improve their schools
- Specialists to help teachers choose new textbooks and films, plan new courses, try new teaching methods, and set up new laboratories
- Assistance with vocational and career education, programs for retarded and handicapped children, and guidance counseling
- Classes in food preparation, nutrition, menu planning, and food purchasing for cafeteria managers
- Transportation specialists to help local schools set up safe, convenient bus routes and conduct training programs for bus drivers and bus mechanics
- Architects and engineers to work with local school officials in designing, planning, and constructing new schools and athletic facilities
- Georgia Statewide Testing Program to measure the progress of students in grades 4, 8, and 11

The Department of Education directly operates several special schools: the state vocational-technical schools at Clarksville and Americus, the Georgia Academy for the Blind at Macon, the Georgia School for the Deaf at Cave Springs, and the Atlanta Area School for the Deaf. It also is responsible for adult education programs and for Georgia's network of public libraries.

Superintendent of Schools

The state superintendent of schools is the chief education official in Georgia.

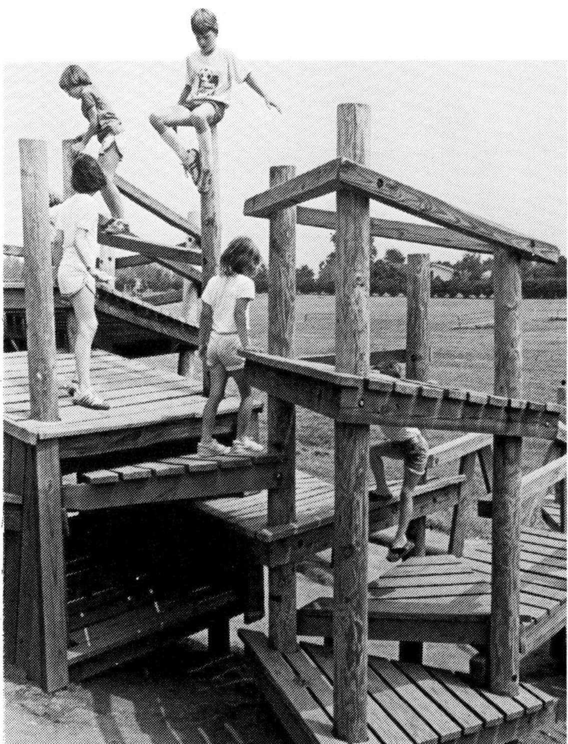

Recreation specialists at the State Department of Education help local school systems plan playgrounds.

The superintendent is nominated in a party primary and elected to a four-year term at the same time as the governor.

Georgia is one of 20 states in which the chief state school officer is elected by the people. In the other states, he or she is appointed by the state board of education or the governor.

To qualify for this office, a person must possess good moral character, high educational standing, three years experience as a teacher, and hold a five-year degree from an accredited college or university. Only someone with professional education experience can become state superintendent.

The state superintendent of schools is the head of the Georgia Department of Education and is executive secretary of the State Board of Education. He enforces the board's regulations and the state laws governing the public schools and makes recommendations to the board on matters affecting public education. He reports each year to the General Assembly on the activities of the Department of Education.

Interview with Dr. Charles McDaniel

In 1977, Dr. Charles McDaniel was appointed state superintendent of schools by the governor to complete the term of a person who had resigned. In 1978, he was elected to a full four-year term.

Dr. McDaniel is a professional educator, a former teacher, counselor, principal, and local school system superintendent.

THINK ABOUT IT

1. In what ways does the state superintendent have to be a politician?
2. According to Dr. McDaniel, why is education the concern of society as a whole and not just the concern of parents?

You recently had to run for office for the first time. What's your reaction to campaign politics?

Running for election meant that I had to be away from this office for about six weeks. Now, I enjoyed the activity of getting out and meeting people. But I didn't like having to ask people to vote for me or to support my campaign with money.

Is it difficult to be a politician and a professional educator at the same time?

It's very difficult.

Don't you, as head of the State Department of Education, sometimes have to go out and get the peoples' support for public education?

Certainly do. And, there's merit in that. I want to get out, shake hands, and meet people at the grassroots level. But, I just hate to put it on such a political level that later those who support me come back and say, "Now, I supported you and I want these favors." That's not the way I want to operate.

And then, when the General Assembly is in session, you have the task of asking the legislators to support public education, don't you?

Yes, and there are trade-offs there. It's a political task. The superintendent is the chief lobbyist among the members of the General Assembly and the governor for the cause of public education.

Is it mostly a question of money for education?

Mostly finances. The number one question is "What will you finance and at what level?" Maintaining a good relationship with the appropriations committees, the leaders of the House and Senate, and the governor is a most important political task.

And, you are all the time competing for the tax dollar with other state agencies.

Right. And, it's fierce competition.

On what kinds of problems do you find yourself spending the most time?

Trouble-shooting. I spend a good deal of time trying to answer parents' complaints about local systems miles away from here. Sometimes it's a local superintendent who calls in because he's having some difficulty with the state fire marshal. And people call who are unhappy with the bus routes in a certain county, so we have our bus folks take a look at it.

These local problems take up more time than I had expected.

So, people in the communities often call you instead of the local superintendent?

Often do. If they're unhappy with what the local superintendent has done, they feel that this is their next appeal even though it is a local problem. If the principal or superintendent doesn't satisfy them, they often bypass the local board of education and call directly here.

It sounds as if you have to be a diplomat as well as a politician.

You have to be diplomatic to work with 187 local superintendents, 236 members of the General Assembly, and 300 or so staff members in this department. But, you also have to be knowledgeable about what needs to be done and what's going on. And, you have to have some sense of direction. You have to set a course that is progressively upward and onward.

Turning from the political aspects of the job, what aspect of being superintendent appeals to you most?

The possibility to bring change. We in public education have had a lot of criticism. I would like to make changes to improve the overall educational program.

But, we can't do everything overnight. I have elected to begin at the early level, in the kindergarten and primary grades.

Sometimes people who do not have children of their own in public school say, "I don't see why I should pay taxes to educate someone else's kids." How would you respond to that kind of question?

I think public education is an opportunity for all of society. Even though I may not have children, I am part of a community whose children need schools.

Or, I may have had the opportunity to educate my children earlier. And, I had a public education myself back in the 1930s and 1940s. Now it's my turn to help give today's children a good education so that they will become responsible citizens.

I think if we neglect the education of today's children, we invite problems for the society of tomorrow.

HIGHER EDUCATION IN GEORGIA

THINK ABOUT IT

1. How do college and university teaching, service, and research influence social and economic conditions in Georgia?
2. How is public higher education organized in Georgia?

In 1784, the Georgia General Assembly set aside 40,000 acres of land "for the endowment of a college or seminary of learning." In doing so, it made Georgia the first state to provide for a public institution of higher education.

By 1980, the University System of Georgia had grown to consist of more than 30 universities, senior colleges, and junior colleges. These institutions are so located around the state that 95 percent of the people live within 35 miles of a college or university. This reflects the great need that people in all parts of the state have today for access to higher education.

The increasing importance of higher education in Georgia is shown in the steep rise in college enrollments. In 1930 there were an estimated 6,000 students attending public institutions of higher education. Fifty years later, enrollment in the university system approached 125,000, an in-

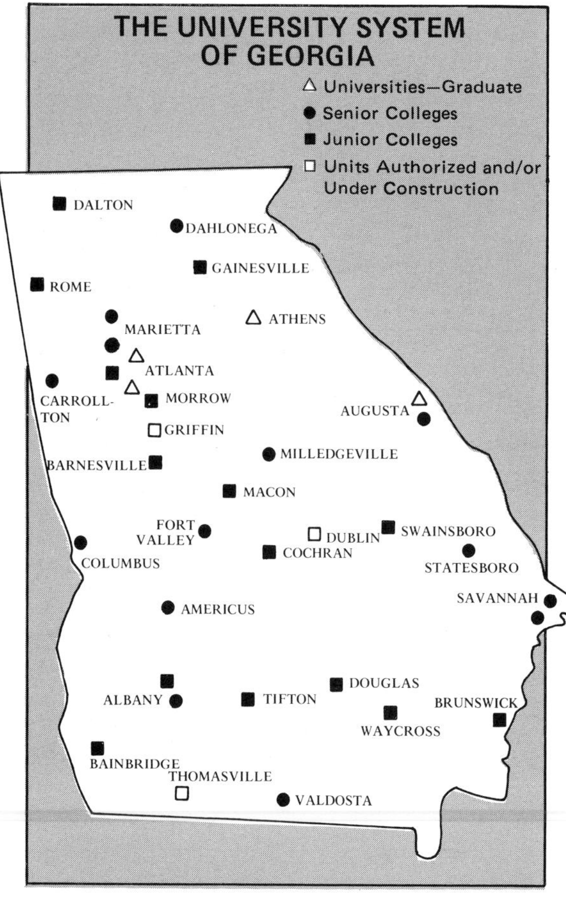

crease of more than 2,000 percent. During the same period, the state population grew by only 85 percent.

To meet this demand for higher education, state funding grew from a little over $2 million in 1930 to almost $400 million in 1980.

What do the people of Georgia get in return for tax money spent on higher education? The university system institutions have three main functions: teaching, service, and research.

Teaching is the primary function of all colleges and universities. It helps develop each student's potential. At the same time, it helps educate Georgia citizens so they will be able to solve the complex problems facing the state.

In addition, the colleges and universities prepare people for occupations in a modern technological society. Nurses, laboratory technicians, data processors, business managers, engineers, lawyers, teachers, foresters, and doctors all receive specialized educations in the university system.

Service is given by all the units of the university system. Generally, service extends the benefits of college teaching to all the people of the state.

Service may take many forms: a demonstration of teaching techniques, a publication reporting on pesticides, a workshop on zoning for city officials. Georgia Tech's Engineering Experiment Station, Georgia State's Urban Life Center, and the Cooperative Extension Service of the University of Georgia College of Agriculture are a few of the agencies set up to help solve problems ranging from animal disease and pollution control to alcohol abuse and mass transportation.

Research is conducted primarily at the four universities. Research is aimed at discovering new knowledge and applying knowledge to solving problems and meeting peoples' needs. Many research projects are directly related to improving the quality of life in Georgia.

For example, one researcher at the University of Georgia has been unravelling the mystery of how insects communicate. This work is a step toward effectively controlling fire ants and other pests which cause huge losses in agriculture.

Other researchers have shown that Georgia's coastal marshlands—once thought to be wastelands—are far more productive than the richest croplands. We now know that fishing and shrimping industries could vanish if the marshlands were filled in. (See Chapter 11 for more on the marshlands.)

Today, researchers at Georgia Tech are seeking ways to harness the sun's energy. Perhaps some day the homes of students

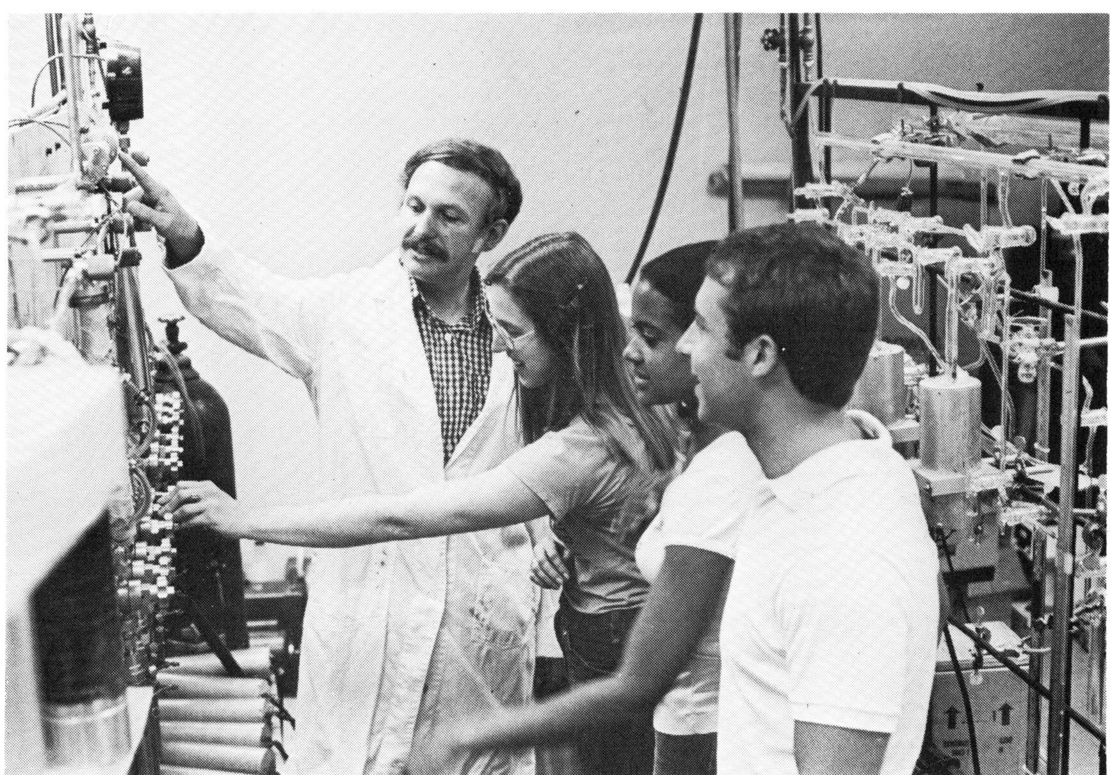

Students at the University of Georgia learn how to conduct research in this geology laboratory at the Athens campus.

reading this book will be heated and cooled by inexpensive solar energy because of this research.

Board of Regents

The Board of Regents controls the university system. It is composed of 15 members appointed by the governor and confirmed by the Senate for seven-year staggered terms.

The board is responsible for the operation and development of the system and each of its units. It has the power to do the following:

1. Establish institutions of higher education
2. Consolidate or discontinue institutions
3. Inaugurate or discontinue courses
4. Add or abolish degrees
5. Employ and remove professors and administrators
6. Set tuition rates
7. Approve budgets of each institution
8. Allocate funds to each institution
9. Approve construction of buildings
10. Purchase property for expansion of institutions

The chief executive officer of the board and the chief administrative officer of the system is called the chancellor. The chancellor is appointed by the regents and serves at their pleasure. He is responsible for carrying out the rules, regulations, and policies of the Board of Regents and generally supervises all units of the system.

Each unit of the system has a president

appointed by the board. The president is responsible for management of his institution's teaching, service, and research activities.

ACTIVITIES FOR CHAPTER 9

Class Discussion

Each year, over 50 percent of the state budget goes to operating public schools and colleges. Public education is often criticized as being too expensive. Some critics argue that private schools could do a better job.

1. In what ways does public education contribute to the well-being of individuals?
2. In what ways does it contribute to the well-being of society?
3. If there were no public education, how might life be different in Georgia? What groups of Georgians, if any, would particularly suffer?

Writing Project

"What does it cost to educate me?" Have you ever asked yourself that question?

There are many other questions to ask in order to find out what it costs to educate just one student. How much are teachers paid? How much are school utility bills? How much does a textbook cost?

Assume you are a member of a taxpayers' committee investigating the cost of education in your school. Your individual assignment is to find and report on the cost of just one "item" in your school. (Examples of items: textbooks, library books, audio-visual equipment and supplies, desks and other furniture, utilities, building maintenance and repairs, salaries, classroom supplies such as chalk, paper, and erasers, athletic and playground equipment.)

For your item, you will need to know certain things. For example: What does each textbook cost? How many are needed? How long will they last? How many are lost or stolen or destroyed?

Write your report on one item. Then combine it with your classmates' reports for a final committee report.

10 Human Development

A woman with three small children is deserted by her husband. She can find no job in her rural county to support herself and her children.

A teen-age boy is paralyzed in an auto accident. Doctors say that with long-term therapy he could lead an active productive life, but his family has no money to pay for therapy.

An elderly man lives alone in a small inner-city apartment. He is often depressed, stays away from his job, and drinks heavily.

What do these people have in common? In each case, they need help. Who has the responsibility to help them?

In centuries past, the family, the churches, and perhaps some private charity organizations looked after the welfare of children and certain adults. However, as early as colonial times, taxpayers assumed some of the support of needy persons.

WELFARE: WHAT IS IT?

Welfare is a word that has different meanings for different people. In its broadest sense, welfare is a basic purpose of all government. The writers of the United States Constitution intended the new government to "promote the general welfare." That is, they expected it to help bring about the general well-being of the nation's people.

In a narrower sense, welfare refers to all kinds of special economic and social services that a government may provide to certain groups of needy persons. These groups include the poor, the aged, the disabled, the neglected, and the abused.

Welfare also means payments to the poor. In this sense, it is often called *public assistance* because it is funded by taxes.

Administering Welfare Programs

Many government services to the needy provide examples of federalism. All three levels of government are involved. Public welfare programs are usually supported by a combination of federal, state, and local funds. For example, the Social Security Act is a federal law, but the state carries out the program. The state also works through local government agencies, such as county departments of Family and Children Services. This helps insure that federal and state aid meets the particular needs of a community.

In Georgia, most welfare programs are administered by the Georgia Department of Human Resources (DHR). One of the largest state agencies, DHR also oversees public health services. It employs almost 20,000 people, and one out of every five dollars in the state budget goes to DHR.

The department serves the public through more than 100 programs. Some programs—such as disease control, immunization, family planning, and environmental sanitation—serve the general public. Other programs—in physical health, mental health, social services, public assistance, and vocational rehabilitation (developing job skills)—help specific groups of needy persons: the young, the old, the handicapped, the poor, the ill.

A few of the programs in the second group are described in this chapter. (DHR's Division of Youth Services, which supports the state's juvenile justice system, is discussed in chapter 17.)

HELPING THE ILL AND THE HANDICAPPED

THINK ABOUT IT

1. What are some ways in which community care differs from institutional care?
2. What kinds of mental health problems are handled in community programs?
3. What is the aim of vocational rehabilitation programs?

Mental Health and Mental Retardation

The lonely, elderly man dependent on alcohol is one of several hundred thousand

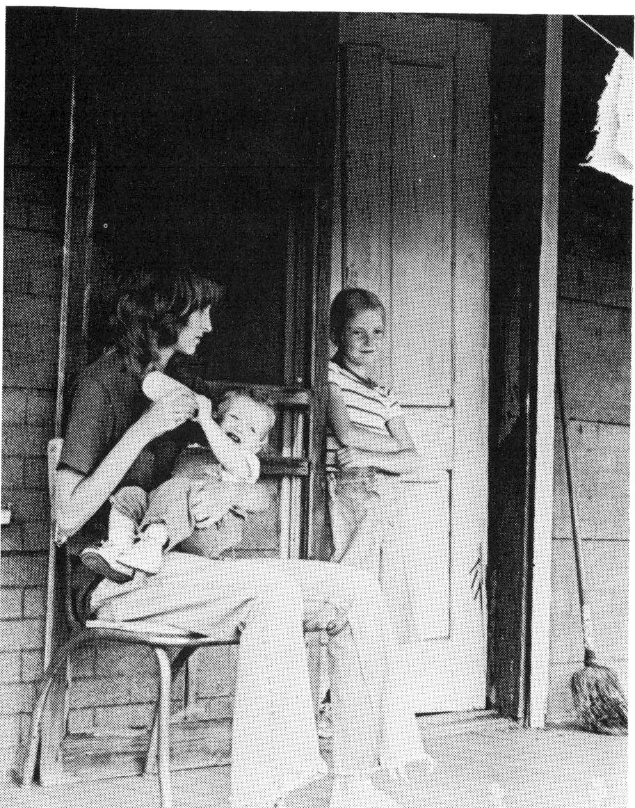

Living conditions for some Georgia families are below the poverty level.

Georgians who are mentally ill or who have serious emotional problems. Thousands of other persons have mental handicaps which require them to have special care and training.

In the past, public treatment of persons with mental illness or mental handicaps was shaped by attitudes of ignorance, fear, and hostility. At worst, such persons were neglected and abused. At best, they might be committed to an asylum to be fed and clothed, but little more.

Today the public knows more about mental health problems. Many people realize that being unable to cope with the death of a loved one, divorce, or other life situations can bring on depression, heavy drinking, and drug abuse in almost any family. And they know that mental retardation can occur in any family.

As a result, public attitudes toward mental health problems have changed. The ways state government meets the needs of the mentally ill and the mentally handicapped have also changed.

From Institutional to Community Care

In 1842 the state of Georgia opened a hospital for mentally ill, mentally retarded, and physically handicapped persons. Located near Milledgeville, this hospital was for many years the state's only facility of its kind.

According to a former DHR official, "It was the dumping ground. The hospital treated not only the sick; it cared for the poor, the hungry, the people nobody else wanted or cared about."

Over the next 100 years, as Georgia's population grew, the number of patients at the state hospital grew. By the late 1940s, it had about 9,000 patients. The average length of stay for a patient was over three years. Many were "put away" in the hospital for the rest of their lives.

In the 1950s, critics pointed out that mental health care in Georgia was just about the worst in the nation. Then, in the early 1960s, plans were made for a new approach to serving the state's mentally ill and mentally handicapped citizens.

This new approach would eventually establish community mental health centers and a system of regional mental health hospitals, treatment centers, and training centers for the retarded.

Services are located close to where people live, making possible early attention and treatment. This avoids hospitalizing most persons who seek help. Also, by staying in the community rather than at a distant institution, such persons can be with their families and keep their jobs.

Alcohol and drug abuse problems are also part of DHR's mental health programs. In Georgia, there are over 250,000 men, women, and children who abuse alcohol. Community-based alcohol treatment programs help some of these persons, but the majority still go untreated. Also, several thousand drug abusers are counseled and treated each year in community facilities as well as regional hospitals.

DHR tries to educate the general public about alcoholism and drug abuse, mainly through its work with schools and civic organizations. However, the use of tax money to treat alcohol and drug

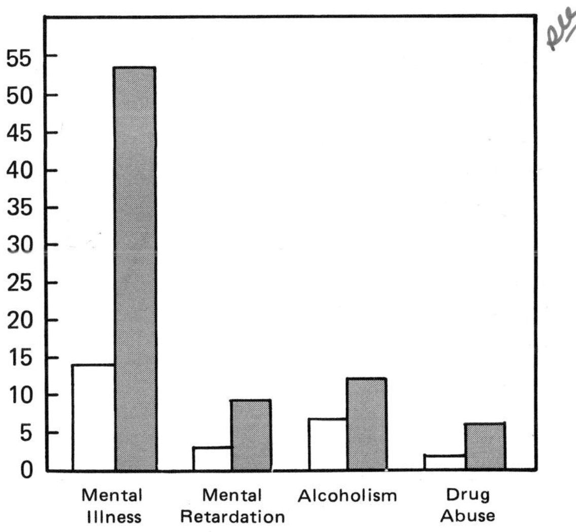

abusers is controversial. While many state officials favor funding for therapy and rehabilitation programs for persons with alcohol and drug problems, many other officials do not. Unless there is more agreement on the need for the state to help treat these persons, DHR's programs will handle only a small percentage of the state's alcohol and drug abusers.

Most of the mentally retarded Georgians who receive services from the state are also helped near their homes at day training centers. Community programs for the retarded focus on helping each individual become as independent as possible. This means providing training in daily living, communication, and job skills.

Of course, for persons who are not able to live in a community or who require regular care, there are hospitals and retardation centers available. These facilities provide special services for severely retarded and more seriously ill individuals.

Vocational Rehabilitation

Until very recently, the public usually regarded physically handicapped persons as being fit only for handouts, for charity. Like the mentally handicapped, the physically handicapped were often "put away" in institutions.

Now, however, there are many tax-supported services which help the paralyzed teen-age boy, the deaf child, the blind adult, and other handicapped persons lead active satisfying lives. Many physically handicapped persons (and mentally handicapped persons) are helped to become self-supporting members of society through vocational rehabilitation programs.

DHR's Division of Vocational Rehabilitation operates rehabilitation centers and other facilities where persons receive medical care for handicaps, physical therapy, and counseling and training for jobs. In some cases, DHR financially assists the handicapped, including the blind and the deaf, to go to vocational schools or colleges. In other cases, it arranges on-the-job training.

Teaching handicapped persons job skills is part of DHR's vocational rehabilitation activities.

Vocational Rehabilitation programs also extend into communities where physically handicapped (and mentally handicapped) persons live. Counselors, social workers, and nurses visit patients in their homes to check their progress and help with problems.

Handicapped persons still suffer discrimination in trying to find jobs, but with the help of vocational rehabilitation programs, fewer of them must be dependent on others for their well being.

PUBLIC ASSISTANCE, PUBLIC ISSUE

THINK ABOUT IT

1. What is AFDC? How is eligibility for this type of public assistance determined?
2. What has contributed to the growth of welfare over the past several decades?

MIDDLETOWN FOLKS TALK ABOUT WELFARE

The Middletown Civic Association holds a monthly "Public Issues Forum." There, members discuss topics that interest them as citizens and taxpayers. Often government officials are invited to talk at these meetings. At a recent meeting, the topic was public assistance. The guest speaker was none other than—State Senator Tom Cody.

Even before the meeting began, several association members were talking about the issue.

"I'm really looking forward to hearing what Cody says about welfare," said Al Hunt. "I'm sick and tired of paying high taxes to support people who won't work."

"People shouldn't be looking for handouts from the government," agreed his friend Luther. "Somebody should make 'em go out and get a job."

Everyone settled down as the association president, Lucy Reagan, introduced Tom Cody. Tom began his talk with a little background information on welfare in Georgia. "When we talk about welfare in Georgia, we're talking mainly about AFDC. That stands for Aid to Families with Dependent Children. The AFDC program is aimed at helping needy children. Money payments go to eligible families with a child or children."

"What do you mean eligible?" asked a woman in the front row.

"OK, to be eligible, children must be under 18. Second, they must be needy. That is, the family doesn't have enough income to meet living expenses according to DHR's standards. Third, children must be deprived of the care of at least one parent. This may be because the parent died, is never home, or is physically or mentally unable to work. Also, children must be living with the mother, father, or another relative. If both parents are living at home and are able to work, the family can't get AFDC payments. Unmarried adults or married couples without children may not receive this kind of public assistance."

A hand shot up in the back of the room. "Senator Cody, who decides whether a family is eligible?"

"Each county has a local Department of Family and Children Services which determines whether or not a family is eligible. A family can't get AFDC payments if it has more than a minimum level of income or owns more than a certain amount of property."

"Aren't there other kinds of welfare payments?" asked a little old lady wearing running shoes.

"Yes, the state gives aid to the disabled and the elderly, but AFDC is the big one."

Luther Arnold stood up. "It seems to me, I mean from the way I grew up, that people who *can* work *ought* to work." Several people nodded their approval.

"I agree with you," answered Tom Cody. "And welfare programs in

Georgia were started to help people who can't work: children, the elderly, the disabled."

"Don't you agree welfare just encourages people to be lazy?" Al Hunt asked.

Before Senator Cody could answer, the Civic Association president, Lucy Reagan, raised her hand, "Al, I know of a woman in this county on welfare. She has three kids; two of them are only babies. Her husband left her, just went off somewhere, and she didn't have any way to support herself and her kids. So, she applied for AFDC."

"Well, why doesn't she go out and get a job?" Al Hunt asked. "She's lazy, that's why."

"Al, she is working now," Reagan replied. "I believe the welfare office arranged it. Her two little kids are in day care while she's at work."

"She is probably in what is called the Work Incentive Program," added Tom Cody. "People who receive AFDC register for this work program and accept a suitable job if it's available. The agency may also pay for day care until that woman has received several paychecks."

"Well, I guess I can see somebody like that getting some help," admitted Luther Arnold. "But I'm against all those others getting it."

"What others do you mean?" asked Senator Cody.

"Well, I'm wondering just how much you people in state government really know," Arnold came back. "In my store, I've cashed a lot of welfare checks for folks who are just as able as you or me to do a day's work. Now that's just not right! There's too much cheating!"

"There sure is," Sen. Cody agreed. "Welfare fraud is a big problem. No matter how you set it up, somebody's going to figure out a way to beat the system."

"I don't understand why there has to be *any* system," said a young woman sitting near the front. "Why should the state government have to take on the responsibility for poor people? When did we ever get into this welfare business, anyway?"

Tom Cody smiled, "Well, ma'am, I'm sure you're too young to remember the Depression back in the 1930s. Before then, public assistance for the poor was not a major responsibility of state government. Charity was a local effort. But so many people were needing food, medicine, clothing, housing—the federal and state governments had to do more to help the poor. In 1937 the General Assembly established a Department of Public Welfare to manage federal and state funds for public assistance in Georgia. So, that's where it really got started, in the Depression.

Since World War II, public assistance and other welfare programs, such as the Department of Labor's unemployment compensation program, have continued to grow. Some people think its a good thing; others don't."

"Well, there's always been needy people," the elderly woman spoke up. "But years ago, their kin took care of them. Even raised up their children if they had to."

A young man sitting with his wife holding a baby stood up, "Well times have changed since then. People may live far away from their families. And it's harder to find jobs today if you don't have a skill. There are a lot of reasons people need aid."

"So, you're in favor of all these giveaways?" asked Al Hunt.

"No, sir," replied the young man. "I didn't say that. I'm just explaining why I think people have come to rely on government for help they used to get from their families. I can't stand here and say there's no fraud and mismanagement in government welfare programs, but cutting out programs like AFDC isn't going to solve the problems either. We've got to attack some of the conditions that create these problems. And, I think this Public Issues Forum is a good way to start the attack."

SOCIAL SERVICES

People often need other kinds of help besides money. A child without parents, an elderly widow unable to care for herself, a man with a chronic health problem—these people need more than financial assistance. Social services are designed to help these people.

Social services are provided to needy persons by the Division of Family and Children Services of the Department of Human Resources. Working through the county departments of family and children services, the agency provides special services to persons having a variety of different health, family-life, and personal problems.

Annually, the state provides these social services to over 350,000 clients. Of the dozens of specialized services offered to Georgia residents, some of the most common are listed here:

Placement Services: These include arranging and paying for foster care when a child's own parents cannot or will not provide care. Adoption services help find parents for children in need of a permanent home.

Protective Services: Through these services, the agency helps to protect children and youth under

18 years of age and incapacitated and incompetent adults from abuse, neglect, and exploitation.

Supportive Services: These services help people cope with daily living problems and live as independently as possible in their own homes. They include home management, home food delivery, family planning, health problems, employment counseling, and care for the aged.

Interview with Mrs. Nancy Bruce

Each county Department of Family and Children Services is staffed by trained social workers. Because they handle the problems of needy individuals and families on a case-by-case basis, they are often called caseworkers.

Mrs. Nancy Bruce is a caseworker with the Oconee County Department of Family and Children Services. Her office has the usual bookshelves and filing cabinets, but stacked up next to her desk are boxes filled with toys. Many of her clients are children.

Her workday begins at 8:00 a.m. and sometimes doesn't end until long after dark. When she is not behind her desk, she might be found anywhere in Oconee County. Anywhere a person needs help.

THINK ABOUT IT

1. What are some of the different kinds of help a caseworker may be called upon to provide?
2. What does it seem to take to be an effective caseworker?

Mrs. Bruce, how did you get to be a caseworker in Oconee County?

I transferred here from another county where my job was authorizing welfare checks and food stamps. I wanted to be in services where I felt I could do more good. So I transferred here.

You handle specialized social services for children, don't you?

Yes, adoption, foster care, protective services. I go out in cases where there's a report of child abuse, child neglect, or child exploitation. By exploitation I mean using a child to make money.

But, because I'm the only social worker in this county, I have the whole caseload. Anything that comes up, I get it.

What are some examples of the cases that do come up?

All right, I could have a case where an elderly person in a nursing home needs surgery, but he or she has been judged incompetent. Therefore, I either have to find a relative, or the agency would have to become the person's guardian so that he or she could get the surgery.

In another case, maybe a teenager is being abused verbally with possibly some slapping around by a parent. I would have to talk with members of the family to see if there were some way we could work out the situation to ease the pressure.

Sometimes, we're asked by the teenager, "Just get me out of the house. I don't care what happens after I get out of the house." Other times the kid says, "Well, give me some advice. I'd like to try to stick it out and see what we can do."

I might have a family come in that doesn't have any groceries in the home. Maybe the family applied for food stamps, but for one reason or another can't get them right away. In that situation, I would go to a church pantry, which is a local community effort, and get groceries for them.

Then, I might get a call from a family that wants to adopt a racially mixed child. In a case like that I would have to do a study of the family.

I could have a mother come in and say, "Here I am. I have no job, no income, no place to live. Would you put my child in foster care until I can get back on my feet?"

If a person comes in who needs a job, I would call around to see if I could help find him or her a job. Or, if somebody needs a place to live, I would try to find them a place to live.

We have all sorts of things going on.

Of all the different kinds of cases you handle, is there one you most enjoy working on?

Adoptions! Oh yes. When they work out, it's just beautiful. The people are happy. The child is happy to find a permanent place that's all his own. That's one of the most enjoyable parts of the job.

Another one, I would say, is getting to know the elderly. They are so much fun just to talk to, and they so much enjoy having somebody to come and talk to them.

I'd say those two are the best.

There must be an unpleasant part, right?

Obviously. When we get a report of child abuse. I have to go out there and say to the family, "Whether you want me here or not, I'm here." That can be a problem.

You mean when you get such a report you are required to check it out?

I have to go. It's a Georgia law. If there is evidence of some problem—it may not be abuse as reported, but actually neglect—we would probably open a case.

If the family does not want to cooperate with us, we try to let them know that they must. If they still refuse, then we would have to ask the court to order them to cooperate.

How much child abuse or neglect goes unreported?

There are people who know of children being locked in trailers in 95 degree weather and being kept away from food. But they never report it because they don't know how.

Or maybe because they don't think they should get involved?

A child comes to school filthy. I don't mean just dirty, but filthy every day and smelling. That child needs some help. But maybe the child's teacher thinks, "You don't tell people how clean they should be."

So, the teacher just passes it off. But, that's something that needs to be reported. And it might be a symptom of something else that's wrong in the family.

You have to be thick-skinned to survive in your kind of work, don't you?

Yes, you do, because there are a lot of times when you really get hurt. For example, sometimes things don't work out as you hoped for the benefit of a child. Maybe the court doesn't go with our recommendation. That's not to say the court order is wrong, but when we lose a court case, it sometimes hurts.

You have to be able to handle disappointments and take your satisfactions when things do work out.

In addition to being tough, what else do you think it takes to be a social worker?

Well, for one thing, you shouldn't have the idea you're going to go out and solve the world's problems. You can't solve people's personal problems for them.

And it's very frustrating to advise people against making a stupid move and then sit back and watch them make that move. But, I can't make people do what I feel they should do with their lives.

Also, if you are going into protective services you have to love children. It's important when you have a child going into foster care or a strange situation that you build a relationship with that child. It includes hugging and touching that child. He or she may have a runny nose, might be dirty, or might throw up on your clothes. But the child needs that love.

You can go home and wash your clothes. You have to be genuine with children. You can't pretend to love them. They know if you don't.

ACTIVITIES FOR CHAPTER 10

Class Discussion

A. Said one state official, "there are really two groups of poor people: those who deserve assistance and those who don't deserve it. Our main problem is distinguishing between the two groups."

1. What circumstances or personal characteristics might make a poor person "deserving" in the eyes of this official? What might make him or her "undeserving?"

2. If you were in charge of a public assistance program, how would you go about distinguishing between the two groups?

B. With the growth of social service programs, government has become involved in what were once private family matters.

1. Why has this involvement come about?

2. If government didn't get involved, would there be any harm? To whom?

3. Are there any dangers in government becoming too involved in family matters? If so, what are they?

Writing Project

Listed below are some statements which reflect values or attitudes about welfare. Choose the statement (or statements) with which you agree most. Write a one-page essay setting out your personal reasons for agreeing with the statement you choose.

a. "A person who is well off should give to the poor because even they have a right to decent food, housing, and medical care."

b. "The poor do not have a right to get something for nothing, only the right to work."

c. "Welfare programs benefit 'haves' as well as 'have nots' because they work against disease, ignorance, and crime in our society."

d. "Our society was built on individual effort, and giveaway programs weaken it by destroying a person's will to better himself."

11 Resources and Roads

The General Assembly shall have the authority to provide restrictions upon land use in order to protect and preserve the natural resources, environment and vital areas of this State. *–Georgia Constitution of 1976.*

The strength of any society depends on its resources. These resources may be "natural" such as water and minerals or "human-made" such as highways.

Should forests be cut for lumber or preserved for wildlife habitats? Should a factory be permitted to dump waste in a river or should the river be preserved for commercial fishing? These questions are not simple to answer.

People have different interests that influence how they regard natural resources. The operator of a lumber business and a person who likes to hunt may not agree on the proper use of forest resources. The factory owner and a person who makes a living by fishing may not see eye to eye on how to use the river.

Because natural resources are so vital and because all people do not agree on how to use them, government has to help determine how resources are used. Government is supposed to see that resources are used (or conserved) in the best interests of all the people.

Government's role is similar to that of the referee in a football game. It tries to insure fair competition between resource users (or conservers). It enforces rules and tries to keep either side from being cheated.

Competition for resources is fierce. A win or a loss is not only measured in millions of dollars, but also in human welfare and environmental quality. Questions of resource use may take many years to settle.

Sometimes a controversy over resources is mainly an in-state affair. For example, should mine operators be required to reclaim (or make useable again) the land which they strip-mined to extract minerals? Several years ago, the Georgia General Assembly said yes, passing an act to require that strip-mined land be reclaimed.

Some environmental issues spill over state lines. In recent years, the states of Georgia, Alabama, and Florida strongly differed over how to use rivers they share.

Other issues involve not only a state government, but also federal and local governments.

THE GEORGIA COAST: A CASE STUDY

THINK ABOUT IT

1. Who was opposed to the phosphate mining proposal?
2. What kinds of damage did some people predict if the mining took place?
3. Why are marshes valuable?
4. Who could benefit from economic development of coastal areas?

Of all the environmental issues in Georgia which have received public attention in the last several decades, none have been so hotly debated as those centered on Georgia's coast.

In 1947, Gov. M.E. Thompson pointed out that the average Georgian had access to only 3 miles of ocean beach. He led an effort to have the state purchase privately owned Jekyll Island for $675,000. The purchase stirred up political controversy that lasted for years. But today the public has access to almost 100 miles of beaches along the coast, 11 of them on Jekyll Island.

In 1968, a state agency proposed to lease some coastal land to a company which wanted to mine phosphate. The mining operation was predicted to bring $2 million into the state government treasury and millions more into the economy of the coastal region. But, as the newspaper item on page 107 shows, the announcement of the proposed mining lease was not well-received by everyone.

The controversy over phosphate mining focused the public's attention on Georgia's coastal marshes.

Actually, Georgia's marshes are far more productive than the richest farmland in the state. They provide a life support system for many kinds of fish, shellfish, waterfowl, and mammals. Rich nutrients produced by the marshes are even carried far offshore to ocean shrimping grounds.

Photo above shows land in McDuffie County after strip mining. Below the land is in the process of being reclaimed.

The marshes also buffer shore property against ocean storms and serve as a natural treatment facility for dispersing and breaking down pollutants from human activities.

Unfortunately, the marshes are very fragile. They depend on fresh waters from streams and salt waters from the sea to do their work. Anything that blocks the

PHOSPHATE MINING OPPOSED

Adapted from the Atlanta Journal and Constitution, *July 21, 1968.*

Proposed mining of phosphates off the Georgia coast is meeting mounting opposition from conservationists.

The latest group to voice opposition to the project is the 6,000 member Georgia Sportsmen's Federation, the state's largest conservation organization, with more than 60 affiliated hunting, fishing, boating, and archery clubs.

Meeting in Haralson County here, the board of directors of the federation unanimously adopted a resolution opposing leasing of 7,200 acres of Georgia coastline to the Kerr McGee Oil Company for phosphate mining.

The president of the Federation, James (Jim) L. Adams of Stone Mountain, told the directors that the proposed mining was "the gravest conservation threat to Georgia that we have faced."

"It is impossible to calculate the damage that such an operation could do to our natural resources on the coast," Adams said.

He noted that the proposed mining has been opposed by the Georgia Water Quality Control Board's director, Rock Howard.

Howard opposed it on the grounds that it might cause extensive pollution of marine life in the coastal area, threatening a multimillion dollar commercial and sport fishery.

The project has also been opposed by noted conservationists and scientists, including world renowned ecologist Dr. Eugene P. Odum of the University of Georgia's Zoology Department, who fears that the underwater dredging several hundred feet below the sea floor might cause saltwater intrusion into the freshwater supply of the coastal area, especially of Savannah.

Adams said that very little information about the project was known because the Kerr McGee Company had declined to supply additional details, including when mining would actually start, how large an area would be mined, how deep dredging would go, and how extensive the operation would be.

Phosphate deposits off the Georgia coast within the three mile limit are believed to lie under a hundred or more feet of mud, sand, and rocks. This would have to be dredged up first and deposited in nearby areas.

Company officials have said that the project would include filling in saltwater marshes with some of the materials.

However, ecologists say that this would destroy the aquatic food supply of many marine organisms valuable to man, including shrimp, oysters, crabs, and fish.

flow of water, such as dredged, filled, or raised land, may destroy the marshes.

The Kerr McGee controversy was not quickly settled. Scientists conducted studies of the economic benefits and the environmental damage phosphate mining could cause. Business interests said economic development should include tourism and recreation as well as mining. Groups of citizens organized to "Save Our Marshes." State agency officials disagreed among themselves on the best course of action.

As more and more people agreed on the need to conserve marshlands, the Georgia General Assembly enacted the Coastal Marshlands Protection Act of 1970. This law said in part

> . . . it is in the public interest that the State of Georgia regulate the use of the coastal marshlands. . .
>
> . . . it is the intent of the General Assembly that any use of the marshlands be balanced between protection of the environment on the one hand and industrial and commercial development on the other.

The controversial phosphate mining lease was eventually rejected by the state,

Marshlands such as these in Glynn County are a valuable resource to the state. Industrial activities near them must be carefully planned to avoid disrupting the ecological balance.

but an even larger problem remained.

In 1977, 30 years after Gov. Thompson's Jekyll Island purchase, another Georgia governor addressed a coastal resource problem. Gov. Busbee noted that Georgians still had valuable untouched resources in almost a half-million acres of marshlands, the coastal islands, the beaches and dunes, and the great coastal underground water system.

But, he also pointed out that

> . . . the people of the area have a per capita income which is much lower than the national average. To them, industrial and economic development are very welcome. The shipping industry provides about $1 billion of income to the area each year. But, this industry cannot operate without dredging and filling in coastal waters.
>
> The recreation industry brings in over $500 million in income annually. But, it depends on the marshes, barrier islands, and beaches. Commercial fishing, offshore oil and gas exploration, mining, power generation, and paper processing are other activities which appear to be essential to the area's prosperity.
>
> Georgia's coastal area has two kinds of valuable assets:
>
> (1) Natural resources are valuable because they are relatively untouched, and (2) The economic potential of the region is valuable because, if developed, it will improve the welfare of the people on the coast. The problem is that increasing the value of one of these assets may decrease the value of the other.
>
> Everyday, decisions have to be made between these two alternatives—economic development and conservation of resources. Maintaining a reasonable balance between them is the concern of the state. [*Adapted from* Governor's Policy Statement, 1977.]

GOVERNMENT AGENCIES AND NATURAL RESOURCES: ENFORCEMENT AND ASSISTANCE

THINK ABOUT IT

1. What are some ways in which the Department of Natural Resources protects the public? protects resources?
2. How does this agency promote the use of resources?
3. How does the State Forestry Commission aid the forest products industry?

Once decisions are made regarding natural resources, how are they carried out? Who enforces the laws which regulate resource use? Who assists the economic development of resources?

In Georgia two agencies, the Department of Natural Resources and the State Forestry Commission, have the main responsibilities for natural resources. The following reading presents an overview of their work.

The Department of Natural Resources and the State Forestry Commission work for both economic development and conservation of resources. On the one hand, they enforce laws protecting and regulating the use of resources. On the other hand, they promote and encourage the use of resources.

Department of Natural Resources

The most important function of the Department of Natural Resources (DNR) is protecting the public's health. Water resources are a main concern. DNR sets standards for water purity, regulates public water systems, and conducts tests of drinking water. It also works to insure clean air. Sewage treatment plants, sanitary landfills, and other waste disposal facilities are regulated by this agency.

This agency also enforces a wide range of laws. These laws protect the coastal marshlands and endangered plants and animals. They also regulate surface (strip) mining and the construction of dams. DNR provides assistance to local governments, industries, and private citizens trying to solve their own environmental problems. It conducts geologic surveys, locates and analyzes mineral deposits, and identifies underground sources of water.

The public's recreational use of the natural environment is also a major concern of the department. It registers boats, issues licenses to fish and hunt, and maintains boat launching ramps on lakes and rivers. DNR conservation rangers enforce state game and fish, boating, and water safety laws.

Of course, hunting and fishing wouldn't be very worthwhile if there were nothing to hunt or fish. So, DNR works to improve wildlife resources by (1) operating fish hatcheries and stocking lakes, streams, and ponds; and (2) conducting research on wildlife diseases and breeding. It also assists private landowners in wildlife management.

To allow Georgians and tourists alike to have outdoor types of recreation in natural surroundings, the Department of

At Ft. Yargo State Park, handicapped people can enjoy water activities by using special ramps and equipment.

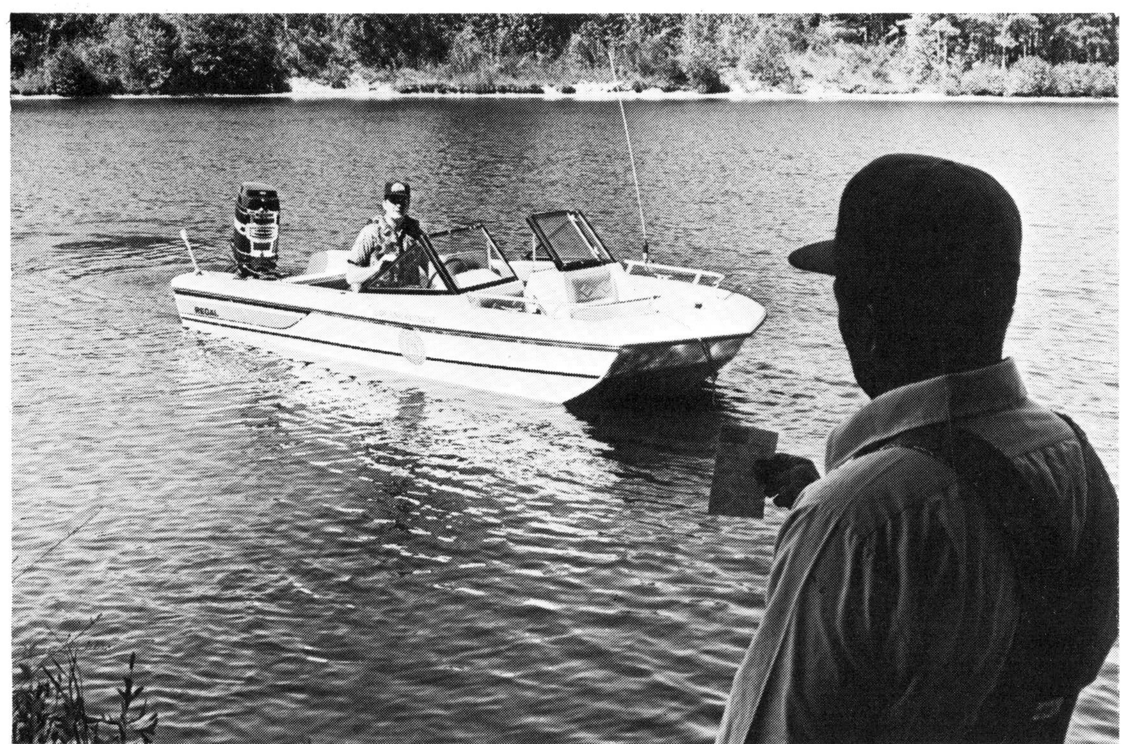

A conservation ranger from the Department of Natural Resources comes by to check the fishing license of this Georgia fisherman.

Natural Resources operates a state system of parks and historic sites.

Historic sites (actually cultural resources, not natural resources) give today's Georgians a glimpse into the lifestyles of earlier residents of the state. They provide information about how the culture of today's Georgians developed. Historic remains are easily destroyed through accident, ignorance, or vandalism. Therefore, state government takes on the responsibility to preserve, restore, and maintain them for the public's benefit.

State Forestry Commission

Forests, one of Georgia's most valuable natural resources, are the responsibility of a separate agency—the State Forestry Commission.

The earliest settlers found most of Georgia covered with trees: cypress along the coastal marshes, pines across the sandy plains, hardwoods in the mountains. However, in the nineteenth century most of the forest land was destroyed to make way for cotton fields.

Today, about two-thirds of Georgia is once again covered with forest land. Georgia is one of the leading states in producing lumber, pulpwood, and products such as turpentine and rosin that are obtained from pine trees. As the costs of gas and oil rise, attention is being focused on the state's forests as a renewable source of energy.

The Forestry Commission works closely with the forest products industry to develop these resources. The commission manages state forests and tree nurseries, makes tree seedlings available to private landowners, and provides technical assistance to the forest industry.

The State Forestry Commission's activities also include the protection of forest resources.

To prevent, detect, and combat fires on state and privately owned forest land, the commission depends on fire towers, aircraft, special equipment, and trained fire fighters. During a drought, the commission may prohibit outdoor trash burning anywhere in the state.

Whenever insect pests or tree diseases threaten the forests, quarantine and other control measures may be ordered by the commission.

The bulk of the State Forestry Commission enforcement work is carried out around the state by forest rangers and patrolmen. They also assist landowners in caring for and protecting their own trees.

TRANSPORTATION

Transportation is a resource as vital to a people's economy as natural resources. Without good transportation, resources and goods cannot be distributed when and where they are needed, and the economy suffers.

Transportation may make use of natural resources, such as rivers and harbors, or man-made resources, such as railroads and highways.

Transportation by water, air, and rail is provided almost totally by private companies. (Georgia is one of the few states to own a railroad, the Western & Atlantic, now leased to a private company.) However, these forms of transportation are regulated in the public interest by the federal government and, to a smaller degree, by state government.

State government has been most involved in transportation in the area of road and highway building. The following reading focuses on how Georgia's present highway system came about.

The Growth of Georgia Roads

THINK ABOUT IT

1. What forced state government to become heavily involved in road-building? When did this happen?
2. What role did the federal government play in developing Georgia's highways?
3. How has road-building been controversial?

For most of Georgia's history, state government was not directly involved in much road construction. Until the twentieth century most people traveled only a few miles, mainly by horseback and horse and wagon. The few Georgians who ever journeyed very far from home took the train. Road-building was left to local governments.

Then, in the early 1900s, the automobile arrived on the scene. Although some streets and roads in and around cities could handle this new form of transportation, the few roads connecting one part of the state to another were totally inadequate. After a good rain they were impassable.

In 1916, the U.S. Congress began to grant financial aid to the states for highway construction.

Fire tower

The Georgia General Assembly set up a State Highway Commission to supervise development of a state network of roads. The greatest need was for paved "all weather" roads. During the next 20 years, state government's main effort was to "get Georgia out of the mud."

To pay for this, the General Assembly placed taxes on motor fuels and earmarked the revenues for road construction. Additional help came from the federal government during the 1930s when it increased its role in highway building and granted more funds to the states.

During World War II, 1941-1945, materials for roadbuilding were unobtainable. Only essential road work was done. At the end of the war, however, a new era in highway construction began for the nation and for Georgia.

The interstate highways and urban expressways now so familiar to all motorists were begun in the decade following World War II. At the same time, paving of rural roads picked up at a new pace.

In the 1960s and 1970s, more highways were needed to handle increasing traffic.

By 1980, the boom in highway-building was over. The surface of the state was criss-crossed with roads and highways.

The table opposite shows how the number of vehicles and the state highway system grew in Georgia over a period of 70 years.

The arrival of the automobile thrust new responsibilities for planning and financing roads on state government. And the growth of Georgia's highway system was the source of political controversy.

In the 1930s and 1940s, as the building of paved roads went forward, arguments continually arose over "who's going to get the roads?" Certainly all parts of the state couldn't get paved roads at the same time.

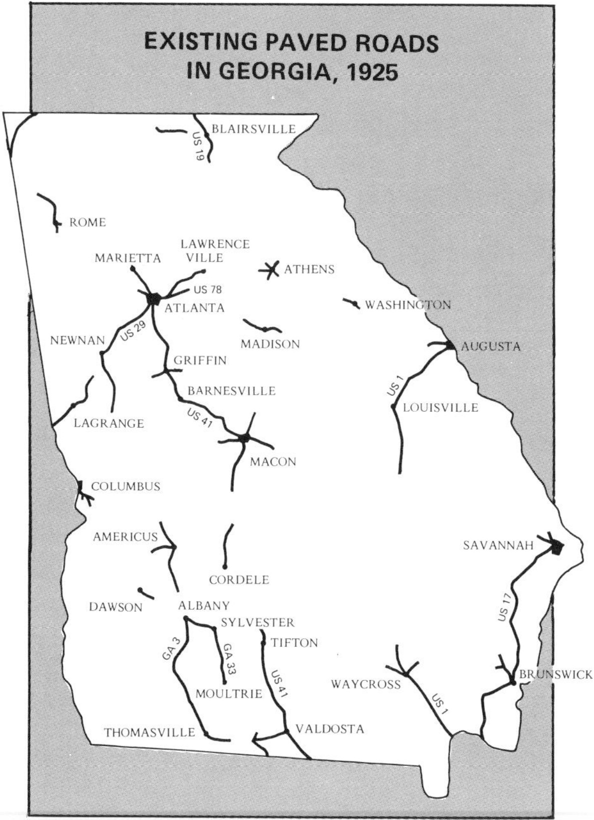

At sessions of the General Assembly, roads were a hot political issue. Some governors saw to it that roads were handed out in return for political favors. A legislator who voted against the governor might

GROWTH OF GEORGIA HIGHWAY SYSTEM, 1910-80

Year	Motor Vehicles Registered in Georgia	Mileage of State Highway System
1910	4,490	0
1920	146,000	4,800
1930	344,883	7,124
1940	510,428	11,908
1950	897,518	15,202
1960	1,512,118	15,959
1970	2,801,265	17,650
1980	3,800,000 (est.)	18,000 (est.)

In addition, there are almost 95,000 miles of streets and roads that are not part of the state highway system. These are primarily the responsibility of local governments.

By land, by water, by rail, by air—four kinds of transportation. State government is involved in all of them.

find his district left out of the State Highway Department's paving plans.

Today, state highway decisions are less influenced by politics. Since 1950 the Department of Transportation (formerly called the State Highway Department) has been governed by a board elected by the General Assembly. This board chooses the commissioner of transportation.

Still there is controversy. In the 1970s, concern for the environment led many citizens to question the need for more highways: "Those road-builders would pave over the state if we let them." Several major highway projects were cancelled because citizens opposed them. Then, as energy shortages became a reality and gasoline prices soared, more people began to agree that more public transit systems—buses and rapid rail—were needed, not more highways.

Presently the Department of Transportation is getting involved in planning all methods of moving goods and people: aviation, railroads, and waterways, as well as highways. But its major concern is still roads.

ACTIVITIES FOR CHAPTER 11

Class Discussion

A. In the last 200 years, living patterns of Georgians have changed greatly.

1. What are some ways that resource use is related to population growth?
2. What are some ways resource use is related to the way people live?

B. At one time, state government had no agencies such as the Department of Natural Resources, the State Forestry Commission, or the Department of Transportation. They, too, came about as the result of change.

1. What changes in Georgia's population, economy, and technology have influenced the creation of these agencies?

2. How might the activities of these three agencies be influenced by scarce energy resources?

Writing Project

The citizens of Coastal City have split into two groups over the issue of economic development. There's a good chance an oil refinery would be built there if the community wants it. One group, however, wants to keep the natural environment much as it is. The other group wants the better jobs and better housing that the new industry would provide.

Assume you are the editor of the Coastal City Times. You decide to write an editorial on the issue, either (1) supporting one of the groups or (2) trying to bring them together. Assignment: Write the editorial. Be sure to support your opinions. (Optional assignment: Draw an editorial cartoon on the same subject.)

omit

12 State Government and Private Enterprise

Under the Georgia Constitution, the General Assembly enacts laws which affect not only the private lives of Georgians, but also the private enterprise of Georgians. These laws regulate businesses, professions, and trades. They are examples of the state's police power.

Why should government concern itself with private enterprise? It does so mostly to protect the rights of all the businesses in the marketplace and to protect the public.

For example, a large supermarket chain might use its wealth to influence milk producers not to sell to small food stores. In this case, one large business would be preventing food store owners from exercising their right to do business.

Or, a meat processing plant might ship contaminated meat to food stores around the state. Consumers, not suspecting the meat was spoiled, might buy it and get sick.

Today, the regulation of private enterprise is a major role of all state governments. This role takes such forms as

- issuing business and occupational licenses,
- taxing the sale of certain products,
- inspecting facilities and products,
- chartering corporations and granting franchises, and
- prohibiting certain business practices and types of businesses.

State governments also cooperate with federal agencies in enforcing federal laws. These laws affect interstate commerce, resource use, environmental protection, and the manufacture and sale of certain products such as explosives, alcohol, drugs, and tobacco.

STATE AGENCIES AND REGULATION

How does Georgia enforce regulatory laws? Practically every agency of state government is in one way or another involved in regulating or serving private enterprise. The chart on page 116 lists some of the ways state agencies regulate private enterprise.

PROTECTING THE PUBLIC'S HEALTH AND SAFETY

Not all private enterprise is regulated to the same degree. Businesses such as clothing and furniture stores are relatively

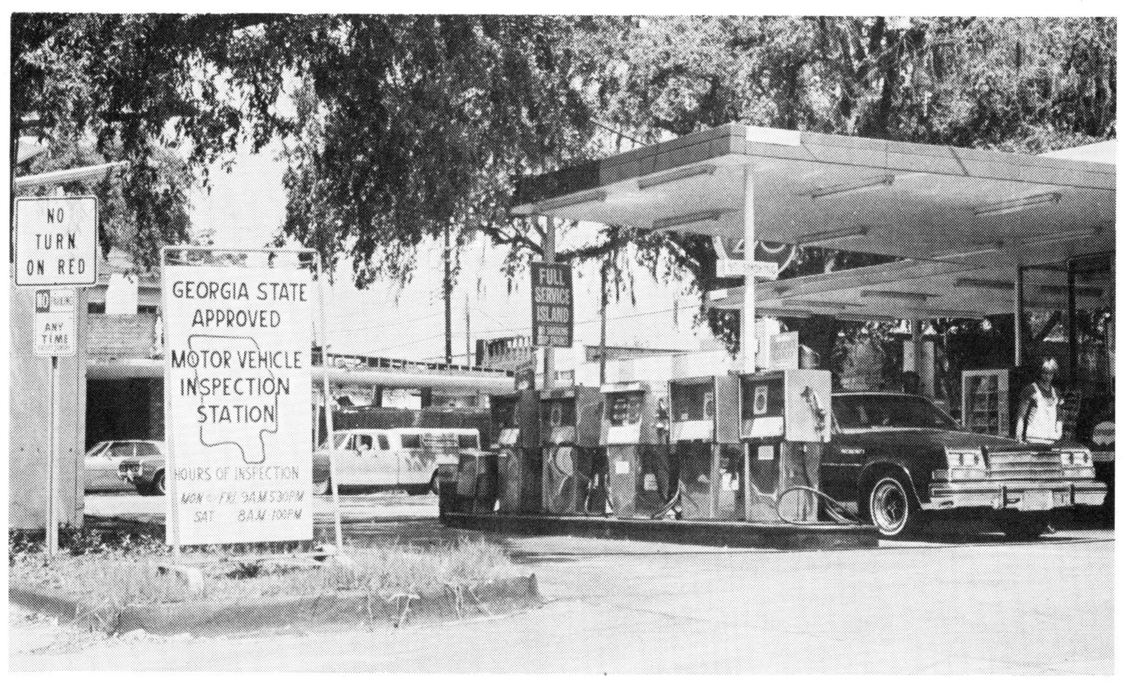

How many regulatory signs can you spot in this picture? What state regulations not shown in the picture affect the business at this gas station?

Some State Agencies and Their Regulatory Activities

Georgia State Agency	Examples of Regulatory Responsibilities
Department of Agriculture	Licenses and inspects dairies, livestock companies, meat-processing plants, soft drink bottlers
Department of Human Resources	Issues permits and inspects restaurants, hotels, hospitals, nursing homes, and day care centers
Department of Labor	Enforces child labor and wage and hour laws; administers unemployment insurance; regulates private employment agencies
Department of Natural Resources	Issues permits and regulates commercial fishing, mining, oil and gas well drilling, waste disposal companies
Public Service Commission	Grants franchises to and sets rates for public utilities and transportation companies
Department of Revenue	Regulates manufacture, distribution, and sale of alcoholic beverages and tobacco products; collects state taxes

free from state government regulation. Of course, they have to meet fire and safety regulations, and they come under the Georgia Fair Business Practices Act (see page 122). However, other businesses, such as those manufacturing or selling alcoholic beverages, are very tightly controlled by the state.

What's the difference? Generally, businesses that are believed to affect most directly the public's health and safety are the most regulated.

Business Licensing

Business licensing is one way in which the state regulates private enterprise.

State licenses are required for certain kinds of businesses, such as food stores and liquor stores. In addition, cities and counties usually require all businesses to have locally issued licenses to operate within city or county boundaries.

In the following reading—"The State and Mr. Dudley's Store"—the case of the regulation of one business is presented. It illustrates several ways in which state government regulates and at the same time serves private enterprise.

THINK ABOUT IT

1. In what ways did state laws affect the way Mr. Dudley ran his business?
2. How did state regulation add to the cost of Mr. Dudley doing business?

THE STATE AND MR. DUDLEY'S STORE

Herschel Dudley runs a food store and gas station in rural southwest Georgia. The local men often gather there to pass the time of day.

"Who's those fellows out front messing around your gas pumps?" snapped a stern-looking old man waving a cane as he came in the door.

Mr. Dudley looked up, "They're from the Department of Agriculture, Mr. Hankins. They come by every so often to make sure the pumps are accurate."

"The government sure gets its nose into everything, doesn't it, Gene?" Mr. Hankins squinted at a round-faced man getting a soft drink out of the cooler.

"Morning, Mr. Hankins," said Gene Fuller. "Have a seat."

"You wouldn't believe how much I'm regulated," continued Mr. Dudley. "First off, I have to have a license from the Georgia Department of Agriculture. When I opened up several years back, they sent somebody called a sanitarian around to inspect this building. He said I had to meet special sanitation standards because I sell fresh meat and make sausage on the premises. Then, some inspectors came by to check the scales I use to weigh meat and produce. Later they even picked up some sausage.

"What for?" asked Mr. Hankins.

"They tested it in their laboratory for weight and to see if it was OK, not contaminated or anything. They even look to see if the sausage is made out of what the label says it is."

"They can make trouble for you, all right," Gene Fuller added.

"Yes sir, if you don't meet the laws, they can take away your license to sell food," agreed Mr. Dudley.

"Don't that beat all," grumbled Mr. Hankins.

"That isn't half of it," replied Mr. Dudley. "Because I sell beer and wine, I've got to meet a bunch of other state laws. And you never know when those boys from the Department of Revenue are going to check on you."

"Department of what?" asked Mr. Hankins cupping his hand behind an ear.

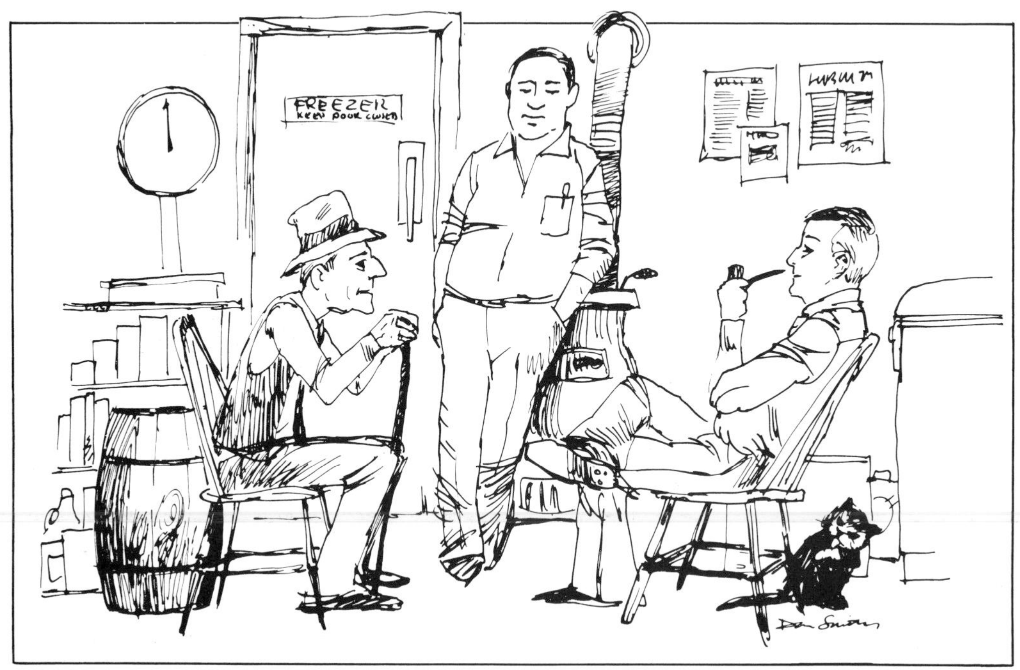

"Revenue," repeated Mr. Dudley. "It enforces the state alcohol laws and has strict regulations. If you don't meet 'em, they can take away your beer and wine license just like that."

"And you can get fined, too, can't you, Herschel?" asked Gene Fuller.

"What for?" snapped Mr. Hankins at Gene.

"Gene's talking about the alcohol laws," explained Mr. Dudley. "If the revenue people find you selling beer on Sunday, election day, after hours, or to minors, why, you've had it."

"Got a lot of extra paperwork, too, don't you?" quizzed Gene.

Mr. Dudley sighed and began explaining, "You said it. There are special state taxes on selling beer and wine. Liquor too. I'm required by law to keep good records of all my purchases from the beer and wine distributor, my stock of beer and wine on hand, and my sales. Each month, I've got to send this information and the taxes I owe to the Department of Revenue."

"And if he doesn't meet all those regulations, he could lose his beer and wine license," added Gene.

"Seems to me like you got to put up with a lot to run a business today," muttered Mr. Hankins. "Is it worth it?"

"Well," said Mr. Dudley, "I pay out over $1,000 each year for license fees. I have to have a county business license and a county beer and wine license, and state licenses from the Agriculture Department and the Revenue Department. It does cost me some to meet all those health laws. They even made me put in a fancy meat cooler. And, I have to hire a bookkeeper to keep my tax accounts straight. But, I guess it's worth it.

"The laws help keep out bad businesses. I'd probably have competition from shady characters who'd gladly rig their scales to make an extra dollar. And I know people who'd sell diseased meat if they could get away with it. I guess the laws protect the honest business owner as well as the customer. Yeah, I guess it's worth it."

Occupational Licensing

Occupational licensing is another way in which state government regulates private enterprises. It is designed to permit only qualified persons to practice medicine, engineering, pharmacy, and other professions and trades. Licensing makes it illegal for anyone who doesn't hold a license to engage in a profession or trade covered by law. Occupations which come under state licensing laws supposedly affect the public's health, safety, and welfare most directly.

How does licensing work? Generally, it begins with the General Assembly passing legislation to regulate the practice of a profession or trade. Under this legislation an examining board, composed of members of the profession or trade, is set up. This board sets qualifications to be met by applicants for a license to practice. Qualifications usually pertain to education or training, experience in the occupation, and perhaps moral character.

In Georgia, most licensed occupations are regulated by examining boards within the Office of the Secretary of State. A few groups are licensed by other state agencies. For example, public school teachers must be certified by the Georgia Department of Education. Lawyers are regulated by the Georgia Supreme Court and its Board of Bar Examiners.

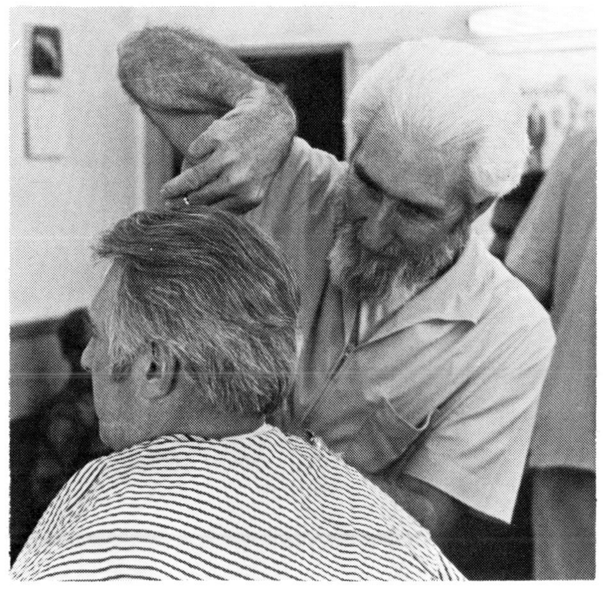

Barbers are one occupation group that comes under state regulation.

Presently, over 40 professions and trades are licensed in Georgia. A partial listing of these shows how state regulation has grown to include a wide variety of occupational groups.

Profession or Trade	Regulated Since
Accountants	1908
Architects	1919
Barbers and Hairdressers	1914
Chiropractors	1921
Dentists	1872
Electrical Contractors	1971
Engineers & Land Surveyors	1937
Funeral Directors (Embalmers)	1899
Lawyers	1897
Medical Doctors	1825
Nurses	1907
Optometrists	1916
Pharmacists	1881
Plumbing Contractors	1968
Private Detectives	1973
Public School Teachers	1919
Real Estate Agents	1925
Veterinarians	1908

All occupations certainly don't need to be licensed. Legislators must draw the line between those groups that clearly need to be regulated in the public interest and those that have little effect on the public's well-being.

REGULATING MONOPOLIES

Mrs. Gonzalez asked her class of third graders, "Where do you usually go to buy bread and milk?" The students gave her lots of names which she listed on the board.

Then she went on to ask them where they would go to buy blue jeans, medicine, records, a pizza, and so forth. Soon, she had on the board lists of dozens of businesses.

She then asked her students what they would do if they needed shoes but the prices were too high at store number one. The students suggested that they could try store number two or store number three. Mrs. Gonzalez discussed how competition among stores selling the same kinds of goods worked to keep prices down to where people could afford to buy them.

"What about electricity or telephone service? Where would you go to buy those things?" asked the teacher. The class could think of only one power company and only one telephone company doing business in their town.

"What if the power company charged so much for electricity that you couldn't afford it? Where would you go to buy electricity?" she asked.

Mrs. Gonzalez' third graders didn't know. Some guessed that they would just have to do without electricity.

The Public Service Commission

Although a community may have dozens of restaurants, gas stations, supermarkets, and department stores, it usually has only one electric company and one telephone company. These one-of-a-kind businesses in a community are commonly called "public utilities."

The following reading describes how Georgia regulates public utilities. It focuses on the role of the Public Service Commission.

THINK ABOUT IT

1. What is a franchise? How does the public benefit from this kind of arrangement? How does a utility company benefit?
2. How does the Public Service Commission serve as a referee between the utility and the consumer?

Public utilities provide services which are, for the most part, necessary to the public's well-being. To a certain extent they are monopolistic. That is, unlike

Crisscrossing power lines could be even more complicated than these if power companies were allowed to compete with one another for business.

supermarkets and shoe stores, they operate with little or no competition.

In a free enterprise economic system, competition is supposed to benefit both the producer and the consumer. It usually means better products at lower prices than if there were no competition. But, among public utilities, competition would probably not work.

Imagine four or five power companies all stringing lines along the same street competing for the homeowners' dollars. What would happen if three or four gas companies all started digging up the streets to put down their own gas mains? Probably mass confusion. Certainly wasted money. That is why certain services are provided by public utilities.

Who decides which company gets to provide the service? Governments may grant a public utility a *franchise*—or special privilege—to do business without competition. Only the company which gets a franchise may then string its power lines or put down gas mains. Government may decide to grant only one bus company the privilege of providing bus routes in a given area.

Governments grant these monopolistic arrangements because they are supposed to be in the public interest. That is, the consumer should benefit from the service, say electricity, made possible by the arrangement.

A company which is granted a franchise has to guarantee a specified level of service. That is, the state specifies that the company must provide the service at all times to all people desiring the service.

The Georgia Public Service Commission is the state agency charged with overseeing these kinds of arrangements granted to public utilities. To prevent a public utility from charging outrageous rates for its electricity or telephone service, the commission acts as a kind of referee between the consumer and the utility.

The commission is composed of five members who are elected statewide to serve staggered six-year terms. The members choose their own chairman. The commission employs a professional staff of engineers and specialists to help it carry out its duties.

The actions of the Public Service Commission probably affect the finances of each family in Georgia more than any other state agency. Practically all families are served every day by some utility company whose charges are regulated by the commission.

Under laws passed by the General Assembly, the Public Service Commission fixes rates for railroads, truck lines, bus lines, telephone companies, electric power companies, and gas utility companies. This power extends to other public utilities and transportation companies as well.

Before fixing the rates these companies may charge, the commission is required by law to make investigations and hold public hearings. In this way, it is supposed to determine what is fair and reasonable both to the public and to the utility companies.

The commission also regulates the quality of service a utility must provide. It attempts to make sure good service is delivered to all citizens on an equal, nondiscriminatory basis. For example, the commission not only approves what fares a bus line may charge, but also how often the line must run to give adequate service.

Just as a football team may dispute the calls a referee makes in a game, utilities and consumers may dispute decisions of the Public Service Commission. A utility wants to increase profits and a consumer wants to keep his or her monthly bill as low as possible. They are not likely to agree on a proposed rate increase.

Any citizen of the state who deals with a public utility has the right to contact the Public Service Commission to investigate disputes over rates or service which the citizen may have with the utility. He or she has the right to go in person, write, or telephone the commission for relief. Thousands of citizens do so every year.

PROTECTING AGAINST FRAUD

FACTORY FRESH
19" Color TV
$279.95
Shady Deal Appliance Store

A woman bought one of these advertised TVs. When it quit working after one week, she discovered it was actually a used TV. The store refused to replace the TV or refund her money.

What can this woman do? Does Georgia law cover situations like this one?

For many years no executive agency had the power to protect citizens who found themselves in a situation like the one described above. State agencies such as the Department of Agriculture and the Public Service Commission did protect the public against unwholesome food products and unreasonable utility rates. But generally, it was up to consumers themselves to get satisfaction–such as a refund of their money or an exchange of goods–from a merchant.

In 1975, the General Assembly passed the Fair Business Practices Act. This act prohibits the use of unfair or deceptive practices in retail business. It is enforced through the Office of Consumer Affairs, a state agency.

What are unfair business practices? A few examples follow:

1. Selling used products as new
2. Claiming products have characteristics that they do not have

3. Misrepresenting the age or condition of goods
4. Charging for repairs that are not made
5. Advertising that services are free when they are not
6. Not having advertised merchandise on hand

The Office of Consumer Affairs works to prevent these kinds of practices by receiving consumer complaints, conducting investigations, working out settlements between consumers and retailers, and if necessary, by starting court action. It also provides advice to consumers and releases information to the public about unethical business practices in Georgia and the nation.

A closer look at the work of the Office of Consumer Affairs is provided by its administrator, Tim Ryles.

Auto repair is a major complaint coming into the Office of Consumer Affairs.

Interview with Tim Ryles

Tim Ryles is administrator of the Governor's Office of Consumer Affairs. He advised George Busbee on consumer issues during Busbee's 1974 campaign for governor. The following year, Governor Busbee appointed Mr. Ryles to administer the Fair Business Practices Act of 1975.

THINK ABOUT IT

1. What does Mr. Ryles think of the notion "let the buyer beware?"
2. What are some ways in which the Office of Consumer Affairs may help an individual consumer? The general public?
3. According to Mr. Ryles, why isn't consumer education the answer to consumer problems?

Mr. Ryles, what is the main task and main goal of the Office of Consumer Affairs?

Our primary task is to protect business and consumers against unfair practices. That's clearly spelled out in the law.

In actually carrying out the law, our goal is to make decisions that are fair to all parties. The emphasis is on fairness in the marketplace. That's our main concern.

Not too many years ago, most people assumed that the consumer alone was responsible to make sure he or she wasn't being cheated. Has that changed? Why has state government taken on the responsibility for looking after the consumer's well-being?

Georgia was one of the last state governments to do that. And, we're not looking after the well-being of the consumer. We're dealing with lying, cheating, and stealing in the marketplace.

What about the old saying "let the buyer beware?" Isn't the buyer responsible for making sure he's getting what he paid for?

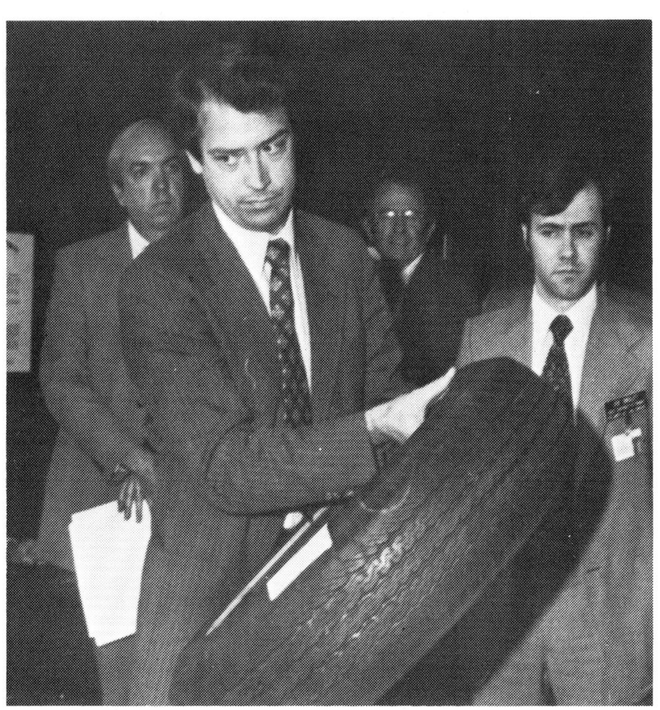

At press conference, Tim Ryles shows tire slashed at a service station on I-75.

The idea of "buyer beware" is not basic to our business system. The founding fathers never mentioned it. It is a principal that was established by judges in the nineteenth century. They decided that the interests of commerce, of corporations, were more important than the protection of the individual.

But things have changed since then. Today we recognize the important role of government in protecting people against fraud. We see that the individual cannot protect himself against huge multinational corporations, modern advertising, and marketing techniques. The technology of food production, of manufacturing in general, is such that the individual is practically helpless.

The Fair Business Practices Act says, "let both the buyer and the seller take care." Take care to be honest. And, let's reward honesty in the marketplace.

How does your office operate? Do you go out looking for unfair business practices, or do you wait until you receive a complaint?

Most of our work is in response to complaints. But, we do engage in what we call "initiatory enforcement."

For example, we take television sets with marked parts into TV repair shops. We have them repair our TV sets. Then we check to see if they charged us for work they didn't do or for parts they didn't put in. We've prosecuted people for violating the law through that.

We rig automobiles and go to auto repair shops. Particularly we've done this along Interstate 75. We've had them cut our tires. We've had them spray oil on our shock absorbers and then tell us we needed new shock absorbers and other parts that we didn't need.

We have gone to health spas, posing as consumers, and made cases against them for unfair practices. We've also gone onto car lots, posing as consumers, to see if the odometers have been rolled back.

So, we're a fairly agressive office in looking at things and doing our own work.

What are the most common kinds of complaints you get?

Every fifth call we get is about a car. A warranty problem, a service problem, a repair problem, a deceptive ad or sales practice.

How do you decide whether or not a business is engaging in some practice unfair to the consumer?

We have a system for recording the complaint and recording the evidence. We look at all of the contracts, sales pitches, advertisements, whatever may be involved. After we have inspected that evidence, we might contact the business. Or, we might do an undercover investigation of the business.

Our aim is to enforce the law. We are just as interested in disproving the evidence as we are in proving that the evidence shows a violation.

If you find that a consumer has a legitimate complaint, how do you help that person?

We have the authority to go into court to sue in order to get a person's money back. If we can show intent, we can also sue for up to $2,000 in civil penalties for each intentional violation.

In some of our cases, there is no clear violation of the law. Then we may mediate the dispute. For example, we've taken on some cases involving dry cleaner disputes in which a person has taken clothing in to be dry-cleaned and it was damaged. Instead of having a law suit, we will try to help the consumer and the business reach an agreement that is satisfactory to both.

What is your most difficult problem?

I think the more difficult problems occur when one business tries to use government to put a competitor out of business. We have to be very sensitive to that. We have to be sure the information is accurate. We also have to look for motivation.

Are there some things the consumer can do for himself to avoid getting into a bad situation?

Yes there are, but consumer education is not the answer to some of our problems. People ought not let anyone convince them that the answer to their problems is simply better information.

To protect yourself against auto repair fraud, you'd have to know everything there was to know about an automobile. You'd have to know everything there was about a TV to protect yourself against TV repair fraud. You'd have to know about chemicals in food to protect yourself against cancer-producing ingredients in your food supply.

If you tried to be well-informed on all these subjects, you'd never have any time for anything else.

ACTIVITIES FOR CHAPTER 12

Class Discussion

A. Government regulation in Georgia dates back to colonial times, but there is much more today than in the past.

1. What changes in the way people live have probably contributed to the growth of government regulation?
2. Does government regulation favor business or consumers? Or both? Explain.

B. Occupational licensing is debated almost every year in the legislature. While some members of an occupational group may favor regulation, other members may oppose it. Consumers may also be on both sides of the issue.

1. Could licensing cut down on competition? Could it increase costs to consumers? How?
2. Consider all the occupations in your community. Divide them into two groups: those you feel should be licensed and those you feel don't need to be. What reasons are there for licensing or not licensing an occupation?

Writing Project

"General Assembly repeals all laws regulating private enterprise!" The headline says it all. It's the year 2,000, and resentment over government regulation had reached a peak. The governor announces, "State government is getting out of the business of business."

How did the repeal of these laws affect average Georgians? How are their lives changed?

Assignment: Write a story describing how the average consumer in 2,000 would have to behave differently from today's consumer to make sure he or she got a good deal. Be sure to include specific examples such as food shopping, getting a tooth filled, or having a telephone installed.

omit

13 Financing State Government

Taken together, these headlines convey one message: government costs money.

To serve the people, governments have to spend money. Like a business, a government must pay salaries, purchase supplies and equipment, and pay for utility service. It must pay for maintenance and repairs, and finance the construction of buildings. The amounts of money government spends for each of these purposes are called *expenditures.*

Also like a business, government must have income. A business's income comes from the sale of goods and services. Government's income comes from taxes (and other charges such as license and admission fees). Monies from these different sources are called government *revenues.*

This chapter tells how government gets and spends its money.

What determines the size of state government's expenditures? What determines the size of its revenues? Government expenditures and revenues are tied to the amount of services government provides. If many services are required, spending will be high and so will taxes. Fewer services require less spending and fewer taxes.

Just as a husband and wife have to work out a budget for a family to live on, the governor and the General Assembly of Georgia have to work out a budget for state government to live on. A budget is a plan for raising and spending money.

Both the family and the government face a similar problem: how to balance the budget. That is, how to make sure that the amount of money paid out is not greater than the amount coming in.

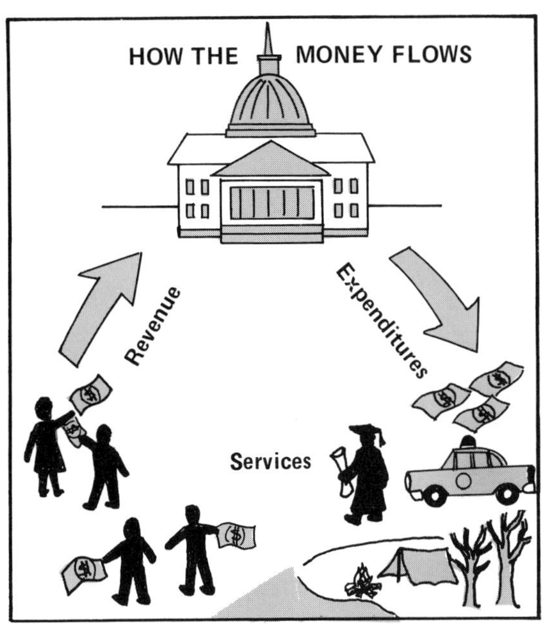

Government has to face rising costs just as the family does. And, it has to deal with the demands of a growing population just as a family has to adjust to the costs of additional children. In Georgia, during a recent 10-year period, state government's budget tripled in size, from $674,802,000 in 1967 to $1,902,800,000 in 1977.

A budget is designed to cover a specific period of time. A family's budget may be figured on a weekly or monthly basis. The state's budget is figured on a yearly basis.

The year-long period between each settling of the state's accounts is called the *fiscal year.* The fiscal year used by the state of Georgia begins on July 1 and ends on June 30. The fiscal year is designated according to the calendar year in which it ends. For example, fiscal year 1980 ran from July 1, 1979, to June 30, 1980.

BUDGET MAKING AT THE CAPITOL

The process for making up the state's budget is described in the following reading.

THINK ABOUT IT

1. What is the role of the governor? The General Assembly?
2. How do the governor's policies and the revenue estimate affect the budget proposal?
3. For what purposes does state government spend the most money?
4. From what sources does most of the money for state government come?

In Georgia, the governor and the General Assembly share the job of making up the budget. The governor's job is to work out a proposal for state government spending. The General Assembly's task is to make that proposal into law.

Role of the Governor

The budget-making process begins when officials in each state agency estimate how much money their agency will need in the coming fiscal year.

By September 15th of each year, agency heads must submit detailed budget requests to the governor. The actual work of analyzing and approving the agency requests is carried out by the Office of Planning and Budget, a unit within the governor's office.

The Office of Planning and Budget may cut or increase an agency's budget request. Two important factors used in shaping the governor's final budget proposal are (1) the governor's policies and (2) the revenue estimate.

The Governor's Policies

The policies of the governor determine the framework in which spending decisions are made for the executive branch. This framework consists of seven major areas. All the activities of executive branch agencies fall into one or another of the areas listed on page 128.* The portion of

**The executive branch spends about 99 percent of the entire state budget.*

state funds spent on each of the seven areas is shown in the "pie chart" below.

Seven Major Policy Areas

1. Intellectual Development
   - –elementary and secondary education
   - –university system
   - –libraries, scholarships, arts, and humanities
2. Economic Development
   - –trade, industry, tourism
3. Human Development
   - –physical and mental health, labor
   - –social services, public assistance
4. Natural Environment
   - –resource management, environmental quality
   - –public recreation, energy
5. Transportation
   - –highways and roads
   - –air, rail, and waterways
6. Protection of Persons and Property
   - –law enforcement, corrections
   - –consumer protection
7. General Government
   - –administrative services, retirement systems, personnel

The governor's overall policies in these seven areas do not change very much from year to year. However, he may have certain priorities–programs or activities he feels should have special attention–in a given year. For example, the governor may decide that a special effort should be made to improve the state's prisons. Or he may give special attention to a highway repaving program.

Which areas usually receive the most money? Look at the chart below to see how the state's expenditures have been divided in recent years.

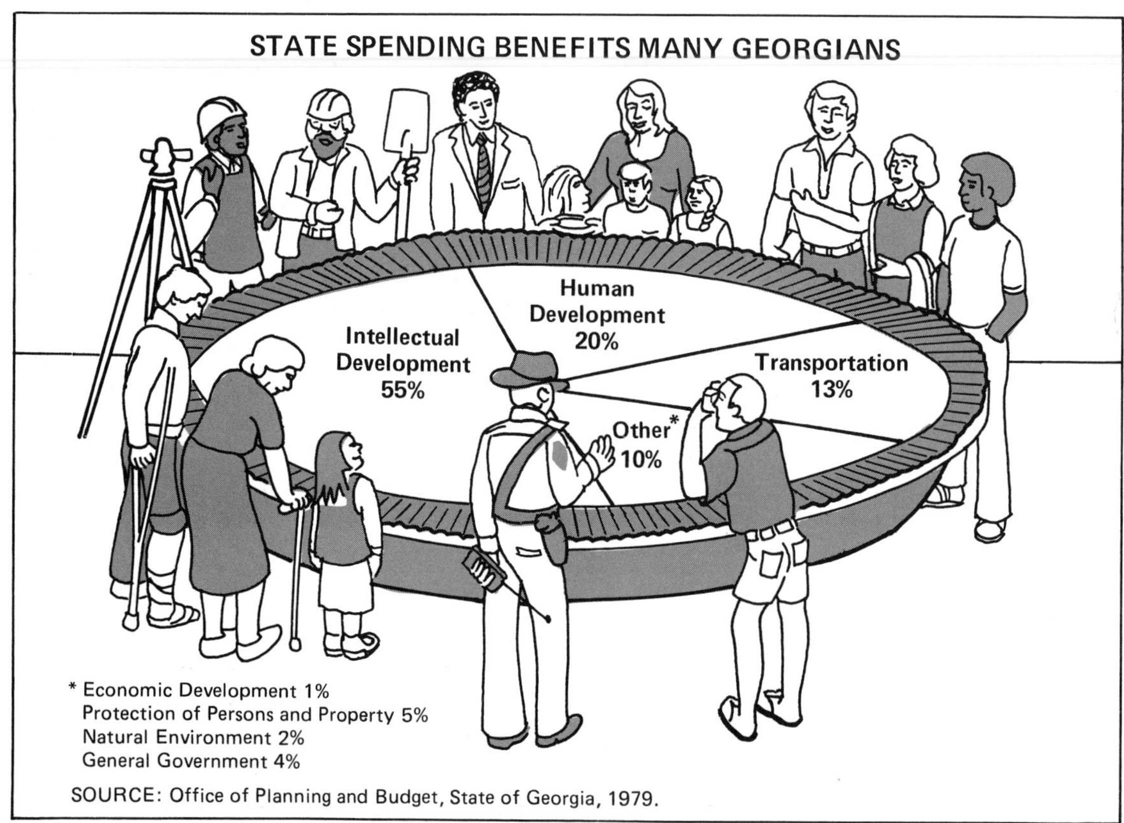

Revenue Estimate

By law, Georgia's state government may not spend more money than it takes in each year (see "The State's Debt," below). The budget has to be balanced.

Therefore, in working up the budget proposal, the governor needs to have an estimate of what the state's revenue will be in the next fiscal year. This revenue estimate is based on what experts think will be the amount of tax money collected. Of course, the revenue estimate is only a prediction. If the state's economy slumps, tax collections will be less. If the economy booms, tax collections will be greater. The size of the budget is limited by the size of the revenue estimate. Having a reliable prediction is very important.

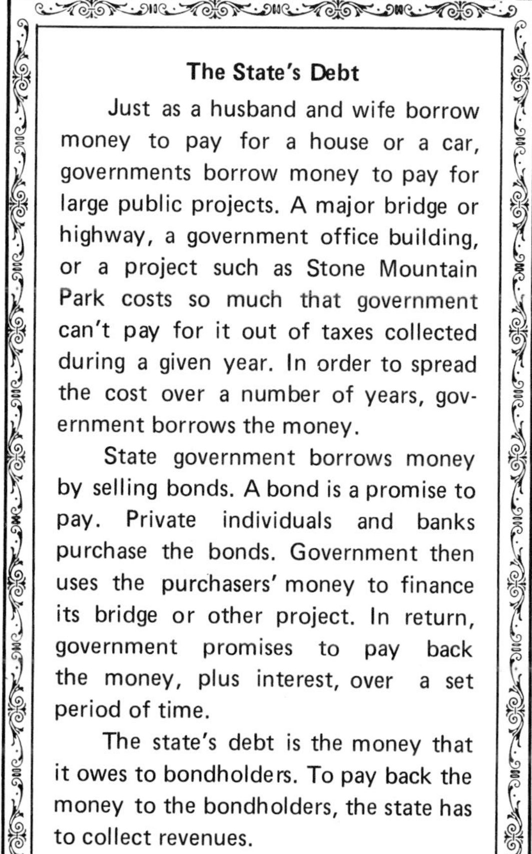

The State's Debt

Just as a husband and wife borrow money to pay for a house or a car, governments borrow money to pay for large public projects. A major bridge or highway, a government office building, or a project such as Stone Mountain Park costs so much that government can't pay for it out of taxes collected during a given year. In order to spread the cost over a number of years, government borrows the money.

State government borrows money by selling bonds. A bond is a promise to pay. Private individuals and banks purchase the bonds. Government then uses the purchasers' money to finance its bridge or other project. In return, government promises to pay back the money, plus interest, over a set period of time.

The state's debt is the money that it owes to bondholders. To pay back the money to the bondholders, the state has to collect revenues.

Role of the General Assembly

After the governor, with the Office of Planning and Budget, has worked on the budget proposal for several months, he submits it to the General Assembly. This must be done by the fifth day of the session in January.

The governor's budget proposal is then introduced as a bill into the General Assembly. This *appropriations* bill originates in the House of Representatives and then moves to the Senate. It is handled in much the same way as other bills.

In each house, it is referred to an appropriations committee where it is usually amended. Legislators may amend it further during floor debate in each house.

The task of passing the appropriations bill is usually long and drawn out. A conference committee is almost always needed to iron out differences between the House and Senate versions of the bill.

After the General Assembly passes the budget, the governor gets another crack at it. The governor has the power of the *item veto*. This enables him to strike items from the budget.

The appropriations law—the state's new budget—goes into effect at the start of the fiscal year, July 1.

If there is a possibility that the budget is out of balance, the governor may call a special session later in the year to "fix" the budget.

Lobbyists and interest groups pay a lot of attention to the appropriations bill. Public employees, whose wages depend on state spending decisions, are also active. Other private citizens, as well as corporations and organizations, lobby for increased funding of programs in which they have a special interest.

Every year, the General Assembly's debate over appropriations usually takes more time than any other issue. Often this debate keeps legislators working into late March.

Budget decisions are often controversial. For example, questions of whether to spend more or less money for welfare and the schools affects the citizens who use these services. They also concern the social workers and school teachers who provide the services. And these decisions interest the taxpayer, who will have to pay the bill.

TAXES

In the fall of 1978, Sen. Tom Cody was running for re-election. In a "meet-the-candidate" gathering at the county courthouse, he talked with an audience of citizens about campaign issues.

"As far as I'm concerned there's only one issue," spoke out a man in work clothes. "And, that's the one your opponent's talking about—taxes! She says she'll cut my property taxes when she's elected. Property taxes are eating up all my profits. It ain't fair. And, if you don't cut 'em, I'm going to have to quit farming and take a job at the carpet mill."

"Yes, sir," replied Tom Cody. "I think I understand your problem. But, let me first say that the state gets almost no revenue from property taxes. Property taxes go mainly to support your county and your local schools."

"Well, where does the General Assembly get all the money it's spending?" asked a middle-aged woman. "It's coming from the taxpayer isn't it?"

"You're right, it is," answered Cody. "But at the state level most of the revenue comes from the sales tax and the state income tax."

"Shoot, I don't mind the sales tax so much," said a man in a business suit. "It's only 3 cents on the dollar and everybody, even renters, has to pay it. It's the fairest tax there is. I'd even raise it."

"But that would just hurt us old folks more," snapped an elderly woman in the front row. "Me and my husband have to live on social security. We can barely live as it is. I don't think it's fair to have a sales tax on everything you have to buy, especially on food. People need that to survive."

"I agree, ma'am," said Tom Cody. "The sales tax falls hard on low income people. I'm not in favor of raising it any. As for taking it off food, you know that would mean a big loss in revenue for the state. We'd have to turn around and raise the tax rate somewhere else. Maybe the income tax. . . ."

"Wait just a minute!" interrupted the man in the business suit. "I paid out $200 more this year than last year in your state income tax. You raise the tax rate and no telling what I'll have to pay next year. It's not fair to people who are trying to earn more money to have the government take it away from them."

A young woman holding a baby asked, "What about increasing the tax on gasoline?"

"No, no way!" came a chorus of replies from the audience.

"There's your answer to that one," grinned Senator Cody. "With the price of gas what it is, no legislator could vote for raising the gasoline tax and hope to be reelected."

"Raise the tax on liquor!" shouted an old man rising to his feet.

"Just a minute, Albert," said another old man. "Let's be fair. If you want to up the tax on my beer, let's up the tax on your cigarettes, too."

The rest of the audience laughed, a few clapped their approval.

"You see?" asked Tom Cody. "There's no simple answer."

"There is so a simple answer," growled a man in the back row. "Just cut the !&*!&*! spending!"

"I'm for cutting the spending too, sir," replied Cody. "But where would you start? The schools? Roads? State parks? The State Patrol? You'd have to cut out something."

"Ain't no simple answer is there?" chirped the old woman in the front row.

"Ain't no simple answer," echoed Tom Cody.

PAYING TAXES

Paying taxes rests on the idea that everyone should pay his or her fair share of the cost of government.

The problem, as shown in the citizens' meeting with Tom Cody, is how to decide just what that fair share is.

One common notion is that a person's fair share should be based on his or her ability to pay. "A wealthy person should pay more than a poor person."

Another common notion is that persons who benefit most from government services should pay the most. "A man with five kids in school should pay more than a man with only one kid in school."

For many years, governments have tried to find a tax that is fair to everyone. But, they have yet to find one tax that everyone agrees is fairest. Instead, governments have used a combination of several taxes, which, taken together, affect all people equally—or nearly equally.

Taken together, these taxes should not especially burden or favor any one group of citizens—not the rich or the poor, not the property owners or the renters, not the business operators or the wage earners.

At the same time, government needs to have taxes that are easy to collect and which provide enough revenue to cover its costs.

Generally, taxes can be classified into three groups according to how they affect people having different incomes:

1. A tax is *progressive* when it takes a larger percentage of income from high income groups than from low income groups.
2. A tax is *proportional* when it takes the same percentage of income from all income groups.
3. A tax is *regressive* when it takes a larger percentage of income from low income groups than from high income groups.

The average citizen pays all taxes. Sometimes this is done directly. The sales tax, the income tax, and the property tax are direct taxes. Sometimes the consumer pays taxes indirectly. Examples of indirect taxes are excise taxes (taxes on the manufacture or distribution of goods) and business profits taxes which are passed on to the consumer as part of the price of goods.

THE TAX BITE

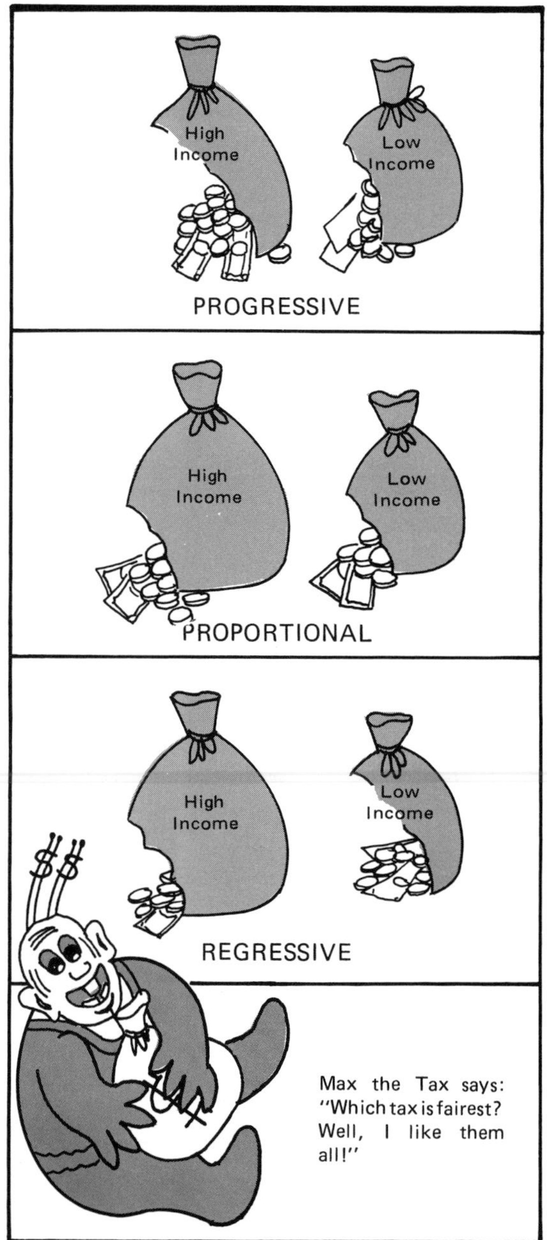

STATE TAXES IN GEORGIA

The question "Which tax is fairest?" has not yet been answered to everyone's satisfaction. In the following reading, the combination of taxes used to finance state government is presented. The reading also describes how some taxes are collected and gives the pros and cons of the major taxes.

THINK ABOUT IT

1. Which taxes bring in the most money? Why?
2. Which taxes are based on the taxpayer's ability to pay?
3. Which taxes do some citizens not have to pay?
4. Which taxes are easiest for government to collect?

Georgia finances state government through a combination of various taxes and fees plus aid from the federal government. The combination of taxes and fees is called the tax structure. It developed, haphazardly for the most part, over a period of many years.

As the state's population grew and the demand for public services grew, state government (and local governments, too) began to tax Georgia residents in a variety of ways.

Property taxes—taxes on agricultural land, urban real estate, merchandise, and personal property including farm animals and vehicles—paid for most of the state's activities through the 1920s.

But there was much dissatisfaction with the property tax. People who owned property felt that they paid more than a fair share of the cost of government. In the 1920s, state government had to find new sources of revenue. Roads needed to be built and schools needed more money. The General Assembly enacted a motor fuel tax and placed a tax on cigarettes. Then in 1929, the legislature passed the state's first income tax law.

The depression forced the state to look for still more sources of tax revenue. Beer, wine, and liquor were taxed.

After World War II, Georgia's population began to grow more rapidly. So did the demand for better government services, especially in public education. To meet these demands, political leaders decided to change the state tax structure.

In 1951, a 3 percent sales tax replaced the unpopular state property tax as a major source of revenue.

Tax Revenues Today

How much money does each tax bring into the state treasury? The amounts vary from year to year depending on the state's economy. For instance, when people earn more income, income tax collections go up. When they spend more, sales tax receipts go up.

The illustration below shows the average percentage of state revenue coming from each tax source. It shows the relative importance of each source.

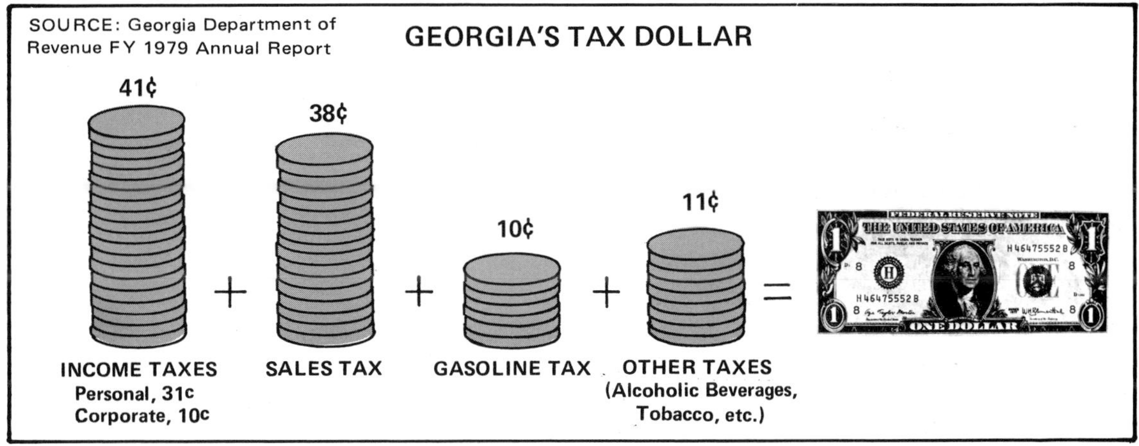

General Sales Tax

The sales tax is the largest state revenue source. It is imposed on the retail sale, rental, or use of goods and certain services.

This tax covers the sale of food, clothing, automobiles, building materials, furniture, sporting goods, and most other goods. It is imposed on entertainment and athletic events, hotel and motel rooms, and restaurant meals.

Some goods are exempt from the tax. For example, there is no sales tax on school lunches, the seed and fertilizer used in farming, and solar energy equipment.

The sales tax is imposed on natural gas, electricity, water, and local telephone services. However, most professional and business services, including those of doctors, barbers, dry cleaners, mechanics, and housepainters, are not subject to the sales tax.

How is the tax paid? The purchaser pays the tax to the seller at the time of purchase. The seller in turn sends the tax to the State Department of Revenue each month.

What is the tax rate? Statewide the sales tax rate is 3 percent. In Fulton and DeKalb counties an additional 1 percent is imposed to finance the Metropolitan Atlanta Rapid Transit Authority (MARTA) system. Also, cities and counties may elect to impose an additional 1 percent local option sales tax to help finance local government.

The general sales tax has certain advantages:

1. It produces a lot of revenue because it covers almost all retail purchases in the state.
2. Every resident and nonresident who benefits from state services helps pay for them.
3. It is relatively easy to collect, and practically no one can avoid paying this tax.

However, the sales tax is a regressive tax. Even though everyone pays the same rate (3 percent or 4 percent), the sales tax takes a larger portion of lower level incomes than higher level incomes. This is because low income families usually spend a larger part of their income on taxable items, such as food and clothing, than do high income families.

Figuring the Sales Tax

On Sales of:	3% Collects—	3% + 1% Collects—
10 cents or less*	0	0
11 cents to 35 cents inclusive	1 cent	1 cent
36 cents to 66 cents inclusive	2 cents	3 cents
67 cents to $1.00 inclusive	3 cents	4 cents

*There is no tax collected on sales of less than 11 cents.

Individual Income Tax

The individual income tax is the second largest source of state revenue. It is imposed on a person's wages, salary, profits, rents, interest, and other forms of income.* Georgia residents, and non-residents who get income from within Georgia, must pay the tax.

How is the tax paid? A person with income must file with the Georgia State Department of Revenue a tax form—called an "income tax return"—by April 15 of each year. However, most wage earners actually pay their taxes before this date. Under Georgia's income tax law, em-

*Essentially, Georgia taxes the same income that the federal government does. The process for paying both taxes is also basically the same with state tax going to the Georgia Department of Revenue and federal tax going to the Internal Revenue Service of the U.S. Treasury Department.

ployers must take out tax payments from the employee's paychecks. This tax money is sent to the Department of Revenue.

Persons who do not have taxes withheld from their wages, for instance farmers and other self-employed persons, may have to make partial advance payments during the year.

What is the tax rate? The individual income tax is based on income. The rate increases as the individual's income increases. There are different rates for single persons and married persons or persons with families to support.

The individual income tax has two important advantages:

1. The tax results in a large amount of revenue because so many wage earners must pay it.
2. It is progressive. People with high incomes pay at a higher rate than people with low incomes.

However, a large number of low income families pay little or no tax. Some critics of the tax say that these are often the very people who benefit most from state services. Also, persons in some occupations (those in which no taxes are withheld by employers) are able to avoid paying all or part of their taxes. These people are able to "hide" their income. This is against the law. If they get caught, they must pay the taxes they owe, plus interest and fines, and may go to jail.

Corporate Income Tax

The corporate income tax is imposed on a corporation's profits. The rate is 6 percent. All corporations doing business or gaining income from property in Georgia must pay this tax.

Motor Fuel Tax

The motor fuel tax is placed on gasoline, diesel oil, or any other fuel used to propel a motor vehicle on the highways. Although paid by the distributors of motor fuel, the tax is passed on to the consumer buying fuel at the pump. The tax rate is computed per gallon of motor fuel.

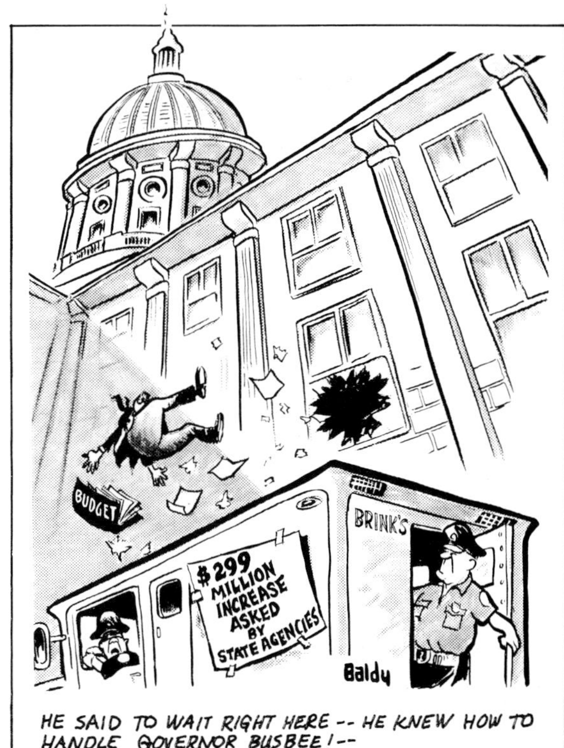

HE SAID TO WAIT RIGHT HERE -- HE KNEW HOW TO HANDLE GOVERNOR BUSBEE!--

Alcohol and Tobacco Taxes

Taxes are imposed on beer, wine, liquor, and tobacco products before they are sold at retail. As with the motor fuel tax, they are passed on to the consumer as part of the price of these products.

Other Taxes and Fees

State government also gains small amounts of revenue from a variety of taxes and license fees.

FEDERAL AID

The federal government is an important source of revenue for state government. Approximately one-third of the cost of state services is met by federal funds.

Federal money comes to the state

under a major program called *grants-in-aid.*

The following reading describes the grant-in-aid program and how it influences federal-state relations.

THINK ABOUT IT

1. What is the purpose of federal grants-in-aid?
2. What arguments are there against grants-in-aid?
3. What arguments are there in favor of grants-in-aid?

The federal government does not give grant-in-aid money to the state to use any way it pleases. Each grant-in-aid, or grant for short, is earmarked for a specific purpose. Georgia receives grants for many purposes including highway construction, elementary and secondary education, mental health care, welfare assistance, unemployment insurance, and environmental protection.*

Grants come with "strings attached." That is, to receive the money, the state government has to agree to certain conditions.

Usually, the state has to put up state funds to match the federal contribution. Then the state has to agree to follow federal regulations in using the grant. Federal agencies supervise how the state spends the money it receives.

For instance, the Georgia Department of Human Resources has to abide by the rules of the U.S. Department of Health and Human Services in spending federal funds for social services. Federal regulations spell out who is eligible to receive services and how services will be delivered to clients. The state may be required to create new jobs to administer the services.

Sometimes federal regulations conflict with state laws. If so, and the state wants to receive the federal aid funds, the state must follow the federal regulations.

Grants help to distribute the nation's income and wealth more evenly among all Americans no matter where they live. Taxpayers in higher income states pay a larger portion into the federal tax system than those in lower income states. Lower income states receive a larger portion of their revenues from federal funds than do the higher-income states.

However, grant programs have long been controversial. Politicians in Georgia as well as other states often criticize the federal government's handling of these programs. Much of the controversy centers around the federal regulations that are imposed on states accepting the money.

How important is federal aid to state government in Georgia? In 1956, federal aid accounted for 19.8 percent of state government's revenue. By 1966, it had grown to 28.5 percent. And, in 1976, federal aid made up 33.0 percent of the state government's revenues. Clearly, over a 20-year period Georgia had come to depend on federal aid more and more to provide government services.

*City and county governments may also receive federal aid. They also receive "state aid" from state government.

ACTIVITIES FOR CHAPTER 13

Class Discussion

A. Consider this statement: "There are three groups of people concerned with the state's budget—those receiving government services, those providing the services, and those paying for the services."

1. To what persons is this statement referring? Be specific.
2. There is a fourth group concerned with the budget—the budget makers, the governor, and the legislators. Which of the first three groups would the budget makers be most likely to listen to?

B. Determining each citizen's fair share of the tax burden has long been a problem.

1. For what reasons do you think a citizen's fair share should be based on his or her ability to pay? Are there reasons why it should not be?
2. What reasons are there for basing a citizen's fair share on the benefits he or she receives from government? If all taxes were based on this idea, would there be any problem?

C. Federal grants-in-aid are based on the idea that each state should be able to furnish at least a minimum level of services. That way public services can be fairly equal from state to state. The problem is that the 50 states are not equal in resources or income.

However, aid programs have made the federal government more powerful within the states. Opponents of federal aid charge that states' rights have been weakened. The states are forced to conduct more and more of their business according to federal regulations. There is also tax money wasted, they charge, because the states have to hire people to enforce federal regulations.

A state doesn't have to accept all the federal aid available. But, what would happen if it didn't?

1. Why might state taxes have to be raised if federal aid were cut?
2. Why might most state politicians be willing to live with federal regulations as the price for accepting federal aid?

Writing Project

"All we need to do to cut these high taxes is to cut the spending, cut out the unnecessary government services."

Assignment: Write an essay either supporting or opposing this idea.

A. If you support the idea: tell where you would cut government services in order to cut taxes. Be sure to consider the effects of these cuts in service on different groups of Georgians. Tell why you think this way is necessary and fair.

B. If you oppose the idea: tell why services shouldn't be cut. Be sure to consider the effect of keeping taxes at their current levels. How would this affect different groups of Georgians? Tell why you think this way is necessary and fair.

IV THE JUSTICE SYSTEM

Protection Against Crime
Courts
Judicial Procedure
Corrections

unit 5

Introduction

Unit 4 of *State Government in Georgia* looks at Georgia's system of justice. This system is based on laws which regulate society. It includes the courts—the judicial branch of government—which apply the law in specific cases, and executive agencies which work with the courts enforcing the law and carrying out court decisions.

Where do our laws come from? The highest law in our nation is the United States Constitution. The diagram below shows our other sets of laws, in their order of importance.

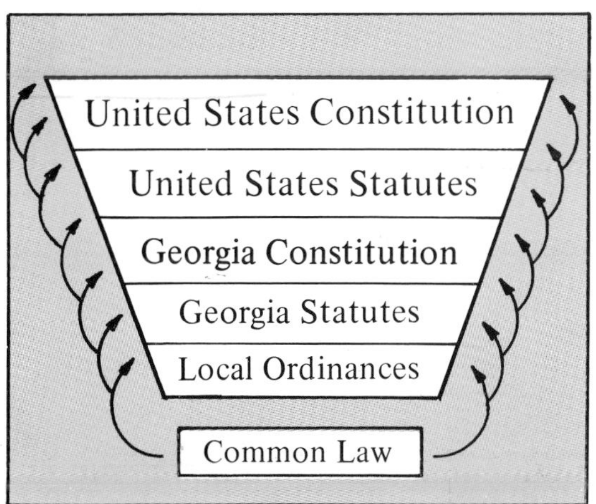

The *United States Constitution* is the "supreme law of the land." As you read in Chapter 1, all other laws must agree with the Constitution.

United States Statutes are laws passed by Congress. United States statutes are written down in the United States Code, a set of books which contain the federal laws.*

The *Georgia Constitution* is superior to any other laws made in Georgia. No state laws may violate the Georgia Constitution. In turn, the Georgia Constitution may not include a law which violates the United States Constitution.

Georgia Statutes are laws passed by the Georgia General Assembly. Georgia statutes are written down in the Georgia Code—books which contain state laws.

Local Ordinances are laws passed by city councils and county commissions. Ordinances cover such subjects as dog control, zoning, parking, and building construction. Ordinances are written down in municipal or county codes.

Common Law is the base of our legal system. Beginning in England and later in America, common law grew out of judges' decisions based on unwritten customs and traditions.

Judges still make common law decisions. Although common law is sometimes referred to as "unwritten," these de-

*Some statutes, federal and state, give executive agencies the power to make regulations that have the effect of law. For example, the Georgia Department of Revenue makes regulations covering the buying and selling of motor vehicles. These kinds of regulations are often called "administrative law."

cisions are actually recorded so that other judges may refer to them.

Common law does not come from legislation, but much of our written law—constitutions, statutes, ordinances—has been taken from common law.

CIVIL CASES AND CRIMINAL CASES

The courts handle two basic kinds of cases—*civil* and *criminal*—plus a special kind—*juvenile* cases.

A *civil case* involves a dispute between private parties. A party may be a private citizen, a corporation, or a government. Typically, in a civil case, one party claims that the other party violated some legal right. Sometimes the claim is that one party caused the other some injury, such as in an auto accident. In a civil case, the court's job is to see that the dispute is settled fairly.

Often judges have to decide civil cases in which written laws do not clearly apply. This is because written laws cannot possibly cover all the disputes that might arise between people. In these cases, the court may have to rely on the common law decisions made previously in similar cases by other judges. In some cases, called "equity" cases, judges have to make decisions on what seems to be fair when there is no written or common law to go by.

A *criminal case* involves a crime—an act that violates the law and for which the law sets a punishment. Generally, crimes are acts that not only are harmful to an individual but also are a threat to the public.

Acting for the public, the government brings criminal cases against persons accused of crimes.

It is important to remember that not all harmful acts (such as causing injuries in an auto accident) are crimes. To be a crime, an act must be defined as such in a law. Federal, state, and local laws define thousands of crimes, from speeding to murder.

A crime is either a *felony* or a *misdemeanor.* Felonies are more serious crimes than misdemeanors. A felony is punishable by *not less* than one year imprisonment, fines, and in certain cases by death. A misdemeanor is punishable by not more than one year imprisonment, fines, or both. Some crimes, such as *assault and battery,* may be treated as felonies or misdemeanors, depending on how severe they are.

A few examples of felonies are murder, robbery, burglary, kidnapping, arson, rape, motor vehicle theft, and possessing and selling certain drugs. A few examples of misdemeanors are abandonment, carrying a concealed weapon, criminal trespass, cruelty to animals, driving under the influence, and shoplifting.

A *juvenile case* may or may not involve a criminal act. But, it always involves a young person.

Each of the four chapters in Part 4 discusses a part of the justice system. Chapter 14 examines those state executive agencies which protect persons and property against crime. Chapters 15 and 16 describe Georgia's courts—the judicial branch of government—and the procedures they use. Chapter 17 looks at state corrections—what happens to persons convicted of crimes.

14 Protection Against Crime

State laws and agencies protect the people in many different ways. Earlier chapters described protection of the public's health, of consumers, of needy persons, and of natural resources. This chapter is about how the state protects persons and property against crime.

As the graph below shows, crime against persons and property is a major problem in Georgia. Protection against crime is a major responsibility of government. This responsibility and the cost of protection are shared by state, federal, and local governments.

CRIME INCREASING: WHEN AND WHERE?

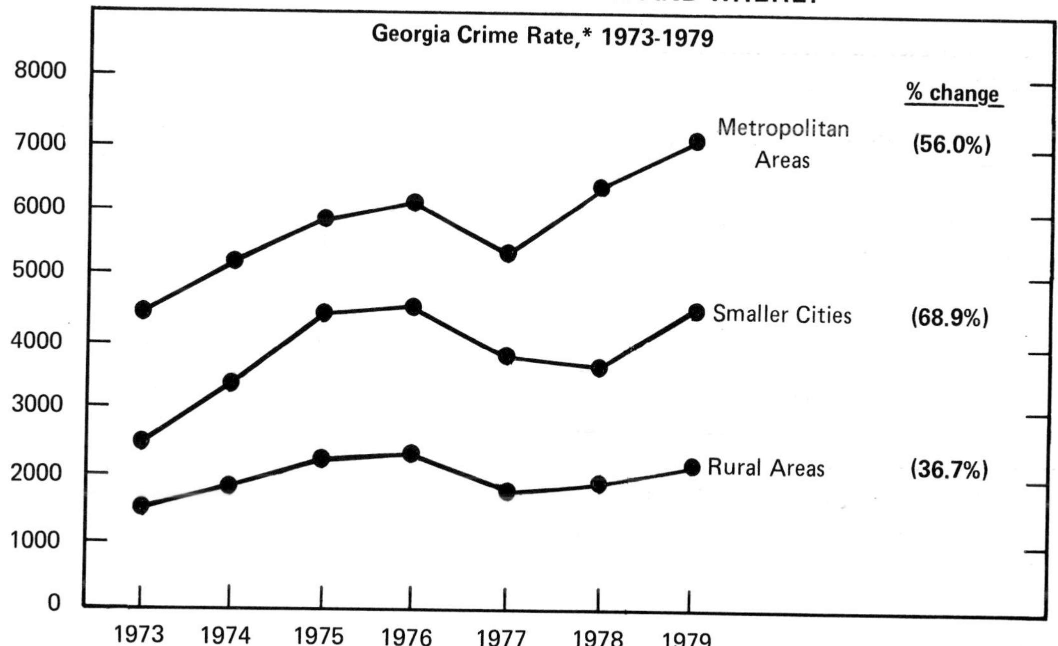

*Crimes per 100,000 people living in each area. Includes selected violent crimes reported (murder, rape, robbery, aggravated assault) and selected property crimes (burglary, larceny, motor vehicle theft).
Source: FBI Uniform Crime Reports.

Protection against crime is, however, largely the job of county and city law enforcement agencies. In most of Georgia's 159 counties, the sheriff is elected to serve as the top law enforcement officer. However, some counties have a county police force in addition to the sheriff's department. Meanwhile, city police enforce the law within municipalities. All local police agencies are responsible for enforcing state laws as well as local ordinances.

So, what is the role of state government? Criminal laws are enacted by state government, and local agencies enforce those laws under the authority of state government. In addition, there are state law enforcement agencies that work with local agencies to protect persons and property against crime.

STATE LAW ENFORCEMENT AGENCIES

In the following reading, the roles of several state agencies are outlined.

THINK ABOUT IT

1. What are the major responsibilities of the State Patrol, the GBI, and the Department of Defense?
2. How did criminal activities change in the 1930s and help create the need for a state patrol?
3. How does the GBI assist local law enforcement agencies?

The Department of Defense

Since colonial times, Georgia has had a state militia, or national guard. This is not a full-time military or police force. It is made up of volunteers who go through short-term military training and continue working at their regular occupations.

The governor is commander-in-chief of the state military forces. He appoints an adjutant general to command the guard and to run the Georgia Department of Defense. In case of disaster, riot, or other emergency, the governor may call out these forces. (They may also be called up by the president of the United States in a national emergency.)

The Civil Defense Division provides a volunteer, non-military force throughout the state to assist victims and to carry out emergency plans in case of natural or man-made disasters.

The Department of Public Safety

With the building of each state's network of roads and highways, there were new traffic laws to enforce. Also, highways provided new opportunities for crime. Local law enforcement agencies needed help in coping with criminals who operated intercounty and interstate.

Georgia established its state police in 1937, in response to these new kinds of automobile-related crimes.

The Department of Public Safety is the major state agency charged with protection of persons and property, particularly on the state's roads and highways. It enforces rules of the road, administers motor vehicle inspection and safety laws, and regulates the licensing of drivers.

The Georgia State Patrol is the main division of the department. Its duty is to protect the public on the highways. The Georgia State Patrol has a force of 750 men and women who regularly patrol interstates, highways, and county roads. It operates through 45 posts at strategic locations throughout the state.

The State Patrol directs most of its efforts toward enforcement of traffic laws and the prevention of accidents, deaths, and injuries. But, it also works at preventing and investigating any type of criminal act committed on the highways. In addition, it has the duty to arrest persons charged with committing those acts.

The patrol cooperates with local police

agencies regarding law enforcement on public roads. Upon the request of local government officials or the governor, the State Patrol may assist in any other types of criminal cases. From time to time, it is called upon to handle riots and other civil disturbances and to help establish order after disasters. Troopers also serve as guards to protect the governor and other officials.

Georgia Bureau of Investigation

The GBI assists local law enforcement agencies in the investigation of criminal cases. Usually, the GBI enters a case after a request by a police chief or sheriff. Sometimes, the governor orders the GBI into a county without a local request.

GBI agents work on many kinds of cases including armed robbery, burglary, forgery and bad checks, gambling, arson, murder, suicide, and other death investigations. Special squads are set up to investigate organized crime and auto theft. The GBI brings to a case trained investigators and special equipment which local police departments normally may not have available.

A special duty of the GBI is to investigate crimes on state property.

A unit of the GBI, the Division of Forensic Science (the "Crime Lab"), carries out scientific examinations of articles used in committing crimes and other items of evidence. It conducts tests for alcohol, drugs, and poisons. It test-fires weapons, identifies bullets and cartridges, and examines fingerprints and bloodstains. In addition, the lab works with local authorities in carrying out autopsies and conducting blood and breath alcohol tests of suspected drunk drivers.

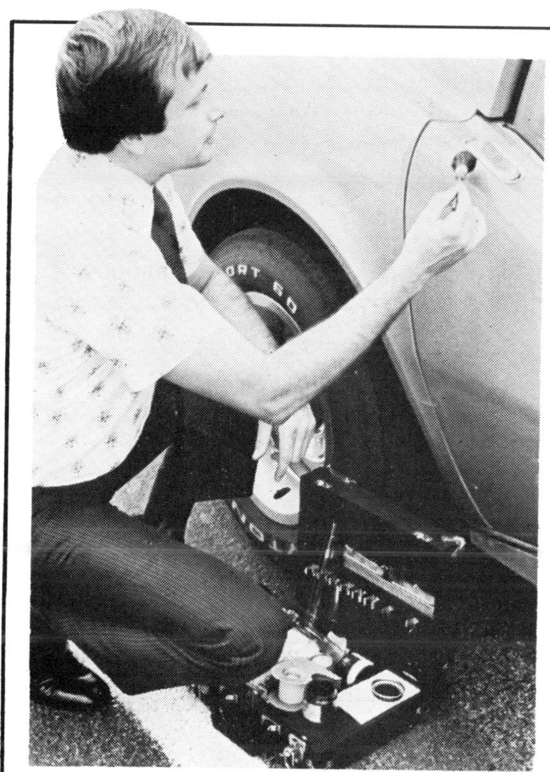

Left: GBI investigator dusts for fingerprints on a stolen auto.

Above: At the crime lab, an agent cleans bones for laboratory tests.

Also within the GBI, the Georgia Crime Information Center serves as the state's central point for collecting, storing, and retrieving crime and law enforcement information.

Local law enforcement agencies supply this center with information, including fingerprints and photographs, about all persons convicted of specific crimes within their jurisdictions. The center also collects information about wanted and missing persons and on stolen vehicles.

The Crime Information Center makes this information available to the courts and to local, state, and federal agencies on a 24-hour-a-day, 7-day-a-week basis.

This means that if a state trooper, for instance, stops a speeder, he or she can find out within a few minutes by radio whether or not the driver is wanted or the vehicle is stolen.

Although the troopers and agents of the Georgia State Patrol and the GBI handle most statewide law enforcement, officers of other state agencies participate in protecting persons and property. For example, Department of Revenue agents investigate crimes involving state liquor laws, and DNR officers enforce hunting and fishing laws.

POST

Nevertheless, county and city officers must handle the bulk of law enforcement in Georgia. To upgrade the quality of local law enforcement, the General Assembly passed an act in 1970 setting up the Georgia Peace Officers Standards and Training Council—called "POST" for short.

POST oversees training programs for state and local law officers in Georgia and sets standards for certifying officers. Each year about 1,500 officers meet POST certification requirements.

INTERVIEW WITH A STATE TROOPER

The lone trooper patrolling the highways does most of the work of the Georgia State Patrol. For many Georgia residents, the state trooper is the one officer of state government they see regularly.

Trooper David C. McCranie is a native of Eastman, Georgia. Prior to joining the Georgia State Patrol he was a police officer for the University of Georgia and for Clarke County.

In the following interview, Trooper McCranie discusses his job and his feelings about being a state trooper.

THINK ABOUT IT

1. Why does a trooper have to be self-sufficient?
2. What other abilities are particularly needed by a trooper?
3. According to Trooper McCranie, why can't government protect people from themselves?

What made you want to join the State Patrol?

Well, I had a lot of friends on the patrol. I liked the way the patrol operates. It's not as restricted as, say, the county police. You're not confined to a small area and you can work special details. I worked the Southern Governors' Conference at Lake Lanier recently, and I was on the strangler case in Columbus. You can move over the state without having to change jobs. Also, there's the pay scale, and there are more opportunities for advancement than with the county police.

What is the most challenging or personally rewarding aspect of being a trooper?

Investigating traffic accidents. That's a primary responsibility of the State Patrol.

You're going to have to work wrecks where there's multiple fatalities. And, it takes a lot of extra work to determine the exact causes of the accident. I've never worked an accident where there's been just one cause. Usually it's three or four things. Determining that accurately is to me very satisfying.

Unraveling what happened? the mystery?

That's right. You do a background investigation on the drivers. Find out where they were, where they had been, whether they had any family problems. You only do this kind of investigation when there are fatalities. I have worked on fatality investigations for three or four days at a time.

On one accident?

On one accident.

So you're pulled off regular patrol?

Right. You have to work the accident when it happens. You can't take off three days and then come back and try to work it. It has to be done right away. That's the most satisfying part of the job.

Is there some duty you'd just as soon not have?

Yeah! To me the most undesirable duties are special details like traffic at the Atlanta 500 or drag races where you get all the drunks. Everybody wants to get out at one time.

Do you consider being a trooper a tough job?

Well, certain parts of it are. Day in and day out, it's not a real hard job. But there are times it's very demanding. Ninety percent of the people you stop are not going to give you any trouble. They know they were speeding, take their ticket and go on. But it's demanding when you do stop people who give you trouble. You have to control your temper and at the same time be forceful enough to convey to them that they have to go with you or do what you ask them to do.

Is there any one kind of enforcement problem you find yourself spending the most time on?

Timewise it's speeding. But the biggest problem is drunk drivers. A lot of them will give you trouble. Speeders may argue with you, but they won't physically give you a problem. A drunk would.

While on duty, you're faced with making quick decisions. Do you have much leeway in making decisions? In deciding how to handle a situation?

Oh yes! For instance, the individual officer determines whether or not a driver is going to get a ticket. And we try to give out as many warnings as we do tickets. A lot of times a warning will do just as well as a ticket.

So a trooper has to be a person who can make decisions on his own?

You have to be. That's why so much time is taken investigating patrol applicants, giving them tests, and putting them into the training program. We go through a school that's equal to almost any state's in the country. It's sixteen weeks.

A difference between the patrol and your local police is that the local officer always has a shift commander on duty. If the officer has a problem he is hesitant about or doesn't know the answer to, he can call the shift commander who's usually got 10 or 12 years more experience than he has. And he'll come over and help out.

With the patrol it's different. You don't always have a supervisor there. You have to make your own decisions. Most of the time, if you had to call a supervisor, you could be 50 miles away from him. You're down at one end of the territory and he's at the other end.

You can't sit and wait an hour for somebody to get down there and help you out. You have to be self-sufficient.

If you have any problem arresting somebody, you can't expect any help. By the time anybody got there, it would be over anyway.

What about criticism? Are you ever accused of not doing your job properly?

Yes. But it's mostly from out-of-staters. If you're from out of state, you have to post a cash bond on a speeding ticket with the county sheriff's department. We don't handle any of that. We just turn them over to the sheriff's department if they are from out of state.

Sometimes, when we're holding a concentrated patrol on an interstate—that's five or six patrol cars working an area—we get a sheriff's car to meet us at one of the exits. We bring people there who are stopped for speeding—to save us and the motorist the trip into town, to the sheriff's office! We get criticism on that because some people think we're in cahoots with the county to raise money, which is not true. These people may call it a speed trap.

But the speed limit on the interstate is the same all over the country. You stop people running 65, most of them running 70, 72, 78, and they call it a speed trap. That's mainly where the criticism comes from.

What makes your day a good day?

Well, a good day is making a lot of traffic stops because you're slowing people down some. Of course, you're slowing the ones you've stopped. Plus everybody that rides by and sees you slows down too—if not for the whole trip, at least for a little while.

If I can get three or four D.U.I's (people driving under the influence of alcohol) off the road on Friday or Saturday night, that's a good night. If you can get them before they wreck, then you feel like you've done something.

Regarding seatbelts, some people say, "the government can put them in, but it can't make me wear them." From your experience investigating accidents, does wearing seatbelts really make any difference?

Yes, no doubt about it. There's no doubt in my mind at all. The wrecks that I've worked where there was very serious injury or death were the ones where people were sitting on the seatbelts, not wearing them.

In most of the injuries that I've worked and most of the deaths, had they been wearing the seatbelts, they wouldn't have gotten hurt or wouldn't have gotten hurt nearly as bad. And the people wouldn't have been killed.

I wear my seatbelt. I never get in the patrol car without the seatbelt. And I wear the one in my private car. There's no doubt in my mind that seatbelts save lives.

Do you think government can really save people from themselves?

No. No way in the world. Take motorcycles and the helmet law. You can show people that in nine out of ten wrecks you'll get killed without a helmet. And, the law says you have to be 16 to drive a motorcycle.

But a year or so ago we had, in Madison County, many wrecks with kids 13 or 14 years old driving motorcycles. Parents let them do it. You can't save them from themselves in a case like that.

You have 12- and 13-year-old boys getting killed. They don't have any business being on a motorcycle. And, they don't have any helmet on when they do get on it.

What good does it do to prosecute the parents when the kid is already dead?

No, I don't think government can save people from themselves. But government can help—such as with a helmet law.

For a young person thinking about a career such as yours, what personal qualities would that person need to be a good state trooper?

You've got to have a good sense of humor. In restaurants, I've had people come up to me in the middle of a meal and sit down and start telling me their problems.

Also, you have to be able to get along with people. You have to be able to talk to them. You have to understand what a person may be going through because they may never have been stopped before and they don't know how to act. You have to kind of help them out. Maybe they're embarrassed or scared of you. You have to talk to them and make them feel better about it.

You're saying that a trooper has to be sensitive? That's something that doesn't fit with the popular "tough guy" image of a state trooper.

Well, you have to be that too. Sometimes when you're nice to people you've stopped, they'll view that as a weakness and start to give you a hard time. So, you have to be able to turn right around and put them where they're supposed to be and let them know they're not going to run over you.

You do have to go out there knowing you're not ever going to back down from anybody.

The worst strain, though, in police work is not physical strain. It's mental strain. Not knowing what's going to happen. You constantly have to be thinking, "Now if he does that, what am I going to do? If this happens, what do I do?"

So, it's more mental toughness than physical. But, you have to have the physical part there when it's necessary.

ACTIVITIES FOR CHAPTER 14

Class Discussion

A. One of the major goals of the GBI is "to reduce the sale and use of illegal drugs in Georgia." In 1978, the GBI made about 800 drug-case arrests and seized about $15 million worth of drugs.

1. Why would illegal drugs be a special concern of a statewide law enforcement agency?
2. How might the GBI be better able to investigate drug cases than most local police departments?

B. An authority on law enforcement observed: "It has been said that a police officer must have the wisdom of Solomon and the patience of Job. He or she must be a teacher, doctor, lawyer, social worker, clergyman, and psychologist. . . . The job is often thankless, often lonely, and usually frustrating because a police officer sees people's problems but cannot always help solve them."
Do Trooper McCranie's comments support this observation? Which ones?

15 Courts

A merchant asks a judge to issue a *warrant* for the arrest of a man he believes robbed his store. A farmer files a *complaint* with the superior court against a neighbor who dams up a creek. A housewife makes out a *petition* with the juvenile court alleging a teenager is harrassing her with obscene phone calls.

What do these situations have in common? In each, a citizen is setting the law in motion. Instead of taking the law into their own hands, the merchant, the farmer, and the housewife are seeking justice through the courts.

The court responds by (1) deciding what the facts are and (2) determining which laws apply. Finally, depending on the case, the court may decide whether an accused person is guilty or innocent of a crime; or who is right and who is wrong in a civil dispute; or whether a young person should be placed under the control of the juvenile court.

What if the court reaches a decision that goes against the wishes of the person who came to the court for help? In some cases, that person may appeal the decision to a higher court. Ultimately, some court will make a final decision.

How busy are the courts? Each year, hundreds of thousands of cases–ranging from traffic offenses to murder–are handled by Georgia's courts.

Does it matter which court handles a particular legal problem? Yes, the different courts are set up to deal with different kinds of cases.

THE GEORGIA COURT SYSTEM

THINK ABOUT IT

1. What is original jurisdiction? What is appellate jurisdiction?

2. Why are there so many different kinds of courts in Georgia?

Juvenile courts, county courts, magistrate's courts, probate courts, superior courts! Why does Georgia have all these and many other kinds of courts?

Different courts were set up at one time or another to handle specific kinds of legal matters. They were given different kinds of authority.

Jurisdiction

A court's authority or power is called *jurisdiction.* The Georgia Constitution and state laws spell out what jurisdiction each court has.

The two basic kinds of jurisdiction are *original* jurisdiction and *appellate* jurisdiction.

Original jurisdiction is the power to consider a case for the first time. A court with this kind of jurisdiction, often called a "trial" court, makes the original decision in a case.

A court's original jurisdiction may be limited to hearing only certain kinds of cases. For example, in criminal matters a "state" court is limited to hearing only misdemeanor cases. It may not try felony cases.

Appellate jurisdiction is the power to review the decisions of other courts. In an appellate court, the original decision in a case may be upheld or overturned. For example, the Georgia Supreme Court may hear an appeal from a person convicted of murder in a superior court. If it finds errors in the superior court trial, the supreme court may throw out the conviction.

Growth

Georgia's courts were set up by the General Assembly to meet the particular needs of local communities. As a result, the Georgia court system grew, rather haphazardly, to include over a dozen different kinds of courts.

Courts went by different names in different communities. Some existed in only certain counties. One court's jurisdiction sometimes overlapped with the jurisdiction of another court.

By 1979, the system looked like the chart on the next page.

Trial Courts in Georgia

The superior court is the state's main trial court in all 159 counties. In fact, in many counties it is the only court where a citizen can have a jury trial.

The superior court is the highest-ranking court in Georgia with original jurisdiction. It can consider practically all kinds of civil and criminal cases. It is the only court that can try felony cases, divorce cases, cases involving titles to land, and equity cases.

The superior court also has appellate jurisdiction: it can hear appeals from courts of limited jurisdiction and can review and correct errors in those courts.

The superior court was first set up under the Constitution of 1777. To provide justice in each county, the judges had to "ride circuit"—travel by horseback to hold trials where and when they were needed.

Today, the state is divided into 42 superior court circuits. The superior court must sit (or hold sessions) in each county at least twice a year. Each circuit has at least one superior court judge.

The juvenile court has original jurisdiction in matters involving persons under 17 years of age. It may also retain jurisdiction over delinquents until they reach age 21.

In some counties, the juvenile court has its own judge who handles only juvenile

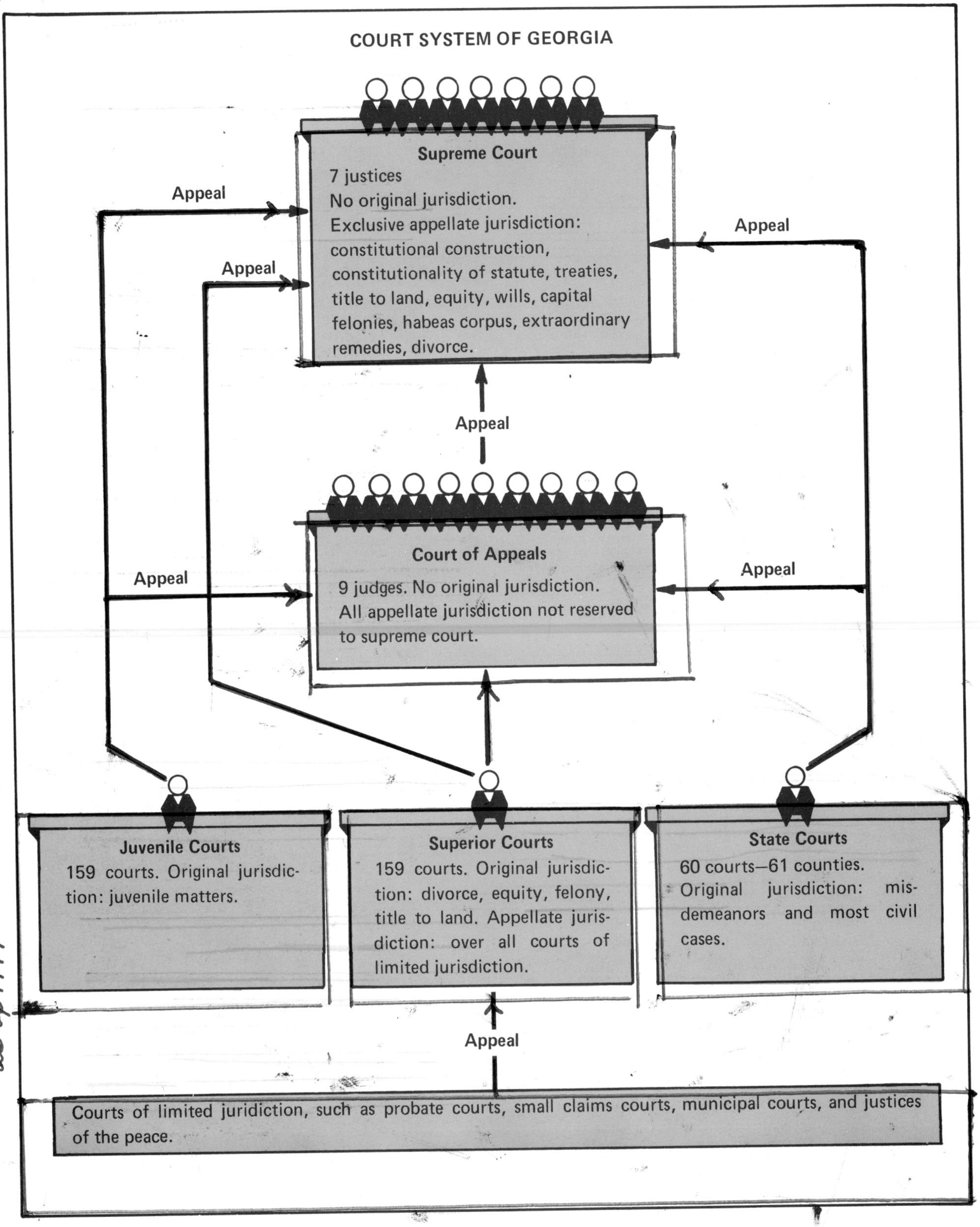

COURT SYSTEM OF GEORGIA

Supreme Court
7 justices
No original jurisdiction.
Exclusive appellate jurisdiction: constitutional construction, constitutionality of statute, treaties, title to land, equity, wills, capital felonies, habeas corpus, extraordinary remedies, divorce.

Appeal

Appeal

Appeal

Appeal

Court of Appeals
9 judges. No original jurisdiction.
All appellate jurisdiction not reserved to supreme court.

Appeal

Appeal

Juvenile Courts
159 courts. Original jurisdiction: juvenile matters.

Superior Courts
159 courts. Original jurisdiction: divorce, equity, felony, title to land. Appellate jurisdiction: over all courts of limited jurisdiction.

State Courts
60 courts—61 counties.
Original jurisdiction: misdemeanors and most civil cases.

Appeal

Courts of limited juridiction, such as probate courts, small claims courts, municipal courts, and justices of the peace.

matters. In others, the superior court judge serves in special sessions as juvenile court judge. Some juvenile cases are heard by "referees" appointed by the judge. Generally, separate juvenile courts are found in the more heavily populated counties.

The juvenile court hears cases in which young people are alleged to be delinquent, unruly, or deprived. *Delinquent juveniles* are those who commit acts, such as robbery and auto theft, which would be criminal offenses if committed by an adult. *Unruly juveniles* are those who are unmanageable by their parents or who run away from home or refuse to go to school—acts that would *not* be offenses if committed by an adult. *Deprived juveniles* are those who are neglected by parents or who have no parents and are in need of some kind of help, guidance, or supervision by the court.

Under certain circumstances, a juvenile's case may be transferred from juvenile court to superior court. For example, if a 16-year-old is alleged to have committed murder, the juvenile may be transferred to superior court for trial as an adult.

The state court is found in only 61 counties. It serves mainly to take some of the caseload off the superior court in densely populated counties.

State court jurisdiction is limited to misdemeanor criminal cases and civil cases. It is the only court, other than the superior court, that can provide a jury trial.

The probate court has existed in each county since the early days of the state. It was formerly known as the court of ordinary. In most counties, the probate court handles violations of state traffic laws and game and fish laws.

It also handles wills and the disposing of the estates of deceased persons.

The probate judge can appoint guardians for persons of unsound mind and hold hearings for committing persons to hospitals for mental illness.

There are other *courts with limited*

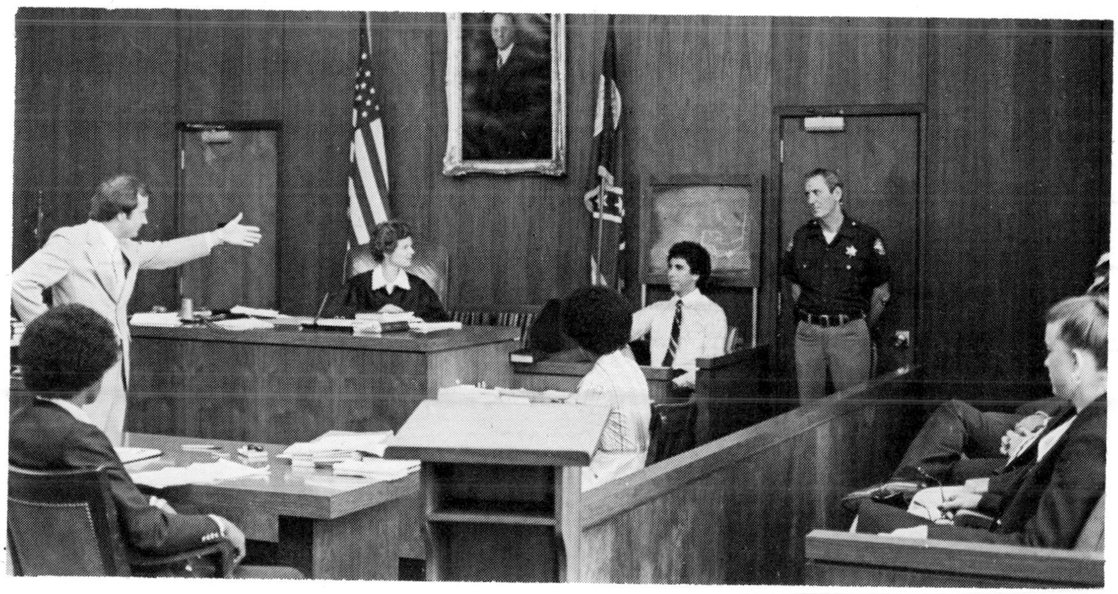

Prosecuting attorney questions a witness in this state court scene.

jurisdiction. The judges in these courts issue arrest and search warrants. Also they handle such things as violations of city or county ordinances and traffic cases.

Appellate Courts in Georgia

The Georgia Supreme Court is the highest court in the state—the "court of last resort." It has the final authority in all legal disputes except those reviewed by the United States Supreme Court.

The supreme court has no original jurisdiction, only appellate jurisdiction. It hears cases on appeal from the superior courts, state courts, and juvenile courts. It also considers cases brought from the court of appeals.

The supreme court can review and correct errors of the trial courts in cases involving capital felonies—crimes punishable by death. In fact, all death sentences in Georgia are automatically reviewed by the supreme court.

The supreme court also considers constitutional questions. For example, if in a lawsuit someone alleges that the General Assembly passed a law which violated the Georgia Constitution, the supreme court would have the final say in the matter. Likewise, if a civil case centered on a dispute over the meaning of a part of the Georgia Constitution, the supreme court would make the final decision.

Seven justices serve on the supreme court. They are elected by the people for terms of six years. Or, they may be appointed to the court by the governor after a death or retirement created a vacancy. The justices elect one member as chief justice.

The seven justices sit together when lawyers argue cases before the court. Each case is assigned to one justice for a written opinion. That justice circulates his opinion to the other justices. After discussion, they adopt or reject the opinion by a majority vote.

The court of appeals has appellate jurisdiction in all types of cases except those which must go to the Georgia Supreme Court. Decisions of the court of appeals may be further reviewed by the supreme court. Like the supreme court, it has no original jurisdiction.

The court of appeals has nine judges elected by the people to six-year terms. The judges of the court then elect one member to be chief judge.

The Federal Courts in Georgia

There are three United States *district courts* in Georgia. These courts are not part of the state court system. They have original jurisdiction to hear cases which come under federal, not state, laws.

Appeals from U.S. district courts go to the Eleventh Circuit Court of Appeals of the United States (which covers Georgia, Alabama and Florida). Decisions of the U.S. Court of Appeals may be further appealed to the United States Supreme Court.

Unlike most state judges who are elected by the voters, federal judges are appointed by the president of the United States.

SUPERIOR COURT PERSONNEL

As in any branch of government, the effectiveness of the courts depends on people. In the Georgia court system, there are many kinds of jobs to be carried out.

The following readings focus on the personnel in the superior court. In other courts, there are similar positions.

THINK ABOUT IT

1. How is the superior court judge's role in a jury trial different from his or her role in a non-jury trial?

Seven justices serve on the Georgia Supreme Court—the highest court in the state.

2. How are the responsibilities of grand jurors and trial jurors different? How are they similar?

The top person in the superior court is the judge who conducts the trials. A jury trial begins with the judge supervising the selection of jurors (see page 154).

Once the trial starts, the judge makes sure it is orderly, fair, and that it proceeds according to legal rules. The judge makes rulings about the law, such as, "What evidence can be accepted? What testimony may the jury hear?"

The judge also instructs the jurors on what the law means and how they can apply it in reaching their decision. If the jury convicts a defendant, the judge determines (within limits set by law) what the sentence will be.

In a non-jury trial, the judge has to decide what the facts are, such as, "Did the defendant strike the victim? Did the defendant do so in self-defense?" In a non-jury trial, the judge also makes the judgment.

Superior court judges are elected by the people within a circuit. The term of office is four years (eight years in the Atlanta circuit). To qualify, a person must be at least 30 years old, a Georgia resident for three years, and have practiced law for seven years. (These same qualifications hold for judges of the court of appeals and justices of the supreme court.)

Each circuit also has a *district attorney* who represents the state, or the "people," in criminal cases before the superior court. He or she sometimes represents the state in certain cases appealed to the supreme court or the court of appeals.*

District attorneys are elected by the voters of the circuit for a term of four years. To qualify, a person must be at least 25 years old, a Georgia resident for three years, a resident of the circuit, and have practiced law before the superior courts for at least three years.

Some circuits may also employ a *public defender.* This attorney provides legal assistance for accused persons who

---

*The Attorney General of Georgia, who handles many kinds of legal matters involving state officials and agencies, may also represent the state in an appeal.

can't afford to hire their own lawyer. Where there is no public defender, the court arranges for other lawyers to defend poor persons accused of crimes.

Others who serve the superior court are—

a *clerk* to maintain court records;

a *sheriff* to serve court papers on persons who must come before the court;

a *probation officer* to investigate the backgrounds of defendants and persons on probation and to collect fines and payments ordered by the court;

a *bailiff* to assist in maintaining order in the courtroom; and

a *court reporter* to record trial proceedings.

JURIES

Juries are made up of regular citizens who perform a civic duty when called to do so. Jury duty is different from other civic duties, such as voting. For one thing, jurors are paid. This is to make up for wages a person may lose while serving on a jury. Also, citizens are required by law to serve if called, unless they have good reason to be excused.

Jurors are selected from a list of registered voters in a county. Every two years, a new list is made up so that the same people are not always called to serve on juries.

In each county, the superior court is served by grand juries and trial juries.

The *grand jury* is made up of 16 to 23 citizens. In criminal matters, it determines whether or not persons charged with an offense should be indicted (formally accused of the charges) and required to stand trial.

The grand jury hears evidence and testimony, presented in secret, by the district attorney, the sheriff, and witnesses. If the jurors feel there is sufficient evidence to have a suspect stand trial, it returns an *indictment* (called a "true bill"). If it feels the evidence is insufficient, no indictment ("no bill") is returned and the charges against the suspect are dismissed.

The grand jury may also investigate charges of bribery of public officials and fraud in elections. It may investigate the operation of government services in a county and inspect public facilities.

The *trial jury* is usually made up of 12 citizens. In state court only, 6 jurors are used in some kinds of cases. However, about 40 potential jurors may be notified to appear for jury duty.

For each case, lawyers for the two sides participate in selecting the trial jury. The lawyers and the judge may question each potential juror about his or her knowledge or attitudes about the case. Persons may be excused from serving if, for example, they personally know someone involved in the case or have already made up their minds about the case. Each side is also permitted to strike a certain number of potential jurors from a trial jury without stating a reason.

During a criminal trial, the jury hears evidence presented by the prosecution (the district attorney or assistants) and the defense. It decides whether the *defendant* is guilty or not guilty. To convict someone, the jury's verdict must be unanimous.

During a civil trial, the jury hears evidence presented by the attorneys for the two opposing sides (called the *plaintiff* and the defendant) in a dispute. The jurors decide which side has more supporting evidence. As in a criminal case, the decision must be unanimous.

hung jury

While a trial is going on, jurors are not supposed to talk to anyone outside the jury about it. They must not read newspaper stories about the trial or listen to radio or

sequestered

television accounts of the trial. This is to help the jury focus on the evidence, and to keep jurors free of outside pressures.

The jurors choose one member of the jury to be foreman. When the jury goes to the jury room to make its decision, the foreman leads the discussions, handles the taking of ballots, and signs the written verdict.

INTERVIEW WITH A SUPREME COURT JUSTICE

In 1974, Justice Robert H. Hall was appointed to the Georgia Supreme Court by then-Governor Jimmy Carter. Before that, Justice Hall had served Georgia as an assistant attorney general and as a judge of the court of appeals. Shortly after this interview, Justice Hall was appointed a federal judge by President Jimmy Carter.

THINK ABOUT IT

1. What is involved in appealing a conviction? Why does the process take so long?
2. According to Justice Hall, should the court listen to public opinion in making a decision? Should a justice's personal beliefs influence a decision?

Justice Hall, what takes up most of a supreme court justice's time?

The most time is taken up, I would say, in writing the court's opinions. Each opinion is written by an individual justice. Also, I have to read the other justices' opinions and decide whether I'm going to agree with them or write something in disagreement.

In addition, we have to listen to the oral arguments. Then we all have to sit in conference and discuss the cases we are deciding.

What types of cases are most often appealed to the court—civil or criminal?

About 35 percent of our cases are criminal. Probably today almost every major conviction, that is where a person would get more than a year in prison, is appealed.

After a case comes to the court, how long does it usually take to make a decision?

Well, let's take a criminal case where a person has been convicted. His lawyer files a notice of appeal. It will probably take two or three months after the conviction for the court reporter to get up a transcript (or record) of what took place at the trial.

The transcript is sent to the appellate court. Then it takes the lawyer about three weeks to write up a statement telling why the case should be reversed. Then after receiving that *brief,* the opposing side, normally the district attorney or the state attorney general, would have a similar period of time in which to file a brief.

After a couple of weeks, the case will be sent down for oral argument. The two lawyers will appear on a particular day before all seven justices. After that, on the average it takes up to three months for the decision to come down either affirming or reversing the trial court and the conviction.

So it's about six months to a year between the trial court conviction and the appellate court decision.

If the seven justices widely disagree, is a decision ever put off?

Well, sure. But not for very long. Usually it's only put off for one week to give everybody a chance to think about it some more.

After a split decision, isn't it difficult to get back together again on subsequent cases?

Oh, no! On our court we can disagree rather strongly and then have a friendly lunch together. It's the best way.

What kinds of decisions are the most difficult to make?

I think the most difficult are those criminal cases in which a person has received the death penalty. If you make a mistake, there's no way to correct it. Therefore, the court takes extreme pains to make sure that, when a death penalty is affirmed, there really is no error in the case at all.

Does public opinion ever enter into a decision whether or not to take up a case?

Well, most judges I think would say they hope public opinion did not. But, it's hard to say whether it does. Of course, whatever the law is, it should be enforced regardless of whether the public agrees with it or not. Otherwise you wouldn't have ruie by law but just rule by the mass opinion of the moment.

Sometimes the Georgia Supreme Court has to rule on the constitutionality of laws passed by the General Assembly. Does this kind of decision ever become a political issue?

No. I don't think it ever becomes a political issue. The court is going to rule on the constitutionality of a bill without regard to the politics of it.

For example, we recently struck down part of the law dealing with local sales tax. It was a very unpopular thing with the General Assembly. The court was severely criticized in the press. But I don't think that disturbed any member of this court whatsoever.

But, at the same time, the court will never strike down an act of the General Assembly as unconstitutional unless the court feels it is patently unconstitutional. If there is any doubt whatever, the court is going to try to uphold any act passed by the General Assembly of Georgia.

Does the supreme court have a special role in preserving our traditional separation of powers?

Absolutely. It is the one branch of government that has the primary duty to keep the powers separate. When there is any dispute between the three branches of government, the one branch that has to settle that dispute is the judicial branch.

I think it is the duty of the judicial branch to keep the branches equal. It not only has to protect the rights of the legislative branch against the executive and the executive against the legislative, but also to protect the judicial against either, or either against the judicial.

And that's a tough act.

What was the most controversial decision that you had to make?

Probably the most controversial decision that I wrote was back in the 1960s dealing with a white civil rights worker in Americus, Georgia, who was convicted of stirring up agitation there. He raised the question whether a white civil rights worker could object to the fact that the jury was made up only of whites and excluded blacks.

I was on the court of appeals then, and we decided that he could object. It was the first time this had been said in Georgia.

At that time it stirred up a lot of comment and, perhaps, opposition. Today, if the decision came out, there would be nothing to it at all. Decisions of that type are controversial depending upon the time in which they come out.

Were you personally attacked after making that decision?

No, no. I don't think I received a single letter attacking me. But, I got a lot of complimentary letters from around the country.

What personal qualities does one need to be an effective supreme court justice?

The most important quality is the ability to be impartial. And that goes for any judge—trial or appellate. Regardless of personal beliefs about the law or the parties involved in a case—one party is not a very nice fellow, the other party is a nice fellow—you have to be impartial in deciding cases. We are all human and we all have certain prejudices, but the important thing is to put them aside in every case.

Next, of course, would be training, legal experience. And it also helps to have a personality such that you can get along with other people.

The other six members of the supreme court?

That's right!

ACTIVITIES FOR CHAPTER 15

Class Discussion

A. In order to have justice, good judges and juries are needed. Their selection sometimes becomes controversial, especially when much of the public disagrees with the outcome of a trial.

   1. What advantages are there in having state judges elected rather than appointed for life as in the federal system? Are there any disadvantages in having judges campaign for office?

   2. Why should jurors be picked only from a list of registered voters? Would such a list be representative of all people in a community? Does it matter?

B. In his interview, Justice Hall says that the court has the duty to protect the power of each branch of government against the other branches.

   1. How would striking down an act of the General Assembly be an example of this duty?

   2. In what other ways might the court carry out this duty? Give some examples.

Writing Project

Our belief in the fairness of our justice system rests heavily on trial by jury. The United States Constitution guarantees it in all but minor cases. Yet, some people try to avoid serving on juries.

Is there a better system? Some countries, such as the Soviet Union, don't have juries for their trials. Is there any danger in this?

Write a brief speech on why each citizen should be willing to serve on jury duty. Comment on some of the reasons people give for wanting to be excused from jury duty.

You might prepare for your speechwriting by interviewing some adults. Ask questions such as: Would you be willing to serve on jury duty? Why or why not? Would you be willing to stand trial in a serious matter without a jury present? Why or why not?

16 Judicial Procedure

No State shall . . . deprive any person of life, liberty, or property without due process of law.—*14th Amendment, Constitution of the United States*

A shopper slips and falls in a food store and sues in court for $50,000. Without notifying the store-owner that he was being sued, a judge awards the money to the shopper. Is this fair?

A sheriff is unable to solve a series of break-ins. He decides to lock up a suspicious-looking person just to see if the break-ins stop. Is this fair?

What protects people from these kinds of unfair actions by government officials? The answer: "*due process of law.*"

Due process of law is designed to safeguard everyone against abusive government power. Some parts of due process are specified in the Constitution of the United States (and repeated in state constitutions). Others have been established by the courts.

Originally, the "Bill of Rights" was added to the Constitution of the United States to limit the power of the federal government. Later, the 14th Amendment placed the same limitations on state governments.

Here are just a few of the due process rights and procedures which make up fair treatment in legal matters. A person has a right to—

be notified of charges against him or her,

be provided a speedy and public trial,

be able to confront and cross examine witnesses,

be represented by a lawyer,

have an impartial judge and jury, and

remain silent (not be a witness against himself).

The courts are regularly called on to spell out just what these rights mean. Court decisions have added to due process, making legal procedures fairer. The basic principles of fairness apply in all types of legal matters—civil and criminal. But in some kinds of cases, including juvenile cases, judges and lawyers disagree over what is fair.

This chapter will examine two kinds of cases—criminal and juvenile.* The cases presented are not real, but they illustrate the legal steps that must be followed in real cases in Georgia.

A CRIMINAL CASE

The steps in criminal procedure are not the same in all cases. Felonies and misdemeanors are handled somewhat differently. The following steps would generally apply in a felony case involving a person 17 years old or older who no longer comes under the jurisdiction of the juvenile court.

THINK ABOUT IT

1. How might the "Miranda" warning help to protect Hank's rights as a person accused of a crime?
2. What went on at the initial appearance and the commitment hearing? What was the grand jury's role?
3. Regarding Hank's trial, who was responsible for the following actions?
   a. defending Hank in the courtroom
   b. deciding on Hank's guilt or innocence
   c. determining what Hank's sentence should be
   d. prosecuting Hank in the courtroom
   e. hearing the appeal of Hank's conviction

The Crime

Hank Byrd was 22. He had drifted from job to job and had a few minor run-ins with the law. Recently, he had moved back to his parents' house in a small North Georgia city. He spent most of his time just hanging around.

John O'Brien was 16. He attended the county high school and worked after school at a tire store. He lived with his parents across the street from the Byrds. He had never been in trouble with the law.

One Saturday afternoon, John was in the carport working on his motorcycle when Hank pulled up in his van. Hank wasn't a close friend, but John was impressed by Hank's big talk, his cars, and the money he always seemed to have—even when he was out of work.

"Hey Johnny-boy, I'm ready to go drink some beer and ride around. Want to come along?"

"Sure," replied John. "I'm tired of messing with these carbs anyway."

As they drove up to Jackson's Package Store, Hank asked, "How much money you got, Johnny?"

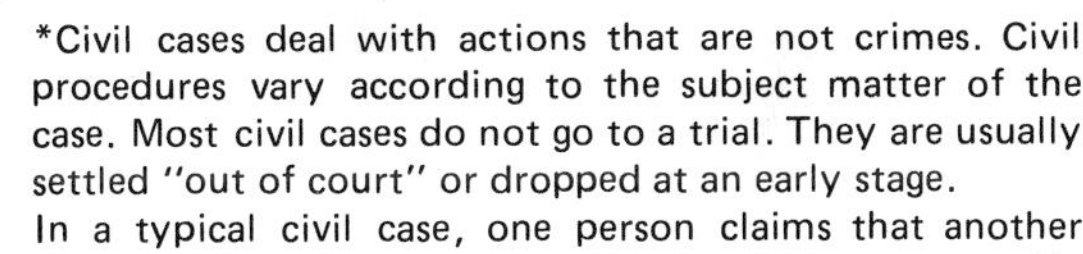

*Civil cases deal with actions that are not crimes. Civil procedures vary according to the subject matter of the case. Most civil cases do not go to a trial. They are usually settled "out of court" or dropped at an early stage.
In a typical civil case, one person claims that another person has wronged or harmed him in some way. He sues for damages—money to compensate him for his loss or injury. The person bringing the lawsuit is called the *plaintiff*; the person being sued is called the *defendant*. The court has to decide whether the evidence is stronger on the side of the plaintiff or on the side of the defendant.

John looked surprised. "Me? Uh, about $3 or $4, I think. What about you?"

"I'm busted," said Hank. "But I've already paid for the gas to ride around, right?"

"Yeah, I guess," John sighed as he handed Hank three bills.

Mr. Jackson was waiting on a customer when Hank and John walked in.

"Be with you fellas in a minute, soon as I help this man load these cases in his car."

As Mr. Jackson carried a case of beer outside, Hank edged over to the liquor counter. Reaching for a bottle of vodka, he whispered, "C'mere! Take this and go sit in the van."

John hesitated, "Hank, I can't. . ."

"Go on," Hank ordered, "he won't see nuthin'."

John took the bottle and crept out to the van.

"Now, what's yours?" asked Mr. Jackson as he came back in.

"Just this, " grinned Hank as he took some beer from the cooler.

"That's $2.90," said Mr. Jackson as Hank handed him the three bills.

". . . plus $6.50!" came a loud voice from behind Hank.

Hank wheeled around to see Mrs. Jackson standing by the door to the back room.

"That other one's got a bottle of vodka from off the shelf," she continued.

"What do you boys think you're doing?" growled Mr. Jackson as he started around the counter toward the front door.

"Move! Or you'll get hurt," Hank snarled as he picked up a beer bottle. Then he swung, knocking the storeowner down. Blood streamed down Mr. Jackson's face.

Hank ran outside and jumped behind the wheel of the van.

"What happened?" asked John nervously.

"Just a little trouble with that old man," replied Hank as the van sped off.

John looked back to see Mr. Jackson stumbling after them. "Maybe we should stop and go back. I don't want to get into. . ."

"Are you crazy?" shouted Hank. "His old lady saw you steal the vodka."

"Me?" cried John. "It was your idea to. . ."

"Shut up and don't worry about it," ordered Hank. "They don't know us."

Four hours later a deputy sheriff picked up Hank and John as they sat in the van at a drive-in restaurant.

What happened to them then? Although they were both involved in the same criminal offense, the process of justice was not the same for Hank and John.

Investigation

The sheriff's department received a phone call from Mrs. Jackson and sent a deputy to the liquor store. There, the Jacksons described Hank and John, the van, and what had been stolen. Mr. Jackson was taken to the hospital.

From the tag number supplied by Mr. Jackson, the sheriff's department quickly found out who owned the van. A judge issued a warrant for the arrest of the two men described by the Jacksons. A deputy sheriff spotted the van parked at the drive-in. Its tag number matched the one supplied by Mr. Jackson. When the deputy approached the van, Hank was drinking from a half-empty bottle of vodka.

Arrest

An arrest is made when someone is taken under control by legal authority. The deputy checked Hank's and John's identification, then searched and handcuffed both of them.

As part of "due process," before any questioning begins, the arresting officer has to advise his prisoners of their rights. This procedure is often called the *"Miranda Warning."* The deputy warned Hank and John of their constitutional rights by reading from a card he carried.

MIRANDA WARNING

1. You have the right to remain silent.
2. Anything you say can and will be used against you in a court of law.
3. You have the right to talk to a lawyer and have him present with you while you are being questioned.
4. If you cannot afford to hire a lawyer, one will be appointed to represent you before any questioning, if you wish.
5. You can decide at any time to exercise these rights and not answer any questions or make any statements.

WAIVER

After the warning and in order to secure a waiver the following questions should be asked and an affirmative reply secured to each question.

1. Do you understand each of these rights I have explained to you?
2. Having the rights in mind, do you wish to talk to us now?

Booking

The deputy brought Hank and John to the sheriff's department at the county courthouse. He told the desk sergeant to "book" Hank. "Booking" made an official record of his arrest. Hank was informed that he could phone his family and a lawyer. He was then put in a cell. (While this was going on, the deputy called John's parents. He then notified a juvenile probation officer to come and take custody of John. John's case is described beginning on page 166.)

Initial Appearance

The morning after his arrest, Hank was taken before the superior court judge for an initial appearance. This has to take place within 72 hours after an arrest with a warrant, 48 hours after an arrest without one. Otherwise, a suspect has to be released.

The judge told Hank what he was charged with and explained his rights. He asked Hank if he had enough money to hire an attorney. Hank didn't think so. The judge said he would appoint a public defender to Hank's case.

Next, the judge set bail. Bail money (or bond) is put up to get an accused person released from jail. Bail is based on the idea that a person is innocent until proven guilty. It is designed to make sure a defendant shows up in court without having to stay locked up. Hank was released after his father came to the courthouse and paid the amount set by the judge.

The judge also set the time for a commitment hearing. (Sometimes this hearing is held at the initial appearance.)

Commitment Hearing

About a week later, the judge held the commitment hearing. Hank was present with the public defender assigned to his case.

The purpose of this hearing was to decide whether there was probable cause to suspect Hank committed the crimes he was charged with–*aggravated assault, aggravated battery*, and *theft by taking*. The hearing also allowed the defense attorney to discover what evidence the state was going to rely on. Based on the evidence presented by the district attorney, the judge decided there was probable cause to suspect Hank.

Grand Jury Indictment (pronounced in-dite-ment)

Before Hank could be tried on felony charges–aggravated assault and aggravated battery–the district attorney (or "D.A.") had to present the evidence to the grand jury. This procedure was not public; neither Hank nor his attorney were present.

If Hank had been charged with only theft by taking–a misdemeanor–the D.A. would not have had to get an indictment. He could have gone ahead by merely filing a "prosecutor's accusation."

The grand jury decided there was enough evidence to indict Hank.

Arraignment

Next, Hank had to go with his lawyer, the public defender, before the superior court judge to plead either "guilty" or "not guilty" to the crimes with which he was charged. He pleaded "not guilty" to the charges.

The judge then set the date for Hank's trial.

The D.A. continued preparing the case for the prosecution. The public defender worked on Hank's defense. Both attorneys had the court issue subpoenas (notices requiring persons, such as the Jacksons, to appear in court to give testimony).

Plea Bargaining

More than three out of four criminal defendants plead guilty. Many of these guilty pleas are the result of plea bargaining between the prosecutor and the defense attorney. Typically, the prosecutor offers the defendant a chance to plead guilty to a crime less serious than the original charge. For example, the defendant might plead simple assault (a misdemeanor) rather than aggravated assault (a felony). In return, the defendant would get a lighter sentence than if he were tried and found guilty of the original charge. If a plea bargain is worked out, there is no trial. In Hank Byrd's case, no plea bargain could be worked out. He had to stand trial.

Trial

The trial opened with the superior court judge announcing that the court was in session and that it would hear "People vs. Byrd." Then the D.A. made the opening statement for the prosecution, followed by the public defender's opening statements for the defense. These statements were not evidence, but only what they expected to prove to the jury.

Both the district attorney and Hank's attorney called witnesses to testify. Both sides cross-examined each other's witnesses.

After the Jacksons and the deputy had testified, the prosecution put John on the witness stand. He testified that Hank gave him the bottle of vodka and ordered him to take it out to the van. He told the court that he didn't want to do it, but was afraid not to do what Hank demanded.

When the defense attorney put Hank on the witness stand, he testified that he took the bottle off the shelf intending to buy it. But John grabbed it and ran out the door. Hank claimed that he started after John to make him come back with the vodka, but Mr. Jackson blocked the door. He denied threatening Mr. Jackson and claimed he swung the beer bottle in self-defense only after Mr. Jackson tried to grab him. "I got scared," Hank testified.

After all the evidence was heard, the public defender and the district attorney made their closing arguments to the jury.

The judge then instructed the jury on how to proceed in making their decision. He explained the questions to be decided and which state laws were involved in the case.

The jury then retired to the jury room to consider the evidence.

Verdict

The jury went over all the facts presented during the trial. The foreman led the discussions and gave all jurors a chance to state their views. After almost an hour, they took a ballot.

By a unanimous vote, the jury found Hank Byrd guilty of the charges of aggravated assault and theft by taking. After the verdict was announced, the judge ordered that Hank be held in the county jail until he appeared before the court for sentencing one week later.

If the jury had not been able to agree on a conviction, the judge would have had to declare a mistrial. In such a situation (sometimes called a hung jury), the district attorney would decide whether to ask for a new trial or have the charges dismissed.

Sentencing

Before sentencing Hank Byrd, the judge ordered a pre-sentencing investigation of Hank's background: his previous criminal record, family life, education and employment records, and so forth. The judge used this information in deciding on a sentence.

The judge sentenced Hank to serve two years in prison plus two years on probation. (See pages 172-77 for more information on how sentences are carried out within the Department of Offender Rehabilitation.) Hank slumped down in his chair. He couldn't believe it—two years in prison! His lawyer tried to reassure him. "We will certainly appeal," he said.

Appeal

Within 30 days, the public defender filed a notice of appeal with the Georgia court of appeals. Later he filed a brief (written statement) listing errors he felt the trial court had made. He asked that the verdict be overturned.

The district attorney then filed a brief citing reasons why the verdict should stand. The two lawyers also presented oral arguments before the court of appeals.

The court of appeals judges did not attempt to substitute their own decision for that of the trial court. Rather, they looked over the complete record of the trial proceedings to see if there were legal errors. They looked to see whether the law was properly applied by the jury in reaching its verdict.

If errors had been made, the court of appeals could have overturned the verdict and sent the case back to the superior court. There might have been a completely new trial.

Because the court of appeals found no errors, it upheld the original verdict. Hank Byrd went to prison.

A JUVENILE CASE

While Hank Byrd's case was moving through the steps in the adult criminal process, John O'Brien's case was being handled in a different manner. The following steps provide a general outline of juvenile court procedure.

THINK ABOUT IT

1. What is a petition? To be filed, a petition has to be endorsed by the juvenile court. How might this requirement protect a young person?
2. What pre-trial steps in the adult criminal process were missing from the procedure used in John's case?
3. How was John's hearing in juvenile court different from Hank's trial in superior court? What were the two parts to John's hearing?

Taking into Custody

As soon as John was brought to the courthouse, the deputy called the O'Briens to notify them that their son was in custody. He gave the reasons and asked them to come to the courthouse.

The deputy also notified a juvenile probation officer who took custody of John. This officer of the juvenile court had the responsibility to decide whether John should be placed in a juvenile detention center or released to his parents. The officer therefore had to make an immediate investigation.

How serious was the offense John was suspected of committing? Did he resist or cooperate with the deputy sheriff? Was he likely to run away or harm someone if released? Would his parents make sure he returned to court when required?

When Mr. and Mrs. O'Brien arrived at the courthouse, the probation officer told them how serious the crime was. He also explained their rights.

The probation officer discussed the situation with John and his parents. He said he would release John in their custody if they would return him to court when directed to do so. They agreed.

Mrs. O'Brien wondered what would happen to John. "Will he go to jail?"

"That," replied the officer, "is entirely up to the juvenile judge. She decides what is best for the child."

"Should we get a lawyer?" asked Mr. O'Brien.

"That's a good idea," replied the officer. "If you can't afford to hire an attorney, the court will appoint one to represent your son."

Meeting with the Lawyer

The next day, John and his parents met with a lawyer. He explained to them what could happen in a juvenile case.

"First, someone will make out a petition alleging that John committed a delinquent act. A delinquent act is one that would be a felony or misdemeanor if committed by an adult. The person making out the petition is asking the court to take some action."

"Well, what action could the court take?" asked Mrs. O'Brien.

"Given the circumstances, I doubt this case would be transferred from juvenile court to superior court," said the lawyer. That usually happens in only the most serious cases. John will probably get a regular juvenile court hearing. And, that's certainly better than a trial in an adult court."

"Why's that?" asked Mr. O'Brien.

"Well, a hearing in juvenile court is something like a trial, but there are important differences. There will be no jury and it won't be public. Furthermore, a finding in juvenile court that a child did commit a delinquent act is not a conviction of a crime. Therefore, it would not disqualify that child from, say, appointment to a government job later on in his life. If he is asked on an application for college or a job whether he has ever been convicted of a crime, he may truthfully reply that he has not."

The lawyer also pointed out that the same child could truthfully state that he had never even been arrested, because a child's being taken into custody is not an arrest. The child is given a chance to start adulthood with a clean record.

Petition

Under Georgia law, legal proceedings against a child begin with the filing of a petition, a written request for action. This petition is filed with the juvenile court.

Any person, including a law enforcement officer, who has knowledge of an alleged delinquent act may make out a petition. However, the petition may be filed only if the juvenile court or a person authorized by the court agrees that it is in the best interests of the public and the child.

In John O'Brien's case, the petition was made out by Mr. Jackson. The juvenile probation officer read the petition and discussed the case with the petitioner, Mr. Jackson. After determining that the case was too serious to be resolved informally, he recommended that the court agree to the petition.

The petition was filed. It explained why John's case belonged in juvenile court. It stated that he was delinquent and was in need of supervision, treatment, or rehabilitation.

Meanwhile, the juvenile probation officer prepared a report for the juvenile court judge. He investigated John's part in the offense. He also investigated John's background. In his report, the probation officer made recommendations to the judge for handling John's case.

The Hearing

John and his parents were issued a summons requiring them to appear before the juvenile court to answer the charges in the petition. The summons included the time, date, and place of the hearing and had a copy of the petition attached. The O'Briens asked their lawyer to represent John at the hearing.

Unlike Hank Byrd's trial, the hearing on John's case was conducted by a judge without a jury. It was not open to the public. Only the parties involved, the attorneys, and witnesses were admitted to the hearing.

The juvenile court judge announced that the purpose of the hearing was to determine whether the statements in the petition were true. She said that the hearing could have two parts. The first part would be similar to an actual trial. The issue would be whether or not John O'Brien committed the delinquent acts that brought him before the juvenile court. If the court found that to be so, then there would be a second part to the hearing. This part would be similar to sentencing in an adult court. The issue would be whether or not John needed treatment, supervision, or rehabilitation by the state. The second part of the hearing, said the judge, could be postponed to a later date.

During the first part of the hearing, an assistant from the district attorney's office introduced the evidence to support the petition. He also called witnesses. Mrs. Jackson said that she saw John take the bottle out of the store. The deputy described how he had picked up John and Hank. On cross-examination by John's attorney, he told how John cooperated while Hank tried to resist arrest.

Hank took the stand and stuck by his story that stealing the bottle was all John's doing. John denied that when he testified, but he did admit taking the bottle to the van.

After hearing all the evidence, the judge found that John had, beyond a reasonable doubt, committed a delinquent act. The first part of the hearing was over.

After a brief recess, the judge resumed the hearing. She stated that the court would immediately proceed to the issue of whether or not John O'Brien was in need of treatment, rehabilitation, or supervision.

John's lawyer introduced evidence to show that John's misdeed was a one-time stunt. He called Mr. O'Brien and the minister of John's church to testify. They said that John was a hardworking and conscientious boy. They thought he would certainly take advantage of a new lease on life if the court gave it to him.

After considering all the evidence in the second part of the hearing, the judge called John to the bench. She said, "The court has found that you committed a delinquent act, a serious crime if you were an adult. There are a number of ways this court could dispose of your case including commitment to the Department of Human Resources, Division of Youth Services. That would mean placing you in a facility for delinquent youth. However, I am of the opinion that after your close brush with the law and your experience in this court you will not misbehave again. I don't think you are inclined to repeat the offense which brought you here. I find that you are not in need of treatment, rehabilitation, or supervision."

John was released to his parents. They as well as Mr. Jackson seemed satisfied with the judge's findings. There was no appeal.

ACTIVITIES FOR CHAPTER 16

Class Discussion

A. Between the time Hank Byrd was arrested and tried, there were a number of procedures the state had to follow. These included (a) giving the "Miranda" warning, (b) informing Hank of the charges against him, (c) setting bail at a reasonable amount, and (d) providing Hank with a defense lawyer.

1. Do these procedures help insure fairness in our legal system? How?
2. Which of these procedures do you feel is the most important? Why?

B. Plea bargaining is *not* a required procedure. Yet, many defendants do plea bargain, thus giving up their right to a trial.

1. Why might a defendant and his or her lawyer prefer plea bargaining to going to

trial? Why might the prosecutor and judge be willing to plea bargain?

2. Should the chance to plea bargain be offered to all criminal defendants? Would there be any danger in this? Explain.

C. At one time there were no special courts or procedures for juvenile offenders. They were treated the same as adult criminals, even put into the same prisons. Later, juvenile cases were handled differently, usually without the due process rights and procedures guaranteed to adults. Then, in 1967, the United States Supreme Court said that due process should apply in juvenile cases.

1. Should juvenile cases be handled differently from adult cases if they involve the same crime? Why? Why not?

2. Should juveniles have the same due process rights as adults? What harm could there be in not having these rights?

Writing Project

Imagine: It's the year 2001. The crime rate has soared. Some police have placed the blame on the legal system. "We could put away all criminals faster if we weren't slowed down by all those due process requirements." Many people agree. The Constitution is amended, eliminating due process.

Assume you are a newspaper reporter assigned to the courthouse beat. A young man named Hank Byrd has just been brought in as a suspect in a liquor store incident. You decide to write up what happens to him.

Assignment: Write a news story in which you tell your readers what happens to criminals now that due process has been abolished.

17 Corrections

About 40,000 Georgia adults were under sentence in 1979 for committing crimes. About 25 percent of these offenders were inmates of the 18 state correctional institutions operated by the Georgia Department of Offender Rehabilitation (DOR) and county jails and work camps. The rest were serving out their sentences under supervision in the community.

Who is the typical offender? He is a male under 30 years old. He most likely comes from a low-income big-city background. When arrested, he was living with parents or a wife. Although he got through the ninth grade, he reads at a sixth grade level. His most frequent crimes: burglary and armed robbery.

Juveniles who break the law do not come under the DOR system. Instead, treatment of juvenile delinquents is the responsibility of the Department of Human Resources (DHR). DHR's Division of Youth Services operates detention facilities—called Youth Development Centers—and community detention programs for persons under 17. But juveniles tried and convicted in superior court may serve time in prisons for adults.

Interior of the Diagnostic and Classification Center at Jackson, a part of the Georgia prison system.

In 1979, about 20,400 juveniles (not all delinquents) were served by DHR programs. Most of these juveniles were supervised in their communities by juvenile court workers. About 2,400 juveniles were committed to DHR for longer term detention.

Who is the typical young person committed to detention? He is a 15-year-old delinquent male. At the time of commitment, he was in the eighth grade. In almost half the cases there was no father in the home.

Why are juveniles handled by DHR, rather than DOR? The special treatment of juveniles is based on the belief that the delinquent child is more in need of supervision and rehabilitation than of punishment. Therefore, DHR facilities are more like schools, less like prisons. DHR's programs are aimed at preventing the young person from becoming a criminal adult.

How does the state respond to adult criminals? That is the main subject of this chapter.

The Georgia Constitution provides that the state can deprive persons of their liberty—it can imprison them. It also provides for the death penalty and for fines. However, it gives those same persons certain protections against the state—no "cruel and unusual punishments" are allowed.

The way in which society responds to the adult criminal is sometimes called "corrections," the "penal system," or just plain "prison." It is the final phase in the criminal justice process that began with arrest by a law enforcement agency and continued with trial in a court.

Corrections is mainly a state government responsibility. It's expensive, and it causes controversy. The following reading examines the different ways the state of Georgia handles convicted criminals.

THE PROPER PUNISHMENT: A CONTINUING DEBATE

THINK ABOUT IT

1. What are the main reasons for imprisonment?
2. What is rehabilitation? Does it work?
3. What are some arguments for and against the death penalty?

What should society do with convicted criminals? Should the punishment fit the crime? Or should the punishment fit the criminal? These questions have been debated for almost 200 years in Georgia. They are still debated today.

Imprisonment

There are four basic reasons for imprisoning persons who commit crimes.

One reason is *punishment*. The criminal "pays" for his crime by serving time, and society "gets even" for the crime.

The second reason is *deterrence*. Imprisonment deters (or discourages) the criminal from more wrongdoing and deters other persons from committing crimes.

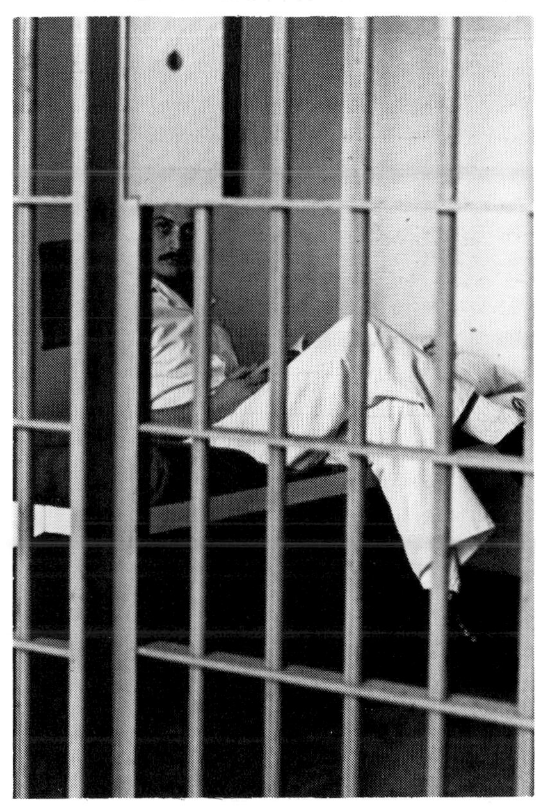

Protection of society is the third reason for imprisonment. A criminal locked up in prison cannot harm law-abiding persons.

The fourth reason is *rehabilitation.* Through treatment and education, a criminal can be reformed and become a useful member of society.

Imprisonment has not always been the accepted method for handling criminals. In the early years of Georgia, persons convicted of crimes were often severely punished. A person might be whipped, hanged, or have his hands and head locked in the pillory before public view.

In 1816, the General Assembly passed a law to replace cruel punishments with long imprisonment in a penitentiary. The state's penitentiary—so-called because prisoners would have time to think about and repent for their crimes—was opened the next year at Milledgeville.

During the Civil War, the penitentiary was destroyed. While it was being repaired, persons convicted of crimes were hired out to private contractors. Thus began the notorious convict lease system.

Soon convicts, leased by the state to the highest bidder, were serving time at work in coal mines, lumber mills, brickyards, on farms, and on railroad construction. The state penitentiary was closed. State government had, in effect, turned over responsibility for handling offenders to private corporations and individuals.

Although the law said that leased convicts were to be properly fed and clothed and humanely treated, they were often cruelly abused. Public sentiment against the lease system arose in the 1880s, but the system wasn't abolished until 1908. Thereafter, offenders served time at a state prison farm or were assigned to the counties to work on public roads. Control of all offenders once again became a public responsibility.

In 1936, a new prison was completed at Reidsville. However, little attempt was made to reform prisoners. Punishment was the main focus. Prisoners assigned to the counties fared little better than under the old convict lease system. They worked in "chain gangs" wearing leg irons and shackles.

Georgia's harsh penal system got national attention. Concerned citizens argued for reform.

In 1943, under the leadership of Gov. Ellis Arnall, Georgia began to reform its penal system. The chain gangs disappeared. In a special session called by the governor, the General Assembly replaced the State Board of Prisons with a new State Department of Corrections, whose director was to

> institute immediately a program of wise, humane and intelligent prison administration which will have for its underlying purpose the *rehabilitation and reclamation of the inmates. . .*

During the following year, a program was begun "to train deserving inmates for future usefulness." Male prisoners could learn to be machinists, mechanics, sheet metal workers, laundry workers, dairy workers, painters, carpenters and so forth—all jobs which helped to make the prison system self-sufficient.

Over the next 30 years, the idea of rehabilitation got more support. Increasingly the offender's age, social background, criminal record, and the circumstances of his or her offense were considered in deciding how to handle the convicted person. Judges gave sentences that were indeterminate (had no fixed end) such as 1 to 5 years, or 5 to 10 years. The offender would get out of prison when corrections officials determined that he or she was rehabilitated. In 1972, the Department of Corrections was renamed

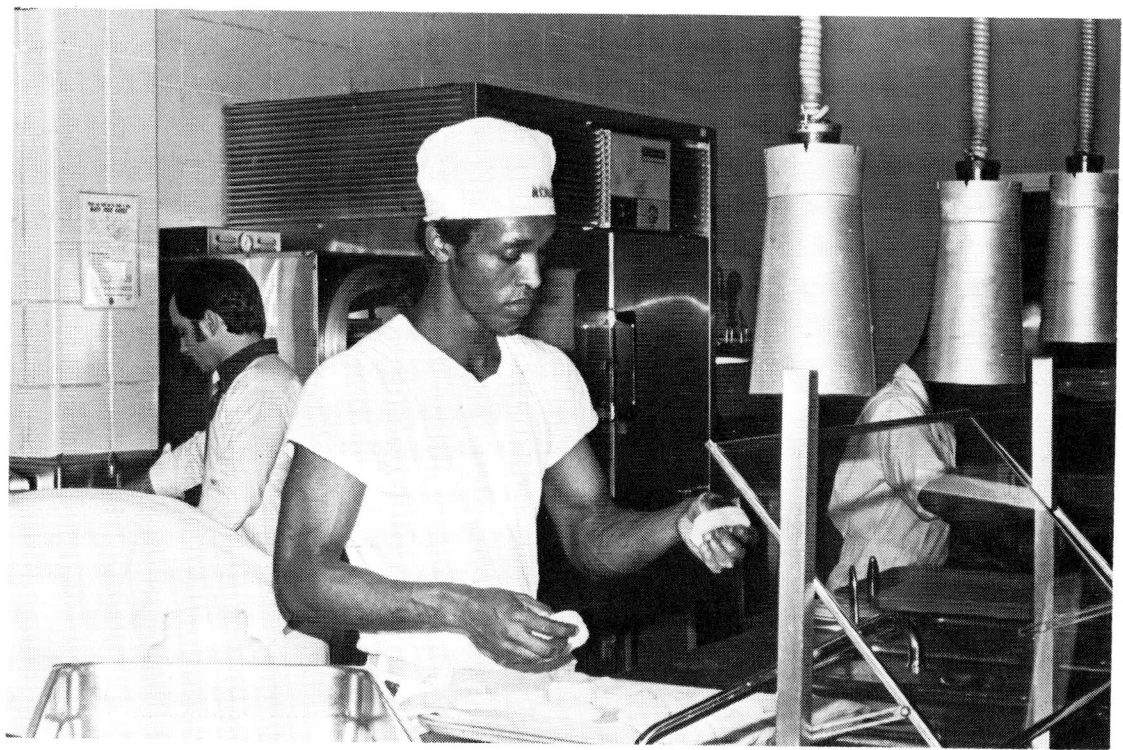

A prisoner gets job training while providing meals for other inmates.

the Department of Offender Rehabilitation.

Today each of the 18 correctional institutions operated by DOR is set up for a special purpose. There are institutions for youthful, aged, and female offenders. Some are for less dangerous offenders, some are for hardened criminals.

At most institutions, job training is available. High school and college level instruction are offered, as well. Each institution has counselors to help inmates cope with daily life, choose educational programs, and handle drug, alcohol, and other personal problems. Religion and recreation are also part of rehabilitation.

Does rehabilitation work? Critics argue that many "rehabilitated" offenders return to crime after their release from prison. They also criticize indeterminate sentences. Such sentences leave the prisoner uncertain of when he is going to get out. They also give prison officials and parole boards (see page 177) considerable power in deciding how much time an inmate serves.

Many corrections officials now agree that rehabilitation works only if the offender really wants to change himself. The best the state can do is help the offender help himself by making available education, counseling, and work experiences.

In 1972, inmates at the Georgia State Prison at Reidsville filed a lawsuit to get prison conditions improved. In 1978, the overcrowded prison was the scene of a riot which left one guard and two inmates dead. Under federal court order to improve conditions, DOR is renovating the prison. However, as the following news article indicates, serious problems still existed in 1980.

REPORT ON REIDSVILLE CONFIRMED

Adapted from the Atlanta Constitution, *February 12, 1980.*

Brunswick — U.S. District Judge Anthony Alaimo issued a court order Monday saying that a 400-page report that found filthy and dangerous conditions, brutality by guards and other inhumane conditions at the Georgia State Prison in Reidsville "is in all respects confirmed."

Confirmation of the report, which came after a meeting between Alaimo, attorneys for inmate plaintiffs and DOR representatives, means that the report is part of official court records in the case.

Completed late last year, the report said guards at the prison inflict brutal, unwarranted beatings and Macings on prison inmates "on a regular and widespread basis." Chemical Mace is a brand of tear gas that is packaged in an aerosol can. It temporarily stuns its victims.

"The beating and Macing of mentally ill inmates and the administration of corporal punishment in general constitutes cruel, inhumane and unusual punishment," the report said.

The report also detailed unsanitary food conditions, faulty plumbing that allowed raw sewage to flow through some cell areas, poor ventilation and exposed wiring that created "great potential" for fire.

The Death Penalty

Capital punishment–the death penalty–is the most controversial part of the punishment debate. Use of the death penalty in Georgia and other states has been challenged in court cases. Some states have rewritten their death penalty laws. Other states have abolished the death penalty.

Between 1964 and 1980, there were no executions in Georgia. But the death penalty is still legal here, and the debate over capital punishment continues. Here are some arguments for and against the death penalty.

Those who favor the death penalty argue that it–

1. deters other people from committing murder,
2. protects society from persons who could never be rehabilitated,
3. is less cruel than life imprisonment, and
4. costs less than keeping someone in prison for life.

Those who oppose the death penalty argue that it–

1. does not prevent capital crimes because the offenders usually don't plan or think about their crime,
2. gives the offenders no chance for rehabilitation and rejects the idea that a person can change,
3. is immoral because no person should have the right to take a life,
4. is more likely imposed if the defendant is poor, uneducated, or black.

COMMUNITY PROGRAMS

The criminal justice system in Georgia provides certain alternatives to imprisonment. These are generally known as community programs. Some are designed for the offender who may not require imprisonment. Others are designed to shorten the time spent in prison.

THINK ABOUT IT

1. What are probation and parole? Who decides whether an offender enters these programs?

2. What kind of supervision does a person on probation or parole have?

Almost three times as many offenders in Georgia are serving out their sentences under community supervision as are serving time in prison. There are two general types of community programs:

1. those which are alternatives to going to prison
2. those which involve release from prison

Alternatives to Prison

Should all persons convicted of crimes be sent to prison? Often a criminal will get a suspended sentence. This means he or she will not have to serve a sentence as long as he or she stays out of trouble. Sometimes the sentence is probated, which means that the sentence is to be served in the community under the supervision of a probation officer rather than in prison. In either case, the judge decides that it's better for the offender and for society not to have him or her serve time in prison.

Probation is a sentence of community supervision instead of imprisonment. Persons on probation are, in many cases, first-time offenders and have never been in prison. Typically their offenses are property crimes, such as burglary, theft, and forgery—not violent crimes.

While serving on probation, the offender must follow specific rules concerning work, travel, family support, and social activities. If the offender violates the law or probation rules, his or her probation may be revoked. Then, the rest of the sentence would have to be served in prison.

Persons on probation can hold jobs. Therefore, they can pay fines and court costs, support their families, and make restitution (or repayment) to victims of their crimes.

In some Georgia communities there are *diversion centers.* Here selected offenders live under close supervision—sort of halfway between probation and imprisonment. They hold jobs which enable them to pay fines and make restitution.

Release from Prison

Parole is a conditional release from prison before the end of a sentence. A prison inmate released on parole, called a parolee, lives under the supervision of a parole officer.

After an inmate has served one-third of his prison term, he is eligible to apply for parole. The decision to grant parole is made by the State Board of Pardons and Paroles. The board examines the inmate's record to decide if he will be released under supervision for the rest of the sentence.

A parolee must obey all conditions of the parole. Otherwise he may be arrested and returned to prison. These conditions require that the parolee (1) make a monthly report to the parole officer; (2) get the parole officer's permission to change residence, change jobs, leave the state, or buy a car; (3) obey a midnight curfew; (4) possess no deadly weapon; (5) not abuse drugs or alcohol; (6) not associate with convicted felons; and (7) not violate any laws.

In addition to parole, another type of early release program is being tried by DOR. Offenders serve the last few months of their sentences in *transitional centers.* Located in just a few communities, these centers provide supervised living, counseling, and an opportunity to get a job and gradually "move out" into society.

STATE BOARD OF PARDONS AND PAROLES

At one time, the granting of paroles was the responsibility of the governor.

Some governors abused this power, so in 1943 the General Assembly created the State Board of Pardons and Paroles to exercise these functions.

The five members of the board are appointed by the governor (and confirmed by the Georgia Senate) for seven-year terms. Membership on the board is a full-time office. Members may not engage in any other business or profession while serving on it.

Interview with a Member of the Board of Pardons and Paroles

Mrs. Mamie B. Reese was appointed to the State Board of Pardons and Paroles in 1973 by Gov. Jimmy Carter and reappointed in 1980 by Gov. George Busbee. In the interview, Mrs. Reese describes some of the duties of a board member and how she views her job.

THINK ABOUT IT

1. What kinds of things enter into the decision whether or not to parole a prisoner?
2. Why isn't "family hardship" alone a basis for parole?
3. What qualities does a board member need to have?

Mrs. Reese, I had thought that you and your colleagues on the parole board would have been lawyers. But I understand that is not the case.

Sometimes people do expect that one or more persons on the board are lawyers. But none of us has a legal background.

Of the five presently serving, one has a background in industry, one in insurance, one is a retired army colonel, and one has come up through the ranks in corrections. First he was a police officer in Athens, then a probation supervisor.

My background is strictly education. I was a high school teacher and then for 25 years I taught at Albany State College.

So, what does it take to be a parole board member?

Well, first of all, the duties of a parole board member include making clemency judgments on approximately 6,000 inmates per year. This is a sensitive assignment in which a decision must be made based not only on our "book of rules," but also on the individual board member's feelings as to whether some relief, by way of clemency, should be granted.

You've got to be able to live with that judgment once it's been made, knowing that not all people will be pleased.

So, there has to be brought to this assignment a sensitivity and a willingness to make a judgment.

What's the toughest part of the job?

Making decisions. As I recall, when I

was interviewing for the appointment, Governor Carter said, "You know, this is a very sensitive role. You've got to make these decisions, and it's not going to be easy."

And I said, "Governor, I learned a long time ago that there's no easy way to say no when a person wants to hear yes."

I guess that's about it. You know they are waiting out there and that they know a decision is about to be made. You have to decide whether it's better to let a person out of prison or keep him in. There is a certain amount of risk with each decision.

What is the process for making a decision? Do you meet and talk with every prisoner whose case comes up, or do you make your decision on the basis of written information?

For each case, we do, of course, have a file of information.

Every prisoner is interviewed by an examining officer prior to any parole consideration. But the board itself does not interview every prisoner coming up for parole. Persons such as those who have been denied parole two or more times are interviewed by one or more board members.

Frequently prisoners ask to talk to a board member. And that is their right. But they have to have a good reason because everybody wants to talk to a board member. We consider such requests on our normal visitation schedule to, for example, Reidsville. But for the most part, the board members are not able to personally interview the 6,000 people who come before us for first-time considerations.

So you actually go to Reidsville from time to time?

We have central interview points where people are brought from surrounding areas. Reidsville is one, Macon Correctional Institution is one, Stone Mountain, Alto, Columbus, Milledgeville—we have about six interview points.

What kinds of questions do you ask before you make your decision?

We ask questions like, What are you planning to do? Where are you going to work? Would there be any objections to your going back into the community where the offense took place. How have you been getting along in the institution? Have you taken advantage of the available programs within the institution?

Do you grant paroles on the basis of family hardship?

The state does not allow us to grant releases based on hardship alone because that affects 95 percent of the people. Most of our inmates are under 30, able-bodied, black males. They do have families. They've left jobs. Most of them are hardship.

Does each board member vote on each case?

Yes. The parole decision is rendered on a majority basis. The vote of three out of five members is needed to grant or deny a parole. I read the file, vote, and pass it on to the next board member.

In some cases we get together. For instance, when an inmate has been denied parole and appeals through his family, the board as a whole may give special consideration to the case. Sometimes the board is asked to consider a case by a principal of a school or an attorney. But an inmate gets no special consideration by having an attorney.

Then we have normal hearing days where people can drop in. They don't have to have an appointment to talk about somebody's case. It may be the family or a community supporter. They have various reasons for coming in.

Some just say, "Well, I think he served

long enough and we want him out." Others say, "We have this family hardship."

Others may bring in a letter from a college admissions office saying, "If so and so is released by September 1st, he can get in the fall quarter at Albany State College. Hope you'll consider this."

Sometimes there's a job opportunity. Let's say a person worked for the Coca-Cola Company prior to the offense and incarceration. Coca-Cola looks at his record and says, "Well, he was a good man. If we can get him back in six months, we'll let him pick up his job." We get that type of thing.

Of course, some people come in simply because they want their loved one out.

So you regularly have relatives and friends contacting you to try to convince you to make a decision for parole?

Right. By telephone, by letter, and by personal appearance.

What about the other side? You have to handle a lot of criticism don't you?

We do get severe criticism, emotional criticism. The families of the prisoners never think you're letting them out too early, but others do protest.

There was a case where we released a man involved in a murder. He had served 12 years, was a weak person who had sort of been led along by another man who had actually used the death weapon. Well, when notice of that release was made public, it upset some people very much. We had protests from the widow of the victim, and a couple of sons.

But most people don't die in prison. Even lifers get out some day. Murderers do get out. They spend about an average of 12½, 13, 14 years. But, I can't see anybody like a mass murderer ever getting out.

What kind of satisfaction have you gotten from this position?

I suppose, after 5 years, the success rate of parole. Contrary to what you hear in the community or read in the papers, our success rate is 90 percent. Only one out of ten violate parole. That is, parole on the first consideration.

Now, it's said that two out of three people who get out of prison will at some time return. But, these are people who "max out"—serve their maximum sentence. You're not talking about parole.

We hear a lot about overcrowded conditions in the prisons. Is that ever a factor in your decision to grant a parole?

Unfortunately, prisons are overcrowded. But, we cannot include that as a basis of release. In light of the overcrowding, we have had some special reviews of certain categories of cases.

If we had more pre-release centers, halfway houses, work release houses, that type of thing, we could get more people out of hard confinement. But, no, we don't release them on the basis that we need another bed.

I'm the first to confess that prison is not the answer. I don't believe in "lock 'em up and build more prisons." We have to find some way to change the person, the behavior of the person—if that's at all possible.

ACTIVITIES FOR CHAPTER 17

Class Discussion

A. Proposals to renovate prisons, employ better trained and better paid corrections officers, and install vocational programs have a high price. It already costs more to keep one inmate in prison than to educate one student at a state university.

   1. What are some reasons for spending more money on corrections? What are some reasons for *not* spending more?

2. Would "prison reform" be a popular issue for a political candidate to run on today? Why? Why not?

B. Several years ago, the director of the U.S. Bureau of Prisons (a federal agency) discussed community-based corrections programs, "While I think they show great promise for a segment of the offender population, the great danger is that these programs will be oversold. . . The history of corrections is littered with the failures of programs that worked on a small scale and then broke down when applied to inmates on a large scale."

1. Which of the following offenders might be a good candidate for a community program? Explain your choice.

   a. a first-time offender convicted of passing bad checks
   b. Hank Byrd, convicted back in Chapter 16
   c. a bank accountant convicted of pocketing $5,000 in bank funds
   d. an 18-year-old convicted for the second time on drug charges

2. How might the offender benefit from a community program? How might the community benefit?

Writing Project

Several times in recent years, DOR has announced plans for diversion centers in certain Georgia communities only to have them scrapped because community residents were opposed to them.

Assume that you are a homeowner. DOR has just announced plans for a diversion center near your home. It would house 25 offenders convicted of property type crimes such as forgery, burglary, and theft. Some of your neighbors are very upset. There is to be a meeting with DOR officials at the courthouse. You decide to go.

Assignment: Write a short statement to give at the meeting. Include the reasons you think a diversion center should or should not be located in your community.

GLOSSARY

Words here are defined according to their usage in this book.

Act. A bill that has become law. A *general* act applies throughout the state; a *local* act applies to particular places. See also Law and Statute.

Administration. 1: A governor's term in office. 2: The group of officials setting policy and managing the governor's programs.

Agency. Any working unit of government, such as a department, bureau, commission, or other division.

Amendment. A change in a constitution, bill, or law.

Appeal. A request to a higher court to review a lower court ruling in a civil or criminal case.

Apportionment. The drawing of election district boundaries according to population. To make sure each legislator represents about an equal number of people, the General Assembly is reapportioned after each United States Census.

Appropriation. An amount of money specified by law—an appropriation act—to be spent for a certain purpose.

Arrest. The seizing of a person by legal authority.

Bail. Money deposited with a court for the release of an accused person, to insure his or her appearance in court.

Ballot. 1: The paper on which a vote is marked. 2: The vote itself, as in "casting your ballot."

Bill. A proposal for a new law or for a change in an existing law, introduced by a legislator.

Budget. The state's financial plan for a fiscal year. It proposes spending within limits of expected revenue.

Campaign. Organized effort to get a political candidate elected to office.

Candidate. A person running for a public office.

Caucus. 1: A political meeting. 2: A political group which meets to decide policies or choose candidates for political office.

Certify. To state officially that someone or something meets a standard or requirement.

Checks and Balances. A system of dividing powers among three branches of government—legislative, executive, and judicial.

Citizen. A member of a state or nation who owes it loyalty and who is entitled to certain rights.

Civil case. Legal dispute involving private citizens, groups, governments, or businesses; does not involve wrongdoings defined by the state as crimes.

Code (Georgia). A set of books containing all state laws.

Committee system. A method for dividing the legislature's work among small groups of legislators.

Complaint. A formal accusation or charge against someone (not a criminal charge).

Compromise. A settlement achieved when each opposing side gives up a portion of its position on an issue in order to reach an agreement.

Constituency. The group of people represented by an elected official.

Constitution. A written plan for operating state or national government; "The supreme law of the land" on which all other laws and government actions must be based.

Court. A place for settling civil and criminal cases; also refers to (1) the meetings or sessions held to settle cases and (2) the judges in those sessions.

Criminal case. A legal action brought by the state against a person accused of a crime.

Defendant. The accused person in a criminal case; the person or business being sued in a civil case.

Democracy. Government by the people; rule by the people.

Democratic Party. One of two main political parties in the United States; the dominant party in Georgia.

Due process. The rights and procedures guaranteed by the U.S. and state constitutions. Due process protects the individual against abusive action by government. It requires fair treatment by all local, state, and national public bodies, including the courts and educational institutions.

Election. The choosing of government officials by vote of the people; called the "general election" in Georgia.

Election district. An area of land, marked off on the basis of population, for the purpose of holding elections.

Executive. The person or branch of government responsible for enforcing laws and carrying out policies and programs authorized by the legislative branch.

Expenditure. Payment of public money for some purpose; an expense.

Federalism. A plan of government in which power is divided between a national government and state governments.

Felony. A serious crime which is punishable by more than a year in prison.

Fiscal year. The 12-month period on which the state's budget is based; begins July 1 of each year and ends June 30 of the next.

General election. The election held statewide every two years in Georgia. Candidates for federal and local offices may be on the ballot, as well as state candidates.

Grant-in-aid. A contribution of money from one government to another to support a particular activity.

Hearing. A meeting in which persons may testify to determine facts; in juvenile court, takes place of trial.

Impeachment. A process for bringing charges against a public official for wrongdoing in office.

Interest group. A group of persons having a special legal, economic, or social concern which could be affected by legislation or by executive action.

Jurisdiction. A court's power or authority. *Original* jurisdiction is the power to try a case; *appellate* jurisdiction is the power to hear appeals from and review a lower court's decision.

Indictment. A formal accusation by a grand jury that a person has committed a crime.

Judicial. Branch of government responsible for settling, according to law, disputes between persons or between persons and government. Also decides whether laws agree with the constitution.

Jury. A group of citizens chosen to hear evidence. A *trial jury* decides the verdict in a case; a *grand jury* decides whether to indict an accused person.

Law. 1: An act passed by a legislature. 2: The whole body of rules contained in statutes, constitutions, and court decisions.

Legislative. The branch of government responsible for making laws.

Legislature. A body of elected public officials which makes laws. Its members are legislators and the laws it passes are called legislation. In Georgia, its official name is the General Assembly.

Levy. To place and collect taxes on persons, incomes, businesses, property, goods, etc.

Lobby. 1: To attempt to influence action of government officials, especially to influence lawmakers' voting. 2: An interest group organized to influence government.

Merit system. A plan for employing and promoting persons in government jobs on the basis of their abilities.

Misdemeanor. A less serious crime which is punishable by not more than one year in prison and/or a fine.

Nomination. The naming, or proposing, of a candidate for public office.

Ordinance. A law passed by the lawmaking branch of a city or county government.

Petition. 1: A written request, often signed by many people, for a government to take some specific action. 2: A formal request to start legal action in the case of a juvenile.

Plaintiff. The party filing a complaint–or charge–in a civil case.

Policy. A plan of action to meet a specific goal; also a position on a specific issue.

Political party. A group whose members hold similar ideas on public issues and which tries to put its candidates in office.

Politics. 1: The way a person or group wins and holds control of a government. 2: The competition between persons and interest groups for influence and power in government. A person involved in politics is called a "politician."

Poll. A place where people go to vote.

Primary. A "first" election to nominate political party candidates to run in the general election.

Provisions. Parts of a law (or articles of a constitution).

Police power. The general power of state government to control persons and property in the interest of public safety and welfare.

Reapportionment. See Apportionment.

Registration. Signing up to vote. Before a citizen may vote in Georgia, he or she must first register to vote.

Repeal. To abolish or do away with a law.

Representative. 1: An official chosen to act for a group of people. 2: A member of the state House of Representatives.

Republic. A form of democratic government in which the people exercise power through elected representatives.

Republican Party. One of two main political parties in the United States.

Resolution. A proposal, similar to a bill, on which the legislature votes to express its opinion or will.

Revenue. Money a government receives as income from taxes, license fees, fines, etc.

Runoff. A second election held when no candidate receives enough votes to win the first election.

Separation of powers. See Checks and Balances.

Session. The official meeting period of the legislature. The Georgia General Assembly meets each year for 40 days.

Statute. Any law (intended to be more or less permanent) passed by a legislature; a written law.

Taxes. Money which government charges people to pay public expenses.

Testify. To make a statement about what you know or to give evidence as in a trial or hearing.

Trial. A formal process of examining facts under dispute in a civil or criminal case.

Verdict. A decision in a trial.

Veto. The governor's written disapproval of a bill passed by the legislature that blocks its becoming law. A veto can be overriden by a two-thirds majority vote in the legislature.

Warrant. A document issued by a judge which gives authority to a law enforcement officer to make an arrest, a search, or seize evidence.

Welfare. 1: The well-being of the people. 2: Government services for the needy. 3: Money payments to the poor.

Witness. A person who testifies at a trial or a hearing.

INDEX

Suggested Films for this course

#	Title	Color	time	rating
J0770	Governer John M. Slaton	C	50	★★★★
2131	How our 2 party System operates	B+W	20	
0194	Bill of Rights of the U.S.	C	20	★★★★
0369	The Congress	B+W	20	
J0415	Debt to the past - govt + law	C	16	★★
2078	The last Ballot	C	40	
0388	The executive power		20	
1962	We the people... story of our Federal govt.			
1189	J-Man in the Middle - The State Legislator	B+W	30	★
0717	The Functions of Congress	B+W	29	
0049	Bill of Rights in Action: Story of a Trial	C	22	★★★★
1417	The constitution - The compromise that made a nation	C	27	★★
0713	From where I sit (on st. Dept decision-making)	B+W	27	
0392	Criminal justice in the U.S.	B+W	32	

UPD 4270 7-80